Narratives of the French and Indian War: 3

Narratives of the French and Indian War: 3

The Capture of Fort Duquesne

Commissary Wilson's Orderly Book

Fort Duquesne and Fort Pitt

A Journal Kept During the Siege of Fort William Henry, August, 1757

Braddock Ballads

LEONAUR

Narratives of the French and Indian War: 3
The Capture of Fort Duquesne
Commissary Wilson's Orderly Book
Fort Duquesne and Fort Pitt
A Journal Kept During the Siege of Fort William Henry, August, 1757
Braddock Ballads

FIRST EDITION

Leonaur is an imprint of Oakpast Ltd

Copyright in this form © 2019 Oakpast Ltd

ISBN: 978-1-78282-788-7 (hardcover)
ISBN: 978-1-78282-789-4 (softcover)

http://www.leonaur.com

Publisher's Notes

Contents

The Capture of Fort Duquesne

By the Right Reverend Cortlandt Whitehead Bishop of Pittsburgh

An Historical Discourse before The Society of Colonial Wars
in the Commonwealth of Pennsylvania

Delivered in Christ Church, Philadelphia, on the One Hundred
and Fortieth Anniversary of the Capture of the Fort, Sunday, November
Twenty-seventh, 1898, upon the occasion of the Unveiling of a
Memorial Tablet of Brigadier-General John Forbes, Commander of
His Majesty's troops in the Southern Provinces of North America.

The proposition was not long ago advanced and enlarged upon in
a monthly journal of this city, that the people of Pennsylvania do not
deal gratefully with their public men in life, and have not done their
duty towards their memories in death. Doubtless many of you have
read the argument. It is asserted that there is lack of unity and homo-
geneity among this people, a natural result of its early history. Different
nationalities, with different religions, and with diverse interests at the
beginning and all along the way, rendered this portion of the United
States far different from such a Commonwealth, for instance, as Massachusetts, where the settlers were of one blood and tradition, profess-
ing in the main one creed.

The Quakers, the Welsh and Church of England people, in and
about Philadelphia; Connecticut people, who later on settled at the
north; the Germans at the south, who formed historically an influen-
tial and in some localities an overwhelming element; the Scotch-Irish
beyond the Alleghenies—these have made up this Commonwealth,
a composite whole, with divisive rather than unifying interests. The
results are various, but especially (as one of your own fellow-citizens
has sought to prove) does this diversity appear in the neglect of our
public men. He avers that there is a disposition not to be proud for the
State's sake, when one of her sons has achieved success or renown, and

BRIG. GEN?
JOHN FORBES
Colonel of the 17th Regt. of Foot
and
Commander of His Majesty's Troops
in the Southern Provinces of
North America.
Born in Petincrief, Fifeshire, Scotland 1710.
Died in Philadelphia March 11th 1759.

Interred in this Chancel.

By a steady pursuit of well conducted
measures in defiance of disease and
numberless obstructions, he brought to
a happy issue a most extraordinary
campaign resulting in the evacuation of
Fort Duquesne, and made a willing sacrifice
of his own life to what he loved more, the
interest of his King and Country.

Erected by the Society of Colonial Wars
in the Commonwealth of Pennsylvania.

that "woe to the man of distinct opinion," is an exclamation which the conduct of Pennsylvania has for many generations made familiar. The words of Horace Binney are cited:

That Pennsylvania is more indifferent to her own sons than to strangers.

And the assertion of Judge Porter:

A disposition has prevailed in Pennsylvania to overthrow rather than to sustain men of distinguished ability.

Every citizen of this great State may well be filled with amazement when he learns that no Pennsylvanian has ever written the biography of William Penn. A Virginian, a Frenchman, a Massachusetts man, and three English writers have thought his life and memory worth recounting. Pennsylvanians have been content with pamphlets, essays and speeches. Moreover, no Pennsylvanian, it is asserted, until within a very recent period, has ever written a biography of Benjamin Franklin. The best editions of his works are from Massachusetts and New York; his best biographers heretofore, New Yorkers.

The names of Robert Morris and John Dickenson and General Wayne appear in a list given by our author, of those who for a century were neglected by their fellow-citizens; and the further names of Mifflin, Armstrong, Clymer, Thompson, Gallatin and others, who still await biographers, men conspicuous before the whole continent in their day, who now stand a chance of being well-nigh forgotten. (*Vide Lippincott's Magazine* for July, 1896, "Pennsylvania and her Public Men," by Sidney G. Fisher.)

It may be that in common with all our fellow-citizens in these United States we are too busily occupied in *making* history to be careful in recording it. (*Vide The American Historical Review* for October, 1898, "The Historical Opportunity in America," by Prof. A. B. Hart.)

All this we should recall to memory, because as citizens of this Keystone State, we cannot resent rebuke from friendly lips, but dispose ourselves the rather to repeat the Psalmist's words, "*Let the righteous smite me friendly and reprove me, but let not their precious balms break my head.*" How shall we amend, if there be not brought distinctly before our eyes, those common faults which, because they are shared by many, are not easily recognised as calling for individual amendment and action? How shall we repent, unless the full measure of our sins of omission, as of commission, be brought evidently to our consciousness? It is quite manifest that this Honourable Society to which it is our privilege to belong, and in whose behalf, we assemble on this occasion, is designed to guard against this forgetfulness and to overcome the indifference of which we have been speaking. This Society was organised because "it was desirable that there should be adequate commemorations of events of Colonial History." It has been:

> Instituted to perpetuate the memory of those events, and of the men, who in military, naval and civil positions of high trust and responsibility, assisted in the establishment, defence and preservation of the American Colonies, and were in truth the founders of this nation. With this end in view, it seeks to collect and preserve manuscripts, rolls, relics and records; to provide suitable commemorations or memorials relating to the American Colonial Period, and to inspire in its members, the fraternal and patriotic spirit of their forefathers, and in the community respect and reverence for those whose public services made our freedom and unity possible.

Therefore, just in proportion as we of this Honourable Society carry on towards perfection, and with true patriotic spirit, the purposes for which this organisation was made, shall we remove more and more whatever of censure may be justly imputed to the citizens of this Commonwealth, for ingratitude toward the heroes of the past, or the truly great and noble of the present.

Strictly in line with this purpose is our commemoration today, (1898). General Forbes, of whom I am to speak, was not one whose deeds are recorded in tomes and folios; nor was the event with which his name is most prominently connected of such a character as to catch the eye of the seeker for startling and exciting historical occurrences. General Braddock is well known to all, because of his direful defeat. General Forbes is not widely, or at least popularly known, because his, although a great, was nevertheless a bloodless and combatless achievement.

But we whose duty it is to rescue the memories of the Colonial Heroes from the obscurity of time, and set their lives and characters, and their very faces, if possible, before the eyes of their fellow-citizens, are well agreed that there are not wanting many qualities in General Forbes' character, and many grand results of his fidelity and courage, which entitle him to high place on the list of those whom Pennsylvania delights to honour. In telling the story familiar no doubt to many present, I can set down nothing of my own, but simply collate what others have written, items of information, which after all are not very numerous.

The year 1757 was the beginning of a new era, as we all know, in the history of England; for that year saw the reins of power fall into the hands of "The Great Commoner," whose biography, it is usual to say, is the history of England, so thoroughly was he identified with the grand events which made this period one of the most glorious in the annals of his country:

> It is scarcely too much to say that in the general opinion of his contemporaries, the whole glory of this year was due to his signal genius; his alone was the mind that planned and his, the spirit that animated the brilliant achievements of the British arms in all the four quarters of the globe. (Parkman, *Montcalm & Wolfe*, Vol. 2, republished by Leonaur as *Musket & Tomahawk* containing both volumes)

Posterity, however, has not failed to recognise the independent genius and sterling worth of those who were his subordinates or allies in carrying out his purposes. His discernment selected Wolfe, but Wolfe would have been a hero anywhere when called to make sacrifices for his country. Pitt by his generous praise in Parliament stimulated Clive to his success in India, nevertheless the genius of Clive would have made itself manifest wherever duty gave opportunity. Pitt's subsidy to Frederick certainly brought the Seven Years' War to a speedier conclusion, but doubtless Frederick even without this aid would have still been Frederick the Great.

Nevertheless, William Pitt is not unjustly described as the "Creator of Modern England." He had a genius for organisation, and when he rose to power he told the Duke of Devonshire, "I am sure that I can save this country, and that nobody else can."

> England hailed with one acclaim the undaunted leader who asked for no reward but the honour of serving her. The hour had found the man. For the next four years this imposing figure towered supreme in British history.

He had, indeed, we are told, glaring faults. He was vain, theatrical, domineering and haughty, nevertheless he had undoubted talent for action and great vigour of mind; he was filled with a burning enthusiasm, possessed of an overwhelming force of passion and intensity of will, hurling in debate fiery shafts of eloquence; and was, moreover, too great for faction and partisanship, and pre-eminently and incorruptibly patriotic. The people trusted him, and he loved the people. He waked England from her lethargy and made the power and glory of England one with his own. He started out not to *curb* France in America, but to *annihilate* her; to crush her navy, cripple her foreign trade, ruin her in India, in Africa, and wherever else east or west she had found a foothold, to gain for England the mastery of the seas, to open to her the highways of the globe, and to make her supreme in commerce and colonisation.

Said Frederick of Prussia:

England has long been in labour, and at last she has brought forth a man.

Said Col. Barre:

Nobody ever entered his closet, who did not come out of it a braver man.

That inspiration was felt wherever the British flag waved. England sprang to new life under the kindly influence of this one great man, universally considered as on the whole the most powerful minister that ever guided the foreign policy of England.

The contentions between England and France had been as follows: 1. King William's War, between 1689 and 1697; 2. Queen Anne's War, between 1700 and 1713; and 3. King George's War, 1744 to 1748. In these the colonists in New England and New York had been engaged. But with 1755 began what is called 4. the "Seven Years' War," in which *southern* colonists also were to be engaged, and which was to put at rest forever the question of who should own the North American Continent. (Fisher's *Pennsylvania, Colony and Commonwealth*.) Disaster had attended the British Arms, and in 1757 the campaign had closed, leaving the affairs of Great Britain in a more gloomy condition than at any former period of the unfortunate and disgraceful war.

The Marquis de Montcalm had captured Fort William Henry on Lake George, and thus the French had complete control of that lake and Lake Champlain and the main passage to Canada. By the destruction of Oswego, they had obtained control of the Great Lakes, and by the possession of Fort Duquesne they maintained their ascendency over the western Indians and held control of all the country west of the Allegheny Mountains. Lord Chesterfield is quoted as saying,

(*Olden Time,* vol. I):

Whoever is in or whoever is out, I am sure we are undone, both at home and abroad; at home by our increasing debt and expense, and abroad by our ill-luck and incapacity. . . . . The French are masters in America to do what they please. We are no longer a nation, I never yet saw so dreadful a prospect.

At this juncture William Pitt put his firm hand on the helm, and set himself to the task of settling, as we have said, the question of sovereignty in North America. In his dealings with the colonists, he reversed the former policy, and instead of making demands and exactions upon them, he announced that he would send troops from the Mother Country to act with the Provincials. Earl Londoun, commander-in-chief in America, (Graham's *History N. America: Braddock,* by J. R. Meesick), is described by historians as inefficient; devoid of genius, civil or military; mutable, indecisive, impotent against the enemy. Franklin wrote:

Like S. George on a sign always on horseback but never advancing.

Pitt is reported to have given as a reason for superseding him early in 1758, that he could never learn what Earl Londoun was doing. General Abercrombie was appointed in his place.

Immediately three expeditions were planned against the enemy. The first against Louisbourg, in Cape Breton Island, where the French were debating boundaries with the English. This expedition was commanded by General Amherst and was eminently successful.

The second expedition was directed against Ticonderoga and Crown Point, commanded by General Abercrombie himself, who was, however, routed after a bloody conflict, the disgrace of which was somewhat relieved by the destruction of Fort Frontignac shortly after.

The third expedition is that in which we are particularly interested today, that which had for its purpose the capture of Fort Duquesne. The conduct of this expedition was entrusted to General John Forbes. He left Philadelphia about the middle of September, 1758, to join Colonel Bouquet, who was in command of the regulars awaiting his coming since July at Raystown, now Bedford. Bouquet, who was a French Swiss, is said to have been the equal of General Forbes in much that constitutes a good commander, a most accomplished and attractive person. To his shrewdness and wariness in dealing with savages, much of the success of the expedition is to be attributed.

Dumas (in his account of Bouquet's expedition against the French, published in Amsterdam, 1769), says of Bouquet that:

He made no claim to the good opinion of others, neither did he solicit it. All were compelled to esteem him.

And although Washington wrote on September first:

All is dwindled into ease, sloth and inactivity. Nothing but a miracle can bring this campaign to a happy result.

At that very time Bouquet was exercising his troops every day in the woods and bushes in a way which made them, later on, more able to meet the Indians and others to great advantage. (*Pennsylvania Magazine*, Vol. III, No. 2. See also appendix A).

There were many delays in the preparations necessary to be made, principally in obtaining wagons and horses, as Colonel Bouquet's letters show. In August or September, Colonel George Washington, who had been engaged in collecting troops from Virginia, North Carolina and Maryland, proceeded to the rendezvous, followed shortly by General Forbes. Being all assembled, heated dispute arose amongst these leaders with regard to the route to be followed in the campaign against Fort Duquesne. Colonel Washington, who had traversed the country twice before, (1753 and 1754), favoured the road which had been used in the ill-starred expedition of General Braddock three years earlier; a road at least familiar, and ready for their wagons, but leading through Maryland and Virginia at times, and rather circuitous, as it seemed.

Washington's reasons for his opinion are given at length in a letter written at Fort Cumberland, August 2, 1758. General Bouquet, on the contrary, favoured a new route, laid entirely in Pennsylvania, and had already, on August 23rd, sent Colonel James Burd forward with some troops and wagons, to cut a road through the forest to Loyal Hanna. After much discussion, General Forbes adopted this latter route, although it required the opening of more than one hundred miles of new road through the wilderness between Bedford and Fort Duquesne. A lion heart and courage unparalleled must have been his, who in physical weakness and distress, and in the face of this great undertaking, through the wilderness, and moreover, with the enervating memory of former disasters in this same region, proceeded to carry out his plans. (*Olden Time*, Vol. 1: *Captain Jack the Scout*, by Chai.

McKnight.)

No wonder that "Old Forbes," as he was familiarly called, was credited with obstinacy, and was also entitled among the soldiers, "The Head of Iron." The army under General Forbes was composed of twelve hundred Highlanders, three hundred and fifty Regulars, twenty-seven hundred Pennsylvanians, sixteen hundred Virginians, and others from Maryland and North Carolina, and a body of Cherokee Indians; making an army of about six thousand men. Slow and tedious was the journey, described, although without much detail, in letters of the time.

On October 14th the main army advanced from Raystown towards Loyal Hanna, arriving about November 1st. On November 18th further advance was made, covering fifty miles from Loyal Hanna in five days, stopping at New Camp, twenty-two miles west of Loyal Hanna, on November 18th, and arriving on November 24th, much discouraged and fatigued, at a point on Turtle Creek, about twelve miles from Fort Duquesne, with the intention, as it seems, of entering into winter quarters, and awaiting supplies from the North or from the East. At least, warned by Braddock's fate, Forbes would not recklessly advance. But news came from Indian scouts that the French were evidently making preparations to depart, and heavy smoke in the direction of the fort, and a dull heavy explosion told of extensive conflagration and destruction.

So, on the morning of November 25, 1758, General Forbes declaring that he would sleep in the fort that night, the army hastily advanced from their encampment, the Provincials in front followed by the Highlanders, and marched with all speed to the point where the junction of the Monongahela and Allegheny had furnished for so long a time an unquestionable vantage in the control of the Ohio. During this day, which was chilly and disagreeable, and, indeed, during much of the march, General Forbes' disease had increased so rapidly that he had to be carried on a litter. This the Indians had remarked and derided. And it is written that:

> To counteract unfavourable impression it was given out by the English that the British chief had a temper so impetuous and irascible and combative, that it was not thought safe to trust him at large even among his own people, but that the practice was to *let him out on the eve of battle.*

As the army approached the fort at about six in the evening, they came to a number of stakes on either side of the Indian pathway, on each of which hung the head and kilt of a Highlander, killed or taken prisoner at Major Grant's defeat on September 14th, a few weeks before. We cannot be surprised that this aroused to fury the "petticoat warriors," as they were sneeringly dubbed by their antagonists; and with loud and bitter cries and with swords drawn, they rushed, like mad boars engaged in battle, past the Provincials, who led the column, eager to wreak their vengeance upon the French. Imagine their disappointment, when coming within full view of Fort Duquesne, they found it desolate, ruined and abandoned—everything burned or blown up, fortifications, ovens, houses, magazines, goods of every sort. The French troops had escaped on rafts and boats down the Ohio River.

There was no blow struck; there were no lives lost in mortal combat; and yet the capture of Fort Duquesne was a most notable event in the history of our country, worthy of commemoration through all the future years.

Of this event Mr. Bancroft says:

Armstrong's own hand raised the British flag on the ruined bastions of the fortress, as the banner of England floated over the waters, the place at the suggestion of Forbes, was with one voice called Pittsburgh. America raised to Pitt's name statues that have been wrongfully broken, (see appendix C), and granite piles of which not one stone remains upon another; but long as the Monongahela and the Allegheny shall flow to form the Ohio, long as the English tongue shall be the language of freedom in the boundless valley which their waters traverse, his name shall stand inscribed on the gateway of the West.

That very night as it would seem, November 25th, Colonel Bouquet, who, as Parkman says, "managed his pen as well as he wielded his arms," wrote to a fair correspondent in Philadelphia, (Miss Anne Willing) as follows:

I have the satisfaction to give you the agreeable news of the conquest of this terrible Fort. The French, seized with a panic at our approach, have destroyed themselves that nest of Pirates which has so long harboured the murderers and destructors of our poor people. They have burned and destroyed to the ground their fortifications, houses, magazines, and left us no other cover than the heavens, a very cold one for an army without tents and equipages. We bear all this hardship with alacrity by the consideration of the immense advantage of this important acquisition. The glory of our success must after God be allowed to our general who from the beginning took those wise measures, which deprived the French of their chief strength, and by the treaty of Easton kept such a number of Indians idle during the whole campaign, and procured a peace with those inveterate enemies, more necessary and beneficial to the safety and welfare of the Provinces than the driving the French from the Ohio. His prudence in all his measures in the numberless difficulties he had to surmount, deserves the highest praise. I hope that glorious advantage will be improved and this conquest properly supported by speedy and vigorous measures of the Provinces concerned. I wish sincerely that for their interest and happiness they may agree on that point. (*Pennsylvania Magazine*.Vol. III. No. 2.)

The twenty-sixth was observed as a day of public thanksgiving for success, and Mr. Beatty, the chaplain, was appointed to preach a thanksgiving sermon. (Haslet. *Olden Time*.Vol. I.) The connection between the seaside and the land beyond the mountains was established forever. A vast territory was secured. The civilization of liberty, commerce and religion was henceforth to maintain undisputed possession of the Ohio.

The reasons for the evacuation of Fort Duquesne, as given in a letter of George Washington, are three: the weakness of the French in the failure to receive reinforcements; the want of provisions, which had likewise failed to reach them; and the defection of the Indians, who had been treated well by Forbes and others earlier in the year, and who had begun to perceive a sort of intuition where victory would eventually lie. And he sums up some of the results by saying:

This fortunate and indeed unexpected success of our arms will be attended with happy effects; the Delawares are suing for peace, and I doubt not that other tribes on the Ohio will follow their example. A trade free, open and on equitable terms, is what they seem much to desire, and I do not know so effectual a way of riveting them to our interests as by sending out goods immediately to this place for this purpose. It would, at the same time, be a means of supplying the garrison with such necessaries as may be wanted. And I think that other colonies, which are as greatly interested in the support of this place as Virginia, should neglect no means in their power to establish and maintain a strong garrison here. Our business without this precaution, will be but half finished, while on the other hand, we shall attain a firm and lasting peace with the Indians, if this end is once accomplished. General Forbes is very assiduous in getting these matters settled upon a solid basis and has great merit for the happy issue to which he has brought our affairs, infirm and worn as he is. (*Olden Time*.Vol. I.)

Colonel Bouquet wrote:

After God, the success of this expedition is entirely due to the General, who by bringing about the treaty with the Indians at Easton, has struck the blow which has knocked the French on the head. In temporizing wisely to expect the effects of that treaty, in securing all his posts and giving nothing to chance, and not yielding to the urgent instances for taking Braddock's Road, which would have been our destruction—in all of these measures, I say, he has shown the greatest prudence, firmness and ability. Nobody is better informed of the numberless difficulties he had to surmount than I am, who had an opportunity to see every step that was taken from the beginning, and every obstruction that was thrown in the way. I wish the nation may be as sensible of his services as he really deserves and give him the only reward that can flatter him, the pleasure of seeing them pleased and satisfied. (*Olden Time.* Vol. I.)

To go even further back than General Forbes himself, we may well, in this city and presence, give praise where praise is due, and quote from Sargent's *Braddock's Expedition*, (also republished by Leonaur as *Braddock's Campaign, 1755*), these appreciative words:

It must not be forgotten that it was to the presence and kind words of the Quakers who first set on foot these negotiations, that the merit of prevailing upon the Indians to leave unopposed General Forbes' route to Fort Duquesne, and the consequent fall of that important post, are justly due.

Concerning General Forbes, Parkman writes:

If his achievement was not brilliant, its solid value was above price. It opened the great West to English enterprise; took from

France half her savage allies and relieved the western borders from the scourge of Indian war. From southern New York to North Carolina the frontier population had cause to bless the memory of this steadfast and all-enduring soldier. So, ended the campaign of 1758. The centre of the French had held its own triumphantly at Ticonderoga, but their left had been forced back by the capture of Louisbourg, and their right by that of Fort Duquesne, while their entire right wing had been well-nigh cut off by the destruction of Fort Frontignac. The outlook was dark; their own Indians were turning against them. (*Musket & Tomahawk*).

William Pitt himself wrote under date of January 23, 1759, as follows:

I am now to acquaint you that the king has been pleased immediately upon receiving the news of the success of his arms on the River Ohio, to direct the commander-in-chief of His Majesty's forces in North Carolina, and General Forbes, to lose no time in concerting the properest and speediest means for completely restoring, if possible, the ruined Fort Duquesne to a respectable and defensible state, or for erecting another in the room of it, of sufficient strength and every way adequate to the great importance of the several objects of maintaining His Majesty's subjects in the undisputed possession of the Ohio, of effectually cutting off all trade and communication this way between Canada and the West and Southwest Indians, of protecting the British Colonists from the incursions to which they have been exposed since the French built the above fort, and thereby made themselves masters of the navigation of the Ohio. (*Olden Time*, Vol. I.)

Thus, did General Forbes end forever the attempt of the French to press downward from Canada into the Mississippi Valley; and the possession of the great West by the Anglo-Saxon race was forever assured.

To return to our narrative, so small was the stock of provisions remaining for the maintenance of the soldiers that they could not think of pursuing the French. A few days were spent in treating with the Indians, and then the return journey began. General Forbes, emaciated and worn, was carried on his litter to Philadelphia, where he arrived January 17, 1759. Guns were fired and bells were rung in token of the people's admiration of a brave and victorious soldier. But sorely afflicted by a complication of disorders, he did not long survive to enjoy the gratitude of his countrymen. On the 15th of March, 1759, the *Philadelphia Gazette* has notice of his death as follows:

> On Sunday last, the eleventh, died of tedious illness, John Forbes, Esq., in the forty-ninth year of his age, son to —— Forbes, Esq., of Pittencrief, in the Shire of Fife in Scotland; Brigadier General, Colonel of 17th. Regiment of Foot, Commander of H. M. troops in the Southern Provinces of America; a gentleman well known and esteemed and most sincerely and universally regretted. In his younger days he was bred to the profession of Physics, but early ambitious of the military character, he purchased into the Regiment of Scot's Grey Dragoons, where by repeated purchases and faithful services he arrived to the rank of Lieutenant Colonel.
>
> His superior abilities soon recommended him to the protection of General Campbell, the Earl of Stair, the Duke of Bedford, Lord Ligonier, and other distinguished characters in the army, with some of them as an Aid, with the rest in the familiarity of a family man. During the last war he had the honour to be employed in the post of Quartermaster General in the Army, under His Royal Highness, the Duke, which he discharged with accuracy, dignity and dispatch. His services in America are well-known. By a steady pursuit of well-concerted measures, in defiance of disease and numberless obstructions he brought to a happy issue a most extraordinary campaign and made a willing sacrifice of his own life to what he valued more, the interests of his King and his Country.
>
> As a man he was just and without prejudice; brave without ostentation; uncommonly warm in his friendships and incapable of flattery, acquainted with the world and mankind, he was well-bred, but absolutely impatient of formality and affectation. As an officer he was quick to discern useful men and useful measures; generally seeing both at first view according to their real qualities; steady in his measures and open to information and counsel; in common he had dignity without superciliousness, and though perfectly master of the forms never hesitated to drop them when the spirit and more essential part of the service required it.

A few hours before his death, he avouched with emphasis, that he died contented, as he had got possession of Fort Duquesne, and made the accursed French rascals run away.

Bishop White is quoted as saying that he remembered as a boy going to gaze at the body of General Forbes as it lay in solemn state in the city of Philadelphia. On the 14th of March, 1759, attended by military honours, as befitted his rank and distinguished services, he was laid to rest in the chancel of Christ Church, where we are assembled today, (1898). We have come this morning, on this one hundred and fortieth anniversary of the fall of Fort Duquesne, to continue those honours, with perhaps even better appreciation of the man and his worth and services than could have been possible by his contemporaries. We hail him as the leader by whom God established for this country and for our Anglo-Saxon race so very much of good which only later years have made manifest.

We revere his name as forever associated by God's providence with the onward march of liberty and civilization in this western land. We honour him for his loyalty to his flag, for his endurance of pain and hardship, for his bravery in the face of obstacles natural, barbarous and inimical, all of which qualities we are the better able to understand and commend because of what our own eyes have seen and all the American people have learned anew to value, in the conduct of our own soldiers and sailors during the exciting months of our recent war with Spain. All honour to those who, whether in the days gone by, or in our own present experience have shown us how true are the familiar words, "*Dulce et decorum est pro patria mori.*"

Well may we sing in the words of that fine hymn written by your honoured chaplain for this occasion:

When the souls of men were tried
In old time or latest day,
They who for our land have died—
Count them not of common clay.
God of battles, in Thy keeping
Guard the weary soldier sleeping.

God of battles, whom we trust,
Keep our nation from its night;
And may voices from the dust
Make us staunch to toil for right,
God of battles, in Thy keeping

Guard the weary soldier sleeping.

I do not know why we should not, in our repeated thanksgivings for the "many mercies vouchsafed this nation and people," have in memory the deliverances and conquests of the olden time. I do not know why we should not, in our grateful acknowledgments of victories recently gained, include also those of the Civil War, and of the Revolutionary War, and of all the struggles in the history of our country, back to the perilous days at the beginning on which such wondrous issues hung.

APPENDIX A: COLONEL BOUQUET.

Dumas says:

Respected by the soldiers, in credit with all those who had a share in the internal government of the Provinces, universally esteemed and loved, he had but to ask and he obtained all that it was possible to grant, because it was believed that he asked nothing but what was necessary and proper, and that all would be faithfully employed for the services of the King and Provinces. (*Pennsylvania Journal*, October 24, 1765, obituary notice.)

This gentleman had served His Majesty all the last war with great distinction. He was promoted from merit, not only unenvied but with the approbation of all who knew him. His superior judgment and knowledge of military matters, his experience and abilities, known humanity and remarkable politeness, and constant attention to the civil rights of His Majesty's subjects, rendered him an honour to his country and a loss to mankind.

Bouquet remained in Pennsylvania until 1763. Fought the Indians at Bushy Run, twenty miles from Fort Pitt.

In 1764 he advanced through Ohio to forks of River Muskingum, one hundred and fifty miles west of Pittsburgh, and made peace with the Indians.

On March 3. 1765, he was naturalised by the Supreme Court of Pennsylvania. Promoted Brigadier General February, 1765. Bouquet expected to be called to England, but he was ordered to Pensacola to take command of the king's forces in Southern Department of America. He arrived at this most unhealthy post on August 23, 1765, the deadliest season of the year. He took the fever and on September 2nd was dead.

Braddock's road is supposed to have been originally what is Nemacolin's trail, the Indian Chief. The Ohio Company opened the road in 1753 as far as Will's Creek, near Fort Cumberland. George Washington repaired it as far as Gist's, in the direction of Connellsville; and in 1755, it was widened and completed to within six miles of Fort Duquesne, by General Braddock. Washington had made a trip by direction of Governor Dinwiddie, of Virginia, starting on October 30, 1753, through the western wilds to the junction of the Monongahela and Allegheny, and down the Ohio to Logstown, the exact location of which no one seems to be able to determine.

Thence he had journeyed to Fort Le Boeuf, now Waterford, and thence back again to Philadelphia, arriving in January, 1754. Another trip he made reaching Connellsville, April 20, 1754, and Great Meadows, May 28th, meeting the French in an engagement June 11th, in which Jumonville was killed, seeking refuge afterwards at Fort Necessity, whence he retired July 4th. Braddock's expedition in the spring of 1755 met with disaster in the engagements of July 5th and 9th, and General Braddock died on July 13.

The arguments for opening a new road were that the safety of the settlers in the western part of Pennsylvania required means of prompt communication with the colonists at the east, a spacious military road to communicate with the quarter whence were to be had supplies and succour, a road also straight and comparatively easy for emigrants. Moreover, Braddock's road had led to defeat, and it seemed as if a new road unconnected with unfortunate memories, would be better for the soldiers. (*Olden Time*. Vol. I.)

What is called "Nemacolin's Path" was a great Indian trail, which led east from the "Forks of the Ohio," through southern Pennsylvania. At the instance of the Ohio Company, Nemacolin, well-known Delaware, who resided at the mouth of Dunlap's Creek Fayette County, "blazed" the forest path from Wills' Creek to the Ohio, which was the original tracing of that great highway now known as the National or Cumberland road. In 1753 it was well-marked and cleared of bushes and fallen timber, so as to make it a good pack-horse road. "Gist's plantation" was located on this road, which afterwards became Braddock's road; but as Judge Veech forcibly contends, that was a misnomer; it should have been called Washington's road, for he made it to Gist's; from Gist's to Turtle Creek, it was Braddock's. (Captain Jack the Scout.)

The *New York Herald* of December 11, 1898, has the following concerning these statues:

Over the shattered and decapitated statue of William Pitt, now in a New York museum, Professor Dicey, of Oxford University, proposes that the ties between this country and England be more closely bound. The eminent professor of English law, in the course of a lecture delivered before the students of Columbia University, paid a tribute to William Pitt, afterward Earl of Chatham. He eulogised him as England's greatest Prime Minister, and then reminded his audience of the debt which the United States owed to the great Premier. William Pitt vigorously championed the cause of the colonists in their contention that taxation without representation was unjust, and practically caused the repeal of the Stamp Act, which was especially obnoxious to our forebears.

History tells that upon this action, in 1766, bells were rung and there was great rejoicing. In the colonies of New York and South Carolina it was proposed to erect statues to the great Premier. Large popular subscriptions were made, and the order for the statues was given to one Whilton, a British sculptor. The two statues, one a replica of the other, were brought to this country in 1769. The New York statue was erected at the northeast corner of William and Wall Streets in 1770.

Then, six years later, came the American Revolution. The leaden statue of George III., in Bowling Green, was converted into hostile pellets. The British took charge of affairs here in 1776 and remained until 1783, when they provided New York with a day for feasting and celebration, which has always been religiously observed.

While they were here soldiers removed the head of the statue of William Pitt. Professor Dicey says he is certain that Hessians did it. The head was seen several years afterward in the Blue Bell Tavern, up Kingsbridge way, where it looked down serenely upon rosy faced persons who drank ale from pewter mugs and smoked long clay pipes.

Members of the New York Historical Society have been hunting for that head in the last quarter of a century, for it disappeared from the Blue Bell Tavern.

Professor Dicey proposes that the American people get another head for their statue of William Pitt, and also give him arms for his sides.

The old statue is of marble and of heroic size. The head and neck are entirely missing. The figure is draped, leaning against part of a tree trunk. It is in the possession of the New York Historical Society.

To effect the restoration it would be necessary to send the artist to Charleston, S. C, where the duplicate is intact, with the exception of the left arm. The English besieged Charleston in 1780, and William Pitt's statue had a narrow escape. The head of the old statue in the South is perfect. There are old prints in existence which would show the trend of that missing arm.

Charleston removed her Pitt statue to one of her parks a few years ago.

Commissary Wilson's Orderly Book
Jeffrey Amherst

PREFACE

The manuscript of *Amherst's Expedition against Ticonderoga and Crown Point* was found among the papers of my late grandfather, Frederic de Peyster, Esq., who was in the possession of a large amount of very valuable original matter connected with the history of the city and province of New York. Deeming it of great importance that our Colonial History should be fully made known to the world, as the province of New York was so long the principal theatre of the contests between the mother country and France for the possession of North America, this volume has been printed at the expense of the publisher and myself in pursuance of an arrangement made with the former by me.

J. Watts De Peyster.

Rosehill,
Trivoli, Dutchess Co., S. N.Y.,
29th Oct., 1857.

INTRODUCTION.

As early as 1753 preparations began to be made between Great Britain and France for a struggle to gain a predominance in North America. The defeat of Major Washington by the French and Indians at Little Meadows, of the British under Braddock at the Monongahela, of the French under Baron Dieskau at Fort George by the Provincials, the capture of Oswego by the French under Montcalm, the defeat of Abercrombie by the French at Ticonderoga, the capture of Louisburgh by Amherst, were some of the principal events of the campaigns of the four years preceding the one undertaken by Major-General Amherst in 1759.

★★★★★★

Jeffrey Amherst was descended from an ancient Kentish family, and born at Riverhead in England, 29th January, 1717. He early devoted himself to the profession of arms, receiving an ensign's commission when only fourteen years of age. At the age of twenty-five he acted as *aide-de-camp* to Lord Ligonier, in the Battles of Dettingen and Fontenoy, and afterwards served in the staff of the Duke of Cumberland, in those of Laffeld and Hastenbeck, (*Enc. Americana.*) From that date his promotion was very rapid. In 1756 we find him in command of a regiment of foot; and in 1758 he received orders to return to England, being appointed to the American Service, with the rank of major-general. He sailed from Portsmouth on the 16th of March, having the command of the troops destined for the siege of Louisbourg, on the 26th of July following he captured that place, and without farther difficulty took entire possession of Cape Breton.

After this event he succeeded Abercrombie in the command of the army in North America, (*Allen.*) The capture of Fort Du Quesne, Niagara, Ticonderoga and Crown Point in due time followed. General Amherst, now feeing that the whole continent of North America was reduced in subjection to Great Britain, returned to New York, and was received with all the respect due to his public services. The thanks of the House of Commons had already been transmitted to him; and among other honourable Testimonies of Approbation, in 1761 he was created a Knight of the Bath, (*Chalmers,*) Although he had been appointed commander-in-chief of all the forces in America, and Governor-General of the British Provinces, he resigned his command shortly after the conclusion of peace between Great Britain and France, and returned to London in December, 1763, where honours and favours awaited him.

In 1770 he became Governor of Guernsey and its dependencies, and two years afterwards was sworn of the Privy Council. In 1776 he was advanced to the Dignity of the Peerage, when he took the title of Baron Amherst of Homesdale in the county of Kent; and in 1787 received another patient as Baron Amherst of Montreal, (*Rose.*) From 1772 to 1782 he officiated as Commander-in-Chief of the English forces, serving the latter part of which period he acted as eldest general on the Staff of England.

In 1782 he received the Golden Stick from the king, but on the change of administration, usually called that of Lord North, the Command of the Army and the Lieutenant-Generalship of Ordinance were put into other hands.

In 1793 he was again appointed to the Command of the Army; but in 1795 he was superseded by the Duke of York, then in his 31st year, who had never seen any service. The government upon this occasion, with a view to soothe the feelings of the old general, offered him an earldom, and the rank of field-marshal, both of which he rejected; but in the following year accepted the latter. He died 3rd August, 1797, in the 81st year of his age. Lord Amherst was as a man of a collected and temperate mind, without brilliancy or parade; a strict officer, yet the soldier's friend. He was twice married, but left no issue, and was succeeded in his title and estates by his nephew, the son of the brother whom he had employed in the reduction of Newfoundland.

★★★★★★

Encouraged by the acquisition of Cape Breton and other conquests, the Colonies, on the application made to them through their governors, by Mr. Pitt, prepared vigorously for this campaign; and the vast and bold plan was formed of completing the conquest of Canada during this year. Three expeditions were accordingly planned to effect this object; one under General Wolfe was to ascend the St. Lawrence and reduce Quebec; another under General Prideaux was to proceed against Niagara; and a third under General Amherst was to march against Ticonderoga and Crown Point; and having accomplished their conquest, to rendezvous at Montreal.

Having finished the preparations for the expeditions against Quebec and Niagara, General Amherst transferred his headquarters from New York to Albany, where his troops were assembled by the last of May. Yet notwithstanding the continued exertions of the general, the summer was far advanced before he could cross Lake George, and he did not reach Ticonderoga until the 22nd of July, although he experienced no opposition of any consequence, from the enemy, because their forces were too small to descend that post, much less to attempt ulterior operations. The forces under the immediate command of this general exceeded twelve thousand men, the greater part of which were Provincials, furnished by the Colonies of New York, and New England.

On the appearance of these forces before the lines at Ticonderoga, the enemy, the very next day, abandoned the fort. This step they were compelled to take, in consequence of the feebleness of the garrison, occasioned by the withdrawal of the greater part of the troops to Canada, for the purpose of repelling the invasion expected on the side of Quebec. The plan of the campaign on the part of the French seems to have been to delay the invading army as much as possible, by the appearance of defence, but not to hazard any considerable diminution of their strength, by defending places until they should be so completely inverted, as to render the retreat of the garrison impracticable.

The hope seems to have been entertained, on their part, not without reason, that by retreating from post to post, and making a show in their enfeebled state, of intending to defend each, the advance of the Anglo-American Army might be retarded until the season for action on the lakes should pass away, while their force would gradually be so concentrated as to enable them to maintain some point which would arrest the progress of the army under Amherst, down the St. Lawrence to Quebec. (*Macauley, Hist. N. Y.*) In pursuance of this plan, on the 26th July, 1759, the day after the reduction of Niagara, Ticonderoga surrendered, and thus paved the way for the subjection of Canada. (*Chalmers.*) The garrison which evacuated Ticonderoga retired to Crown Point, and General Amherst, having taken possession of this post, which covered the frontiers of New York on this side, ordered the works to be repaired, and allotted a strong garrison for its defence.

The acquisition, however, was not obtained without some loss; among others, Colonel Townshend was killed by a cannon shot, while reconnoitring the works. While Amherst was employed in the repairs of Ticonderoga, he received intelligence about the first of August, that the enemy had abandoned Crown Point. He immediately detached a body of troops to take possession of the place, and on the 4th of the same month, proceeded with the main army, and landed and encamped at the same place. Here he learned that the enemy had retired to the Isle aux Noix, at the other end of Lake Champlain, five leagues south of St. Johns; and that their force, encamped at that place, under the command of M. de Burlemaque, amounted to three thousand five hundred effective men, and that the lake was occupied by four vessels, mounted with cannon, and manned with piquets of different regiments, under the command and direction of M. le Bras, a captain of the French Navy, assisted by M. de Rigal, and other sea officers.

In consequence of this information, General Amherst caused several vessels of war to be constructed, under the superintendence of Captain Loring, in order that he might obtain the command of the lake. These being completed and equipped, the general embarked with the whole army in *batteaux*, on the eleventh of October, and proceeded down the lake some distance, but owing to the tempests which ensued, was obliged to return again to Crown Point, and give over the design of penetrating into Canada for the present. In the meantime, he put his army into winter quarters, and strengthened the works at Crown Point. He also caused a road to be opened from Ticonderoga to Massachusetts and New Hampshire, to the end that communications might be had with those provinces by more direct routes, than by the way of the Hudson and Albany. Captain Loring however, went down the lake and fell in with the French naval Force, which he defeated and destroyed, whereby the command of its waters came into the hands of the invaders. (*Macauley's Hist. N.Y, iii*, 42.)

Thus, terminated the memorable campaign of 1759, alike creditable to the military abilities of General Amherst, and advantageous to the British Colonies, which had been so long harassed by the incursions of the French and Indians of Canada. It will be observed that to the provincial troops employed in this expedition is to be attributed a greater share of renown than is usually awarded to them. By their zeal, discipline and native energy, they contributed in no small degree to the success of the campaign. Among their officers will be found not a few who were trained here for the lasting same which they acquired in the War of the Revolution. The notes which accompany the text, gathered from every available source, although they serve to rescue their memory, leave us to regret that of some of them so little should be known.

Commissary Wilson's Orderly Book

Albany, 22nd May, 1759. Parole, Philadelphia.

Kate Forbes and the Inniskilling Regiments to march tomorrow at 5 o'clock; the Inniskilling Regiments to give 300 men to push up the *batteaux* which they are to load this evening; two companies of the Royall Highland Regimentare also to receive *batteaux* and load them with provision and baggage; the baggage of the whole to go by water, the Inniskilling taking care of the hospitall baggage and that of the officers that are going to Fort Edward. Kate Forbes Regiment will cross the river at their different quarters and joyn the Inniskilling Regiment on their march; ten waggons will be allowed to carry the camp equipage of Predeaux Regiment which are to march under the escort of the two regiments; Collo. Haviland, to command the whole.

★★★★★★

William Haviland was appointed Lieutenant-Colonel of the 27th, or Inniskilling Foot, on the 16th Dec, 1752, which regiment failed from New York with the expedition under Lord Loudoun, June 20, and arrived at Halifax 1st July, 1757, whence it was afterwards sent to the River St. John, but was countermanded on the way, and ordered to New York, in consequence of the siege of Fort William Henry, on Lake George. In 1758 it formed part of the army sent under General Abercrombie against Ticonderoga, and in 1759 accompanied General Amherst up Lakes George and Champlain, in which expedition Colonel Haviland commanded the van, or front column, of the army, composed of the Rangers, Light-Infantry and Grenadiers. On the evacuation of Ticonderoga by the French, he was despatched at the head of these troops in pursuit of the retreating enemy. On the army being divided in 1760, Col. Haviland, now Brigadier-General, was placed in command of the division designed to proceed against Montreal by way of the lakes. This force amounted to 3400 men, and consisted of a part of the 1st Royals, the 17th and 27th Regiments, the Massachusetts Regiments under Colonels Whitcomb and Willard, Colonel Goffe's New Hampshire Regiment, that of Rhode Island under Harris, five Companies of Rangers under Rogers, and a detachment of artillery under Colonel Ord.

He set out from Albany in the Month of June and sailed from Crown Point on the 11th of August; and after successively reducing Isle aux Noix, St. Johns, Fort Therese, and Chambly, crossed over to Longueuil, and entered Montreal with Amherst in September. On the 9th December following, he was appointed Colonel-Commandant of the 4th Battalion of the 60th Royal Americans. In February, 1762, he was Senior Brigadier-General at the reduction of the Island of Martinico; he was appointed Major-General, 10th July, and commanded the 4th Brigade at the siege of Havana, in August following. In 1767, he became Colonel of the 45th; Lieutenant-General the 25th May, 1772; General in the Army, 19th Feb. 1783, and died in September, 1788 (*Army Lists; Beatson's Naval and Mil. Mem.*, III; Knox's *Journal*, I.)

Collo, Haviland to send *batteaux* with the baggage of the officers and hospittal from Fort Miller to Fort Edward, and proper escorts with the waggons to the same place, the whole to carry 4 days provision to the 26th inclusive. A sergeant and 12 men of the Rhode Island Regiment to relieve a party of the Royall Highland Regiment at the Half-Way House on the way to Schenectadie; they are to march tomorrow morning and carry six days provision with them,

Albany, 23rd May, 1759. Parole, Greenwich.

A generall court martiall to set tomorrow at the town house in Albany at 3 o'clock, to try all the prisoners that may be brought before them. Collo. Grant President, Lieut. Collo. Pyfan, Major Ball, Royall Regiment two captains, Royall Highlanders three, Royall Artillery 1, Rhode Island Regt. 3, Massachusetts 1, Lieut. Balfour of the Royall Deputy Judge Advocate.

★★★★★★

Francis Grant, Brother of Sir Ludovick Grant, of Grant, Scotland, after serving in Flanders, became a Major in the 42nd Highlanders. A vacancy occurring in the lieutenant-colonelcy, in December, 1755, the men of the regiment subscribed a sum of money among themselves to purchase the step for him, but it was not required; he had already obtained his promotion (Brown's *Highland Clans*, IV.), and accompanied the regiment to America in 1756, and was present at the bloody Battle of Ticonderoga, July 8, 1758. In the following year he accompanied Amherst in the present expedition, and in 1760 from Oswego to Montreal, in command of the van of the army.

In 1761 he commanded the army sent to the south to chastise the Cherokees (Knox's *Journal*, II.). He served as Brigadier-General, in the expedition against Martinico in 1762, and on the 19th February of that year, became colonel in the army, and was afterwards appointed to the command of the 90th Light Infantry. In August, 1762, he commanded the 4th Brigade at the siege of Havana (Beatson *N. and M. Mem.* III) and went on half pay at the peace of 1763. In November, 1768, he became Colonel of the 63rd; Major-General in 1770; and Lieutenant-General in 1777. He died in the beginning of 1782 (*Army Lists*). Lieut.-Gen. Grant's daughter was married to the Hon. and Rt. Rev. George Murray, fourth Son of the Duke of Athol, and

Bishop of St. Davids (Debrett's *Peerage*).

Henry Balfour became a Lieutenant in the 2nd Battalion of the 1st or Royal Regiment of Foot, 15th March, 1755; Captain 8th October, 1761, and Major 15th July, 1768. He left the regiment in July, 1769 (*Army Lists*).

★★★★★★

The names of the members and dates of their commission, the prisoners names and crimes with the names of the evidences to be given in to the deputy judge advocate this evening at 4 o'clock. The troops when serving in the *Batteaux* Service shall be paid at the following rates for that service. Each capt. shall receive 4 sh. per day, each subaltern 2 sh., every non-commissioned officer and private man 1 sh., the whole New York currency, and the men shall have rum given them, as the service may require and sircumstance will permitt; the commanding officer of any partys ordered on this service is to keep a list of the men, the company they belong to and the days they work, which list he is to certify and give into the major of brigade, who will deliver it to the deputy quartermaster general, that it may be paid. when a regiment or party are going from any camp or quarters to another and that they take provisions with them, it is not to be reckoned as a service to be paid; they are to be paid when sent on purpose for the *Batteaux* Service,

Albany, 24th May, 1759. Parole, Liverpool.

The orders of the fifth of May, releative to deserting, to be read to the Provincial Troops, for which purpose the officers commanding those corps will have their men under arms and read the same to them, and to assure the men that the general is determined not to pardon any one deserter from any of the troops during the campaign, as he is to reward the men to the utmost of his power, when their good behaviour deserves it; 8 sergeants and 18 men of the Royall returned unfit for service to go to Fort Miller, the 2 officers and 46 men of the Royall at the flats to joyn their respective companies; one corporall and 12 men of the Inniskilling that are returned unfit for service are to march tomorrow to Loudon's Ferry where they will apply to the commanding officer for his orders; they will take 2 days provisions along with them.

Albany, 25th May, 1759. Parole, Glasgow

The Rhode Island Regiment to be ready to march on the first Notice; Surgeon McColm of the Royall, to attend the hospitall at Fort

34

Edward, and Mr. Brag, surgeon's mate of the hospittal to do duty with the Royall as surgeon; the Massachusetts troops to furnish 25 men teamsters that are to be sent immediately to Collo. Brodstreet.

★★★★★★

John McColme, was appointed Surgeon of the 2nd Battalion of the Royals, 1st of May, 1744, and continued with the regiment until June, 1767, when his name is dropped from the *Army Lists*.

★★★★★★

Albany, 26th May, 1759. Parole, Guernsey.

The Provinciall Regiments to be very exact when they send any men to the King's Hospittal, that they have proper certificates of their names, regt. and companies, signed by an officer of the companie, specifying the regiment they belong to; as wagons are now much wanted for the service of the troops, all sutlers, merchants, &c., that have passes to follow the army are for the future to make use of only ox teams in the same manner as regt sutlers; orders having been sent to the different posts to stop all wagons; officers are always to pay for horsess they shall press when their duty requires it; those of the regiments are to apply to the major of brigade, the artillery to their own commanding officer, the engineers to the chief engineer, the hospitals to director generall for payment which accompts are to be laid before the comander in chief to allow the same if reasonable; officers not to neglect to give proper certificates to the drivers employed to carry baggage for these troops mentioning the time they have been imployed, complaint having been made of the omission. The general court martial of which Collo. Grant is President to meet again tomorrow at 8 o'clock; baggage and forrage money to be paid to the several regiments immediately; as the Provincials arrive, the commanding officers to apply to Mr, Leak for provisions, that he may be enabled when the whole of each regiment is arrived so to proportion the delivery of provisions that they may all receive it to the same day.

★★★★★★

Robert Leake was born, it is supposed, about the year 1710, at Calder. in Lanarkshire, Scotland. He enlisted in the 1st Troop of Horse Guards in 1741; had his horse shot under him and was severely wounded at the Battle of Dettingen in 1743, after killing a French soldier who was about to seize the colours. He now became an Outpensioner of Chelsea Hospital, and taught school at Campsie in Scotland, but on the breaking out of the Rebellion in 1745, he received a commission as lieutenant of an Independent Company. In February, 1747, he was appointed commissary at Cape Breton and was placed on half-pay in December, 1749, when he returned to England, where he resided until September, 1754, when he was appointed Commissary of provisions to the army under Braddock, and served in America until the peace of 1763, after which he resided in the city of New York. Commissary Leake died on the morning of Tuesday, 28th December, 1773 at his seat in the bowery, and his remains were interred in the family vault in Trinity Churchyard, attended by a great concourse of the inhabitants and the military. John G. Leake, the last of his descendants, died at New York, unmarried, 2nd June, 1827, and to his munificent endowment the Leake and Watts Orphan Asylum in that city owes its existence (Report of the Hon. Charles P. Daly, N.Y. Assembly Doc. 74, for 1844).

★★★★★★

An officer and 25 men of the Royall Highland Regiment with a week's provision to be sent this afternoon to the Widdow McGinness House to protect that settlement; one companie of the Royall Highland Regiment to march tomorrow morning at 5 o'clock; they will take their tents and camp equipage with them,for which a waggon will be allowed on sending to Collo. Bradstreet for it; the officer commanding that company to call upon the generall this night.

★★★★★★

John Bradstreet was born in 1711, and accompanied the expedition against Louisburg in 1745, as lieutenant-colonel in Pepperell's York Provincials, Maine. Of his conduct in the campaign, Gen. Pepperell observes: "No person in the army could possibly have behaved with more zeal, activity and judgment, in the measures taken for the accomplishment of our design, which, added to his particular knowledge in the circumstances of this place, justly entitle him to the esteem and thanks of every well-wisher to the success of the expedition" (1 *Mass. Hist. Coll.*, I). On the 5th of September, 1745, he received a commission of captain in a regular regiment, called Sir William Pepperell's Foot (Parson's *Life of Pepperell*), and as an additional reward for his services, was appointed, on the 16th September, 1746, to the sinecure place of Lieutenant-Governor of St. John, Newfoundland (*London Mag.*, XV; *Gentleman's Mag.*).

Captain Bradstreet remained in garrison at Louisburg with his regiment until 1748, in which year it was disbanded. On the renewal of hostilities in 1755, he was ordered by General Braddock to march with a party of Provincials to Oswego, preliminary to operations against Niagara; and when Shirley succeeded to the command, he made Bradstreet his adjutant-general (1 *Mass. Hist. Coll.*, VII). In the following year he was again ordered to conduct supplies to Oswego. On his return, after having successfully performed that duty, he was attacked on the 3rd July, nine miles south of that place, by a strong party of the enemy, which he defeated (*N.Y. Doc. Hist.*, 8vo, I, 482-487). In March, 1757, he was appointed to a company in the 60th or Royal Americans and became lieutenant-colonel in the Regular Army on the 27th December following, at which time he was deputy quartermaster-general (*Army List*).

He served in 1758, under Abercrombie, in the unsuccessful attack against Ticonderoga, immediately after which he was permitted to march at the head of 3000 Provincials, against Fort Frontenac, which he reduced on the 27th August (Dunlap's *History New York*, I; Knox's *Campaigns*, I). The details of this achievement were published the following year under this title: *An Impartial Account of Lieutenant-Colonel Bradstreet's Expedition to Fort Frontenac; to which are added a few Reflections on the Conduct of that Enterprise, and the Advantages resulting from its Success: by a Volunteer in the Expedition; London*, 8vo. In 1759 he accompanied Gen. Amherst as quartermaster-general in the expedition against Ticonderoga and Crown Point and had his headquarters the following year at Oswego, where the necessaries were provided to facilitate the descent of the army to Montreal; but ill health prevented him accompanying the troops.

In February, 1762, he was promoted to be colonel, and continued quartermaster-general for a few years after (*Army Lists*). In 1764 he commanded an expedition against the Western Indians and negotiated a peace with these tribes at Detroit on the 7th September of that year, after which he returned to the east (Parkman's *Pontiac*). On the 25th May, 1772, he was advanced to the rank of major-general; and after a life of great activity, and after rendering essential service to his country, died at New York, 25th September (Allen incorrectly says October 21), 1774. The civil and military officers, and the 47th Regiment attended his remains to Trinity Church (Dunlap's *New*

York, II, cclii). General Bradstreet's will bears date 23rd September, 1774, and is recorded in the surrogate's office, New York. It is, says Mr. E. F. De Lancey, a model of brevity and clearness and was drawn by the famous William Smith. His surviving children were Agatha Butler and Martha Bradstreet. Further particulars of the family are to be found in Wendell's *Sup. Court Rep.* XII.

★★★★★★

Albany, 27th May. Parole, Namure.

Albany, 28th May, 1759. Parole, Maestricht.

The following detachment to be made from the Provincial Troops, they are to be proper men for the *Batteaux* Service; Connecticut 2 capts., 7 subs., 10 serjts., 240 rank and file; Massachusetts 1 capt., 4 Subs., 5 serjts., 120; New Jerseys 1 capt., 3 subs., 4 serjts., 104; Rhode Island 1 capt., 1 sub., 2 serjts., 54. This detachment to parade tomorrow at 5 o'clock on the road on the right of the Rhode Island Regiment and wait till Brigade Major Moniepenny sees them march off; they are to take their arms, a proportion of necessaries and as many days provision as they have received with them; three wagons will be allowed for the Connecticut troops, 2 for the Massachusetts, 2 for the Jerseys and one for the Rhode Island, for carrying their tents, on sending to Lieut. Coventry; this detachment is to remaine out perhaps for some months, and the officers and men when employed as *batteaux* men will be paid as per orders 23rd May; this detachment to march tomorrow to Schenecktady; an officer of each corps will go forward when the detachment marches and apply to Capt. McClean, who has orders to mark out their incampment.

★★★★★★

Alexander Moneypenny was appointed a captain on 29th Aug., 1756, and on the 22nd Feb., 1757, joined the 55th Foot, and a few days after sailed from Cork for America, in the expedition under Lord Loudoun. In 1758, he served in the unfortunate campaign against Ticonderoga, and on 5th May, 1759, was appointed one of the brigade majors in the army now on the march against Crown Point; and in 1760 accompanied Amherst from Oswego to Montreal (Knox's *Journal*, I; II.). In September, 1760, he joined the 22nd Foot as major, and in 1761 accompanied the expedition against the Southern Indians (*Ibid*, II), after which he returned to Ireland, and was appointed Lieutenant-

Colonel of the 56th Sept. 1, 1762. His regiment was ordered to Gibraltar in 1769, where it remained in garrison until 1776, in September of which year Lieut.-Colonel Moneypenny died, or resigned his commission (*Army Lists*).

George Coventry entered the army as an ensign of the 55th Foot, on Christmas day, 1755, and accompanied the regiment through the campaign of 1757, and after the defeat of the army before Ticonderoga in 1758, was promoted to a lieutenancy (*Army Lists*). On 5th May, 1759, he was appointed Assistant Deputy Quartermaster-General to Amherst's Army (*Knox*, I,). His name is not found in the *Army List* of 1765.

Allan Maclean, of Torlish, Scotland, was, in 1747, Lieutenant in the Scotch Brigade, which also went by the Name of "the Dutch Brigade," from the circumstance of its being at the time in the pay of the states-general. In cutting his way through the French lines at the famous siege of Bergen-op-Zoom, Lieutenant Maclean was taken prisoner, and immediately admitted to parole by General Lowendahl, with this complimentary address: "Had all conducted themselves as you and your brave corps have done, I should not now be master of Bergen-op-Zoom." Having left the Dutch Service, he obtained a company in the 62nd, or First Highland Battalion, on its organisation in 1757. With this regiment, whose number was afterwards changed to the 77th, he came to America, and served under Forbes, at the taking of Fort du Quesne, in 1758, and in the following year was with Amherst. He raised the 114th Highland Regiment in 1759, of which he was appointed major commanding, but it was reduced in 1763, when Major Maclean went on half pay.

On 25th May, 1771, he became lieut. colonel in the army, but was not again called into active service until 1775, when he was sent to embody a corps of Loyalists in America, to support the royal cause. With his warrant and some followers, Colonel Maclean came to New York in the Spring of 1775; next visited Boston, where his scheme got wind; then hastened back to New York, repaired to Col. Guy Johnson on the Mohawk River, and thence proceeded to Oswego, and so to Canada, where he collected, in the course of the summer, a body of men, chiefly Scotch refugees and disbanded soldiers, formerly belonging to the 42nd, 77th, and 78th Highlanders, under the title of the Royal Highland Emigrants. On the approach of the American Army by Lake Champlain, Colonel Maclean was ordered to St. Johns with a party of militia, but got only as far as St. Denis, when he was deserted by his men. Quebec being next threatened by the American Army under Arnold, Colonel Maclean made the best of his way to that city, which he entered on the 12th November, 1775, just in time to prevent the citizens surrendering the place to the Americans.

His conduct during the siege is mentioned in the handsomest terms. But after all his zeal, his corps was not yet recognised, though he had at the outset been promised establishment and rank for it. He therefore returned to England, where he arrived on the 1st September, 1776, to seek justice for himself and men. They were not received until the close of 1778, when the regiment, which consisted of two battalions, one in Canada and one in Nova Scotia, was numbered the 84th. In January, 1780, he was appointed colonel in the army. The Royal Highland Emigrants were disbanded in 1783, and Colonel Maclean died in 1784. (*Army Lists*; Brown's *Highland Clans*, IV; Smith's *Canada*, II; *American Archives*, I.)

★★★★★★

The commanding officers will report to the Commissary of provisions at Schenectadie to what time they are provided and will afterward receive their provisions from the store there. The Connecticut troops will remaine at Schenectadie and the commanding officers of each corps will receive particular orders when they are to march from thence. David Roger, corporal in the Rhode Island Regiment, tryed by a general court martial, is sentenced to suffer death; Samuel Harres of said regiment is also to suffer death; Peter McMain, soldier in Collo. Montgomery's for mutiny is to suffer death. The troops to be out tomorrow at five o'clock to see the execution, and a platoon of the Rhode Island Regiment to be drawn up in the front of that regiment to be loaded with ball for the execution; David Rogers and Samuel Harres to be brought to the right of the line tomorrow at 6 o'clock and in the right of the centre where the execution is to be; a chapline to attend; Brigadier General Gage to command the whole.

Albany, 29th May, 1759. Parole Amsterdam.

All the Provincial troops to be drawn up without arms in the front of their encampments at one o'clock; any soldier that is found out of camp after retreat beating will be severly punished; a detachment of 250 to take *batteaux* this night at 6 o'clock and load them with provisions and set off earlie tomorrow for Halfmoon, where they will deliver them to the commanding officer.

Albany, 30th May, 1759. Parole Albany.

The Rhode Island Regiment to march tomorrow for Fort Edward; they will apply to Collo. Bradstreet for *batteaux*; they will take 20 *batteaux* with provision which they are to load this evening; the regiment to be compleated with 6 days provision.

Albany, 31st May, 1759. Parole, Sommersett.

The Royall Highland Regiment to march tomorrow morning at 5 o'clock to Halfmoon, where they will take the artillery under their charge and escort the same to Fort Edward; the Massachusetts troops are to take 80 *batteaux* this afternoon at 3 and load them with provisions, reserving 6 for their tents and baggage and at 5 tomorrow will proceed to Fort Edward, they are to take 9 days provisions with them; Major Ord to put the stores and artillery in the scows this evening and are to proceed tomorrow to Halfmoon to be escorted to Fort Edward; the regiments of Lyman, Schuyler and Fitch to be readie march on the first Notice; Liman and Fitch to appoint proper Officers to remaine here, to bring up those men who are left behind of those regiments.

GENERAL ORDERS.

Fort Edward, 6th June, 1759. Parole, Gaudalope.

Lieut. Colo. Robison will mark out the camp tomorrow morning at 5 o'clock, that the regiments may take up their ground as they arrive; the regiments are to encamp, the first brigade the Royall on ye right, the Innilkilling on the left and Predeaux in the centre, second Brigade Forbess on the left, Royall Highlanders on the right, Montgomerys in ye center; the grenediers and light infantry form two battalions apart and will be posted from right to left, according to seniority of regiments; a camp will be marked for these corps and their companys will march to their camp as they arrive.

The Provencials are to be encampd Massachusetts on the left, New Jerseys on the right, that is on the left of Forbess, New Hampshire on the right of the Massachusetts, Connecticuts on the left of the Jerseys, Rhode Islanders on the left of the Connecticuts; this is the order of battle for the troops, they may be altered in their camp according to the sittuation of the ground; the houses of office to made in the front, as the deputy quartermaster general will direct; all beatings to be taken from the regiment on the right; the picquit to turn out at retreat beating, their arms to be examined and the men of the picquits to lie in the front tents, that they may be ready to turn out at anny time at a moment's notice. A serj. and 16 men of ye Royal Highlanders to take the general's guard.

GENERAL ORDERS.

Fort Edward, 7th June, 1759. Parole, Predeaux.

The regiments are not to change their encampment untill the ground be quite dry. The regiments upon their arrival here are all to give in a return unto what time they have received their provisions, that the perticular time for their delivery to each corps may be hereafter regulated, it having been reported by the commissarys that there has been a waste; and as the dailie allowance for each man is fully sufficient, if any have drawn for or expended more then the allowance, they must make it good in having the overpluss deducted in the allowance they are hereafter to receive. The regiments are to take for their effectives only, the commanding officers are to certifie the numbers of their respective companys, on the issuing of the provisions, and the officers commanding the regiment to examine and be answerable that ye whole is just. Spruce beer will soon be brewed for the army, it is hoped sufficient for the whole, and will cost the men but a very moderate price.

GENERAL ORDERS.

Fort Edward, 8th June, 1759. Parole, Falmouth.

Field officer for the picquit this night, Lieut. Colo. Saltenstall.

★★★★★★

Richard Saltonstall was the eldest son of Judge Richard S. of Haverhill, Massachusetts. He was born April 5 1732 and graduated with distinction at Harvard College in 1751. He was commissioned. Colonel of the Haverhill Regiment in 1754 and served in the Campaign of 1756 and 1757 against Crown Point. He was at Fort William Henry, when that place capitulated August 9, 1758, and afterwards escaped from the Indians and reached Fort Edward nearly exhausted. He next made the campaign under Amherst in 1759 and commanded the regiment from 1760 to the close of the War. On his return home he was appointed Sheriff of the County of Essex, and held that office until the autumn of 1774, when, being opposed to forcible resistance, he was obliged to take refuge in Boston and sailed for England in 1775. He refused a commission in the British Army but was allowed a pension. He was proscribed by the Law of 1778 and died in England. A monument is erected to his memory in Kensington with the following inscription:

Near this Place are interred the remains of Richard Saltonstall, Esq., who died October 1, 1785, aged fifty-two. He was an American Loyalist from Haverhill in the Massachusetts, where he was descended from a first family, both for the principal share it had in the early erecting as well as in rank and authority in governing that province. And wherein he himself sustained, with unshaken loyalty and universal applause, various important trusts and commands under the crown, both civil and military, from his youth till its revolt; and throughout life maintained such an amiable private character, as engaged him the esteem and regard of many friends.

As a memorial of his merits this stone is erected. (Ward's *Journal* and *Letters of Curwen*; 3 Mass. *Hist. Coll.*, IX).

★★★★★★

For tomorrow night, Lieut. Colo. Ingersall. The field officer will goe his rounde as useual, and report to the deputy adjt. general, before orderly time. One subaltern and 30 men for the general's guard. No man to goe beyond the centinals in the line of blockhouses, upon any account whatever, except when sent out with a covering party. One serjeant and 12 men to mount guard at each of ye provision shades; one subaltern and 30 men as a guard to the *batteaux*. The regiments to change their encampment this day at 12 o'clock.

GENERAL ORDERS.

Fort Edward, 9th June, 1759. Parole, Plymouth.

Field officers for the picquit this day, Lieut. Colo. Ingersall; for tomorrow. Major Graham.

★★★★★★

Gordon Graham of Draines in the Highlands of Scotland, was appointed Ensign in the 43rd Highlanders in May, 1740. He served in Flanders and shared in the defeat at Fontenoy in 1745, after which the regiment returned home. In 1747 he made another campaign in Flanders. In 1749, the number of the regiment was changed to the 42nd and Mr. Graham obtained a company in it 3rd June, 1752, and came to America in 1756, in 1757 he was at the surrender of Fort William Henry under Colonel Munro and was wounded the following year in the attack on Ticonderoga. The major of the regiment having been killed on that occasion, Captain Graham succeeded to the vacancy, 17th July, 1758, and made the campaign of 1759 and 1760, under Amherst. He next served in the West Indies in the expedition against Martinico, and in July, 1762, became lieutenant-colonel of the regiment, which returned to New York and in the year 1763, proceeded to the relief of Fort Pitt, defeating the Indians on the way in the Battle of Bushy Run. Lieut. Colonel Graham's name is dropped in the *Army List* of 1771, whence 'tis presumed he died the year preceding (Brown's *Highland Clans*, IV. Beatson's *Naval and Mil. Mem.*, II).

★★★★★★

The detachment of the Royal in garrison at Fort Edward to encamp at 5 o'clock this afternoon, on the left of the light infantry of the Royal Highland Regiment, which is the ground the Royal is to encamp on. All suttlers who have passes and are not attached to regiments, are to be encamped together on the ground the quartermaster-general will mark out for them, at one o'clock this day; which ground is to be the centre of the army.

And the market to be keepd there for selling whatever these suttlers may bring for the use of the camp. The provost guard will encamp there for to keep good order. No light to be suffered at night, and none of the soldiers permitted to stay there after retreat beating. The suttlers are to encamp on this ground at 4 o'clock this day, and none to be permitted to remain on the glasies of the fort.

The light infantry of the Highland Regiment is to practice fireing ball tomorrow morning at 6 o'clock, near the Royal Block House on the other side the river. The camp not to be allarmd; the subaltern's guard on the *batteaux* to be taken off, and two guards to be posted in lieu thereof; a serjt. and 15 men on this side the river; a serjt. and 15 on the iseland; a standing order that no droping shots be fired. When there are any firelocks which canot be drawn, a report is to be made thereof that they may be collected together and fired off when the camp is advertised of it, that there may be no unnecessary allarm. The Indians to be perticulary acquainted with this order, which if they disobey they shall be severely punished.

AFTER GENERAL ORDERS.

The Royal to furnish 2 subalterns and 70 men, the Royal Highland Regt. 2 captains, 6 subs., and 200 men; the Massachusetts troops one lieut. col., one major, 6 captains, 12 subs., and 600 men; this detachment to take *batteaux* tomorrow morning at daybreak. The Royal will take 10 *batteaux*, ye Royal Highland Regt. 20, and 60 of the 200 men with arms to serve as a covering party. Massachusetts will take as many as they can man. Major Roggers will furnish 40 Rangers, to serve as a part of the covering party. The whole to take provisions for tomorrow with them; they are to proceed to Col. Haviland's camp, opposite to Fort Miller, where the commanding officer will apply to Col. Haviland, who will order the *batteaux* to be immediately loaded, that the whole party may return to Fort Edward without loss of time; for this duty, Lieut. Col. Saltonstall and Major Hawks.

GENERAL ORDERS.

Fort Edward, 10th June, 1759. Parole, Jersey.

Field officer for the picquit this night Major Graham. For tomorrow Major Campbell. colonel of the day, Colonel Grant. All reports from the field officers of the picquit and extaordinarys that may happen in camp are to be made to the colonel of the day, who will report at orderly time to the commander-in-chief. All guards are to turn out to the colonel of ye day, general officers guards excepted. He will goe his rounds, and visit all guards and outposts, to see that the whole are alert, and properly posted, and inform the colonel, who relieves him of the several guards and posts and time that he visited them. Divine Service to be performed every Sunday at the head of the regiments.

A general court martial to sit tomorrow morning at 8 o'clock, to try such prisoners as are on the provost guard. All evedences to attend. Colo. Montgomery Presedent; Lieut. Col. Ingersall, Major Bell, one capt. from the Royal, 2 captains each from the Royal Highlanders, Preaudeaux, and Montgomerys, 2 from the Massachusetts, and one from the Rhode Isleand Regiment. Members, Lieut. George Burton of the Royal, Judge Advocate, to whom the members names and dates of their comissions, and the evidences names are to be sent.

★★★★★★

Archibald Montgomerie, 3rd Son of Alexander, 9th Earl of Eglinton, having obtained whilst Major, Letters of Service, raised in the year 1757, the 62nd, afterwards the 77th Regiment, called after him the Montgomerie Highlanders, of which he was appointed Lieutenant-Colonel, commanding. He made the campaign against Fort Duquesne in 1758, and in 1759 accompanied Amherst. In the Spring of 1760, he was detached in command of a Force sent to chastise the Cherokees. He was promoted to a Colonelcy in the army in 1762; was appointed Equerry to the Queen in 1763, and Governor of Dumbarton Castle in 1764. He represented Ayrshire in Parliament at this time and for several years after. In June 1767 he was appointed Colonel of the 51st Regiment, and on the murder of his brother, by one Campbell, an Excise Officer, succeeded to the earldom; married the Earl of Crawford's Daughter in March, 1772, and in May following, was appointed Major-General; Lieutenant-General in 1777; Colonel of the Scots Greys (2nd Regt. of Dragoons), 2nd Dec, 1795, and died a General in the Army, 30th Oct., 1796. (Browne's *Highland Clans* IV; Entick's *History of the War*, V; Debrett's *Peerage*; *Army Lists*; Knox, *passim*). George Burton entered the army 27th April, 1756, as ensign in the 2nd Battalion of the 1st or Royals, and 14th April, 1759, was promoted to a Lieutenancy. He acted as Deputy Judge-Advocate in this campaign and is out in 1765. (*Army List.*)

★★★★★★

At 6 o'clock this evening, a marquee to be pitched in the centre of the line, where the court martial will assemble. A serjt. and 12 men of Montgomery's Regiment to serve as a guard whilst the court martial is sitting. The Royal Highlanders and Montgomery's Regiments to send as many men this afternoon at 4 o'clock as are necessary to clean the ground where the light infantry is to encamp. Lieut. Col. Robison will take them to the ground; they will receive axes on aplying to the store-keeper in the fort, which they will return when they have finished that work.

The serjts. guard on the *batteaux* on the isleand to be reduced to a corpl and 6 men. As by the order of the 7th it was said that spruce beer would be brewed for the army, it is not thereby intended to hinder any people from brewing spruce beer. All suttlers are at liberty to brew as much as they will. The generals guard, artillery, magazine, provost, and *batteaux* to be relieved every 48 hours.

GENERAL ORDERS.

Fort Edward, 11th June, 1759. Parole, Northfolk.
Colo, of the day, Colo. Grant; for tomorrow, Colo. Schuyler. Field

officer of the picquits, Major Campbell; tomorrow Lieut. Colo. Hunt.

******

Allan Campbell, Son of Barcaldine, entered the army as ensign of the 43rd (now the 42nd) Highlanders, in 1745, and served that year against the Pretender (Browne, IV). He obtained a company, 15th March, 1755, and the next year came to America, where he shared the difficulties and honours of the regiment. In June, 1759, he was appointed major for the campaign under Amherst, and was actively employed at the head of the grenadiers and Rangers, clearing the way for the army up the lakes (Knox *Journal*, I; II). He became major in the army, 15th August, 1762, and went on half-pay on the reduction of the regiment in 1763, having obtained a grant of 5000 acres of land at Crown Point. In 1770, he was appointed Major of the 36th or Herefordshire Foot, then serving in Jamaica; became lieutenant-colonel in the army in May, 1762, and of his regiment in January, 1778; colonel in the army, 17th Nov., 1780; major-general in 1787; and died about the year 1797. His regiment did not serve in America during the Revolutionary War. (*Army List*.)

******

Each regiment will make a path to their front for their picquits to advance whenever they may be ordered. The general will show the commanding officers where he would have their picquits advanced to. And in case of any alarm in the night, and that the regiments should be ordered out, no regiment is on any account whatsoever to fire a shot from their line. The picquits will be ordered out, and they will be supported. Spruce beer will be brewed for the health and conveniency of the troops, which will be served at prime cost; 5 quarts of mollasses will be put into every barrel of spruce beer; each gallon cost nearly 3 coppers. The quartermasters of the regiments, Regulars and Provincials, are to give notice to Lieut. Colo. Robison of the quantity each corps are desirous to receive, for which they must give receipts and pay the money before the regiments marches.

******

James Robertson was appointed Major of the 1st Battalion of the 60th or Royal Americans, in December, 1755, and in May, 1758, was appointed by General Abercromby Deputy Quartermaster-General of the Army in North America. He accompanied the Expedition against Louisburgh in that year as

Quartermaster-General (Beatson's *Naval and Military Memoirs,* III; *Knox,* I), and was promoted to be Lieutenant-Colonel in the Army 8th July, 1758. In 1759 he accompanied Amherst up Lakes George and Champlain, in charge of the quartermaster's department, and on the 29th October of that year was appointed Lieutenant-Colonel of the 55th Regiment. In February, 1760, he exchanged into the 15th, which regiment formed part of the expedition against Martinico, in 1762; returned to England in 1767, and in the following year exchanged into the 16th, which remained in America. In 1772 he became Colonel in the Army.

In July, 1775, was stationed at Boston (*Journal of New York Provincial Congress,* I); was appointed Major-General in America 1st January, 1776, and Colonel commanding 60th Regiment 11th January following; when the army evacuated that city that year, "General Robertson, under an official cover, seems to have been as great a plunderer as any, and to have connived at the rascally conduct of smaller villains. He might possibly answer to himself for the part he was acting, by viewing what he secured as an equivalent for the many thousands he has out at interest and in property in the colony of New York and elsewhere, should the same be seized" (4 *American Archives,* V). He accompanied the army under Howe to Staten Island, and commanded the 6th Brigade on the 1st August, and after wards in the Battle of Long Island, when he shortly after came to New York City. He returned to England in February, 1777 (5 *American Archives* III), and on 29th August of that year became Major-General in the Army. On 14th May, 1778, he was appointed Colonel of the 16th Regiment, and on the 4th May, 1779, received a commission as Governor of New York, and was accordingly sworn in on the 23rd March, 1780 (*New York Council Minutes,* XXVI). He became Lieutenant-General 20th November, 1782; embarked at New York for England on the 15th April, 1783 and died in 1788 (*Army lists*).

★★★★★★

Each regiment to send a man acquainted with brewing, or that is best capable of assisting the brewers, to the brewery tomorrow morning at 6 o'clock, at the rivulet on the left of Montgomerys. Those men are to remain and are to be paid at the rate of 18 pence currency per day. One serjt. of the Regulars and one of the Provencials to superintend the brewery, who will be paid 1*s* 6*d* per day. Spruce Beer will be deliverd to the regiments on Thursday evening or Friday morning. Tomorrow morning, 1 subaltern, 1 serjt. 3 corplls and 32 men to mount guard in the isleand. He will detach a corpl and 6 men to take care of ye *batteaux*; a corpl and 6 men to take care of the whale boats; this guard to be relievd every 48 hours. The whole to take their tents and provision with them, and the guards on the iseland to come off.

Orderly time at 10 in the morning, and the adjutants to attend at 6 in the evening, for whatever after orders there may be. The generals guard tomorrow, Colo. Montgomerys. The picquits and out guards to load with a runing ball, that there may be no waste of amunition.

AFTER ORDERS.

A detachment of one field officer and 6 captains, 12 subalterns, 18 serjeants, with 600 rank and file, to parade immediately after revellie tomorrow, to march to repair the roads. They may goe in their waiscoats but must carry provisions for the day; one half to carry their arms, the other half spades and shovells. Major Graham Field Officer.

GENERAL ORDERS.

Fort Edward, 12th June, 1759. Parole, Pitt.
Colo for the day, Colo. Schuyler; for tomorrow, Colo. Ruggles.
★★★★★★

Timothy Ruggles, Son of the Rev. Timothy R., was born in Rochester, Mass, Oct., 1711, graduated at Harvard 1732, and adopted the profession of the law. In 1736, represented his native town in the Assembly, and soon rose to eminence in his profession. In 1755, he was colonel in the army under Johnson, at the Battle of Lake George, where Dieskau was defeated; was actively engaged in the following campaigns and served as Brigadier in the present expedition. In 1762, he was appointed Chief Justice of the Common Pleas, and was Speaker of the Assembly in 1762-3. In 1765, he was one of the delegates from Massachusetts to the Stamp Act Congress which met at New York, and was President of that body, but dissented from the proceedings, for which he was confuted by the Assembly on his return home. In 1774, he was a Mandamus Councillor, and afterward, having adhered to the Loyalist Party, was obliged to leave the province, and his property was confiscated. He retired to Nova Scotia where he was one of the proprietors of Digby and died in 1798. (Ward's *Curwen*; Sabine's *Loyalists*.)

★★★★★★

Field officer for the picquit today, Maj. Hawks; for tomorrow Maj. Douglass. The Royal, Predeaux, and Royal Artillery to receive provisions tomorrow for 6 days, which will be to the 18th inclusively. Royal and Royal Artillery at 6 o'clock, Predeaux at 7. Block houses to be relieved tomorrow by the line. The one joyning the bridge on the west side by one serjt, one corpl, and 12 men of the Royal; the one joyning the east side of the bridge by one sub., 2 serjts., 2 corpls. and 24 men of the Royal Highlanders; the one in the front of the right of the Royal, one serjt., one corpl. and 10 men of the Royal Highlanders; the one in the front of Montgomerys by one serjt., one corpl. and 10 men of that regiment; the one on the left of Montgomerys by one serjt., one corpl. and 10 men of that regiment; the one in the front of the Jersey Regiment by one serjt., one corpl and 10 men of ye regt.

The one on the hill, or the front of the Massachusetts by one sub., 2 serjeants, 2 corpus and 24 men of the Massachusetts Troops. The officers and serjts. will be stricttly observing of the orders they receive from those they relieve, and such as are wrote up on each block house; they must take care to keep the block houses sweept clean, and are to be answerable for what tools they receive, which is an ax, pick ax, shovel, and buckett for watter, to each block house, which they will deliver over to the officer who relieve them; those guards to be relieved dailie. Predeaux Regiment to be ready to encamp on the first notice.

After General Orders.

It is the generals orders that no scouting partys or others in the army under his command shall, whatsoever opertunity they may have scalp any women or bellonging to ye enemy. They may bring them away, if they can, if not they are to leave them unhurted; and he is determined that if the enemy should murther or scalp any women or children who are the subjects of the King of England, he will revenge it by the death of 2 men of the enemy, whenever he has occasion, for every woman or child murthered by the enemy.

General Orders.

Fort Edward, 13th June, 1759. Parole Louisburgh.

Collo. of the day tomorrow, Collo. Babcock; field officer for the picquit tomorrow, Lieut. Collo. Hunt. The Royal Highland Regiment

50

to strick their tents tomorrow at revallie beating, and to be joyned by a detachment of Provincialls, commanded by a field officer, and consisting of 500 men rank and file. For this duty Lieut. Collo. Pysan, 2 6-pounders, with an officer and 12 men of the Royal Artillery, and ammunition in proportion, will march with the said detachment. Captain Stark, with his company of Rangers, will joyn the detachment from the Four-Mile Post.

******

John Starke was born at Londonderry, N. H., 28th August, 1728, and in 1752 was a captive among the Indians of St. Francis. He served as Captain of Rangers in the French War (Knox 1), and at the opening of the Revolution received a commission as Colonel, and fought at Bunker Hill in June, 1775; went, in 1776, to Canada, and at Trenton commanded the van of the right wing of the American Army. He was also in the Battle of Princeton, but being omitted in the promotions, threw up his commission in March, 1777. He raised a body of troops in New Hampshire, and in August, following, defeated Col. Baum at Wallumschack. After this he was reinstated in the Continental Army, as Brigadier-General. He served in Rhode Island in 1778-9, and in 1780 in New Jersey; in 1781, had the command of the Northern Department, and was one of the Members of the Court Martial on Major Andre. He died, full of years and honours, May 8th, 1822, aged 93 years, and was buried on a small hill on the banks of the Merrimack River, (Allen.)

******

A company of Indians will likewise be ordered to joyn them. Collo. Grant will receive further orders from the generall; a waggon per company, one for the staff, and five waggons for the 500 Provincialls, will be allowed to carry their tents. The officers of the Provincialls, who command those detachments, will send immediately to compleat the men to fix and thirty rounds, if their horns will hold it, if they will only take what their horns will hold, and ball in proportion; the amunition to carefully examined, and if any cartridges may be dammaged comeing in the *batteaux*, most be new made. The arms most likewise be looked over and put in good order. The Royal Highlanders posted in the block houses as per ordered of yesterday, to be releived by Predeaux Regiment immediately. The Provincialls troops are to compleat their provisions to the 19th inclusive. The Grand Parade is on the right of the grenadiers; ordinary guards to mount at 7. Adjutant of the day tomorrow, the Royal; Generals Guard, Massachusetts.

GENERAL ORDERS.

Fort Edward, 14th June, 1759. Parole, Lancaster. Collo. for the day tomorrow, Collo. Montgomery; Field officer of the picquitt tomorrow, Lieut. Collo. Saltenstall. The generall court martiall, of which Collo. Montgomery was President, is desolved. The generall has been pleased to approve of the following sentences: that Anderow Yeats, of Collo. Montgomery's Regiment, receive one thousand lashes with a catt and nine tails. John Hailsworth, of the Rhode Island Regiment, is to receive 500 with a catt and nine tails. That Thomas Smith, of Capt. Crookshanks Independent Company is to receive 1000 lashes with a catt and nine tails. (Charles Cruickshank succeeded Hubert Marshall as Captain of the 2nd New York Independent Company of Foot, 16th April, 1757, *Army List*.)

That Samuel Pearce, soldier in the Rhode Island Regiment, is to receive 1000 lashes with a catt and nine tails. John Joycelen, Rubin Brown, and Abram Naas, are judged to receive 500 lashes each, are pardoned. Thomas, of the Independent Companie, is to receive his punishment in the following Manner: at 12 o'clock this day to be marched by the provost to the right of the line and is to receive a 100 lashes at the head of each of the following corps, Predeaux Grenadiers and Light Infantry, Montgomerys Jersey Regimentt, Lymons, Fitch Rhode Island Regiment, 2nd Battalion Massachusetts, First Battn. Massachusetts. The grenadiers and light infantry supposed one corps.

A mate of the hospital to attend the punishment. the grenadiers and light infantry to be in their waistcoats, leggets with arms and accouterments to be out at 4 this afternoon; the Royall Highlanders and Predeaux Grenadiers on the hill by the blockhouse, on this side the bridge; Predeaux Light Infantry and Montgomerys Grenadiers and Light Infantry on the hill on the right of the blockhouse, in the front of the Massachusetts; the eldest capt. of both those partys will receive their orders from the generall. A quarter before 2 o'clock Spruce Beer will be delivered to the regiments tomorrow; Predeaux at 6 in the morning, grenadiers and light infantry at half an hour after, Montgomerys at 7, artillery at half an hour after, Jersey Regiment at 8, Connecticut Regiment at half an hour after, Rhode Island Regt. at 9, Massachusetts at half an hour after. The quartermaster or an officer of each of those corps will attend Lieut. Colo. Robison at 6 this evening, at the brewerie, to fix the quantity that each is to receive.

52

The quartermaster and camp colourmen of Predeaux Regiment to be readie when Lieut. Collo. Robison calls for them, the grenadiers and light infantry to be readie to change their encampment when ordered.

GENERAL ORDERS.

Fort Edward, 15th June, 1759. Parole, Sussex.

Collo. for the day tomorrow, Collo. —; Field officer for the pic-quitt, Lieut. Collo. Ingersall. The grenadiers and light infantry to change their ground this afternoon at 2 o'clock, to the ground in the front of the blockhouse on the hill, which Lieut. Collo. Robison has marked out. A waggon will be allowed to each company to carry their tents. Predeaux Regiment to strick their tents at 2 o'clock this afternoon and march half an hour after to the Halfway Brook, (in Warren County, N.Y., and is so called as being equi-distant between Fort Edward and Lake George), where the officer commanding the regiment will follow such orders as he will receive from Collo. Grant; 10 waggons will be allowed to carry the tents of the companys, the one to Collo. Eyres and one for the staff.

★★★★★★

William Eyre was appointed, 7th January, 1756, Major of the 44th Foot, which suffered so much in Braddock's Expedition; he built, the same year, Fort William Henry, at the head of Lake George, since celebrated by Col. Munro's gallant defence of that post in 1757. In January, 1758, Maj. Eyre was commissioned "Engineer in Ordinary;" and in July following, Lieutenant-Colonel in the Army, and afterwards Lieutenant-Colonel of the 55th. In the course of Amherst's Campaign, he was engaged in strengthening Fort Edward, and in July, 1759, was appointed Chief Engineer of the Army, and soon after laid out the ground for a new Fort at Ticonderoga.

In the month of October, 1759, he became Lieutenant-Colonel of his old regiment, the 44th. He accompanied Amherst from Oswego to Montreal in 1760, and remained in America until 1764, in the fall of which year he was unfortunately drowned, in the prime of his life, on his passage to Ireland. In his profession as an engineer, he was exceedingly eminent, and an honour to his country, having arrived at that rank solely by his merit. The service and the army to whom he was a shining ornament, sustained a very considerable loss by his death. (Knox *Journal* I; II. *Army Lists*).

★★★★★★

A generall court martiall to sitt this day at 12 o'clock, to try a deserter from Collo. Fitches Regiment, at the Presidents tent. Collo. Schuyler, President; Maj. Campbell, Maj. Hawks, 2 captains of the Royall, 2 captains of Montgomerys, one of the Royall Artillery, 2 of the Massachusetts, and three of the Connecticut troops, members. Lieutenant George Burton of the Royall, Deputy Judge-Advocate. All evidences to attend. (Maj. Hawks is supposed to have belonged to Keene, N. H. A Col. Hawks was in command of Fort Massachusetts, when taken by the French in 1746.—*Hist. Berkshire Co. Mass.*)

AFTER GENERAL ORDERS.

Predeaux Regiment having been countermanded, is to march tomorrow morning. They will strick their tents tomorrow at revallie beating and march half an hour after. The commanding officer will take under his escort the waggons loaded with artillery stores and what cannon may be ordered to be sent forward. He will proceed with the same to the Halfway Brook and follow shuch further orders as he shall receive from Collo. Grant. It having been reported to the generall that some of the waggons have been too much loaded, the generall will have no greater weight put into the waggons than what Collo. Bradstreet directs.

The generall court martiall, of which Coll. Schuyler was President, is desolved.

★★★★★★

Peter Schuyler was grandson of Philip Pieterse Schuyler of Albany, and second son of Arent Schuyler of New Jersey, by his second wife. In 1746, on the projected invasion of Canada, he was put in command of the New Jersey Regiment and was for two years or more stationed at Oswego, N.Y. He returned at the peace of 1748 to private life, but on the renewal of hostilities his regiment was again called out and reached Oswego 20th July, 1755. In December following, he attended the Congress called by Governor Shirley at New York, whence he returned to Oswego where he remained until its reduction by the French, 14th August, 1756, when he was released on parole.

On his return to New York, 21st November, several houses were illuminated; he arrived at his home in Peterborough N.

54

J., 27th November. The capitulation of Fort William Henry having been declared null by the British, Col. Schuyler was in virtue of the condition of his parole, ordered by Governor Vaudreuil early in 1758 to return to Canada. He at once complied but was exchanged in the fall and reached Albany on his return, 17th November, 1758. In the following year he again commanded the New Jersey Regiment, and was placed at the head of the third column in crossing Lake George.

On the 8th and 9th of August, 1760, Amherst's Army at Oswego was joined by "the Jersey Blues, commanded by that brave, expert officer Col. Schuyler. It was a well-disciplined, regular corps, and the men with their blue uniform faced with scarlet, made a respectable appearance." A month afterwards, Col. Schuyler entered Montreal as a victor, where only two years before he had been a prisoner. After the campaign he returned to New Jersey and finally sank to rest at his residence on the Passaic near Newark, on the 17th November, 1762, leaving behind him a high character for bravery and chivalrous honour (*Proc. of N. J. Hist. Soc,* I; Knox *Journal,* I).

✶✶✶✶✶✶

The genl. approves of the sentence of the court martiall, on the tryall of John Williams of Collo. Fitches Regiment, that he is to suffer death for the desertion proved against him. The picquitts of the line to assemble tomorrow at 6 o'clock for the execution of the above prisoner, the commanding officer of each picquitt will march his picquitt to the right of Collo. Fitches Regiment, where the field officer of the picquitts will take the command of the said picquitts and obey shuch orders as he shall receive from the collo. of the day. Collo. Fitches Regiment to be under arms at 6 o'clock; a platoon to be loaded and formed in the front of the regimt. for the above execution; a chaplain to attend immediately on the prisoner. Adjutant of the day tomorrow, Montgomerys; Genlls Guard, New Jerseys.

GENERAL ORDERS.

Fort Edward, 16th June, 1759. Parole, Boston.
Collo. of the day tomorrow, Collo. Lymman.

✶✶✶✶✶✶

Phinehas Lyman, was born at Durham, Conn., about 1716; was graduated in 1738 at Yale College, in which he was afterwards a tutor 3 years; and settled as a lawyer in Suffield. He sustained various public offices. In 1755, he was appointed Major-General and Commander in chief of the Connecticut Forces, and built Fort Lyman, now called Fort Edward, N. Y. When Sir W. Johnson was wounded in the battle of Lake George, the command devolved on him. In 1758, he served under Abercrombie, and was with Lord Howe, when he was killed. He was also at the capture of Crown Point by Amherst and at the surrender of Montreal. In 1762 he commanded the Provincial troops in the expedition against Havana.

In 1763 he went to England as the agent of his brother officers to receive their prize money, also as agent of a company, called the "Military Adventurers," to solicit a grant of land on the Mississippi, and wasted 11 years of his life. Being deluded for years by idle promises, his mind sunk down into imbecility. At last his wife, who was a sister of Dr. Dwight's father, sent his second son to England to solicit his return in 1774. About this time a tract was granted to the petitioners. After his return he embarked with his eldest son for the Mississippi, and both died soon after their arrival at West Florida in 1775. (Dwight's *Travels*, I; III.)

★★★★★★

Field officer of the picquitt this night, Lieut. Collo. Ingersall, Major Campbell for tomorrow. Collo. Whittings Regiment, and the other regiments of Provincials, as they arraive, must immediately put their arms in good repair, their cartridges must be examined into, and if any be dammaged most be new made to compleat their numbers of cratridges; and all the Provincial troops are now to receive by applying to the commanding officer of the artillery, ammunition sufficient to compleat 36 rounds, if they horns will hold it, if not they most take no more than their horns will contain, and ball in proportion. The whole army to receive provisions for seven days; the Regular Regiments will receive theirs on the 18th, and the seven days will be to the 23rd inclusive.

The quartermasters to give in tomorrow night the number of men they draw for, to Mr. Wilson the commissary, who will fix their hour for receiving it next morning. The Provincials to receive theirs on the 19th, as directed for the Regulars, and they will receive accordingly; and it will be for the 26th inclusively. Any regiments that arraive who have received provisions to different times to what the troops here have done, will compleat now to the time as ordered. John Williams of Collo. Fitch's Regt. who was sentenced to suffer death, is pardoned.

The commanding officers of the Provincials Regiments will examine what number of men they have who are not marksmen; some perhaps may not have fired a muskett: a return to be sent to the deputy adjutant-general tomorrow morning at 9 o'clock of their number, that the whole may be ordered out to fire at a mark; and any of the dammaged cartridges may be alloted for this service, of which they will likewise make a report. Adjutant for the day tomorrow, the Royall.

AFTER GENERAL ORDERS.

The first battalion of the Massachusetts troops to be readie to march on the shortest notice.

GENERAL ORDERS.

Fort Edward, 17th June, 1759. Parole, London.

Collo. of the day tomorrow, Collo. —; Field officer of the pickitt this night, Major Campbell; for tomorrow Major Bell. The first battalion of the Massachusetts troops to strick their tents at two o'clock this afternoon, if they receive no orders to the conterary. Three ox carts will be allowed to carry their tents, and the fourth if necessary. The Royall and New Jersey Regiments to be readie to march on the shortest notice. All the species of provisions which the contractors have engaged to furnish the troops, are to be delivered when the several species are in store; but if the more necessary demands for carriages should prevent the most bulkie articels from the army, or that the contractor may not at all times have it in his power to furnish a sufficient supply of every species, in either of the cases, if the regiments chuse it, they may receive one article in lue of another, in the following proportions: if pease are wanting, half the quantity of rice; or a pound of bread or flouer, or the third of a pound of pork, may be received in leu of pease; if pease and rice are wanting, one pound of pork, or two pound 12 ounces of flower may be received in lue of pease and rice; if pease, rice and butter are wanting, one pound and a quarter of pork or three pounds and a halfe of bread and flouer may be received in lue of the pease, rice and butter. If the above proportions are taken in lue of those species that may be in store, the regiments will then give receipts for their full rations. Genls guard, first Connecticut Regiment, adjutant Montgomerys. The first battalion Massachusetts will receive their provisions at Halfway Brook.

AFTER GENERAL ORDERS.

Surgeon McColm of the Royall having represented to the generall that his health will permit in serving the campaign, Mr. Brice, surgeon's mate of the hospitall is to return to the hospitall.

Whenever a flagtrouce or a drummer may arraive from the enemy, with whatsoever party may be sent, they are to be stopt by the first centrys of whatsoever advanced post they may come to, which centrys will give notice to the guard that the officer commanding at the post may be informed of; the officer will send the letter or letters to the generall and will keep the drummer or party with the flagtrouce so that they cannot see any of the post, out works, or camp, till the answer is returned.

If any officer should be sent with a letter, who may say he is ordered to deliver his despatches to the generall himself, and will not give it to anyone else, and is not on any acount whatsoever to be permitted to advance through any of the out post, but shall be keept till he deliver his despatches, and remaines there for an answer. If he persists in not delivering them, is to be keept, and the officer commanding the post to send a report to the generall a proper guard to be always given from the posts for the protection and security of those may be sent.

EVENING ORDERS.

The First Battalion Massachusetts under orders for marching to strick their tents at revallie beating and march half an hour after to the Halfway Brook, where the commanding officer will put himself under the command of Collo. Grant. They are to take under their escort the waggons loaded with provisions which are to set out very early. All the men returned by the Provinces Regiments not to be marksmen are to assembel tomorrow morning in the front of their regiments. They will march by the left to the ground where the Massachusetts fired this evening and will fire 5 rounds a man. Major Roggers will take care the ground in the front is clear. Officers of each regt. to attend and see the men levell well.

GENERAL ORDERS.

Fort Edward, 19th June, 1759. Parole, Westminster.
Collo. of the day tomorrow, Collo. Whitting.

★★★★★★

Nathaniel Whiting, of New Haven, Conn. He served with distinction in the expedition against Cape Breton in 1745, and the same year was commissioned a Lieutenant in Pepperell's Regiment; he remained in garrison at Louisbourg until the regiment was broke in 1748, when he went on half-pay. In 1755, he was commissioned Lieut. Colonel of the 2nd Connecticut Regiment for the expedition against Crown Point and was present in the engagement near Lake George, when Colonel Williams was killed, and having succeeded in the command ably secured the retreat of his men into the camp, where he also fought with Johnson. In 1758, he was again appointed Colonel of the 2nd Connecticut Regiment and shared Abercrombie's defeat at Ticonderoga; in 1759 accompanied Amherst up the lakes, and in 1760, from Oswego to Montreal (Parsons's *Life of Pepperell*; Trumbull's *Conn.*, II; Knox, II; *1 Mass. Hist. Soc. Coll.*, VII; Dwight, III).

★★★★★★

Field officer for the picquitt this night, Major Bell; tomorrow. Major Baldwin. The largest working party will be required tomorrow, as the cattle will rest, and the roads must be repaired. The number will be given in this evening, as the cattle and carriages will be put this night about three-quarters of a mile from the camp, from Light Infantry towards the lake. Gagges Regiment will furnish one captain 2 subalterns, non-commissioned officers in proportion, and 100 men; Light Infantry, the Royall one subaltern and 30 Light Infantry, of the Royal Highlanders one subaltern and 30 men; Predeaux one subaltern and 24 men; Montgomerys 1 subaltern and 30 men; Royal Grenadiers 1 subaltern and 30 men; Royal Highlanders one subalternand 30 Men; Predeaux one subaltern and 24 Men; Montgomerys one subaltern and 30 men; the whole will take their tents, as they will remain there till Wednesday, as a guard to the cattle and waggons, and they will be posted this afternoon at 5 o'clock. Lieut. Collo. Amherst will shew the ground. Capt. Kennedy, of Brig. Gen. Gages, will command the whole.

★★★★★★

William Amherst, brother of Sir Jefferey, was born in 1732, and on 21st September, 1757, became lieutenant and captain in the 1st Regiment of Foot Guards. In 1758, was appointed *aide-de-camp* to the commander-in-chief in the expedition against Louisbourg; in the present campaign was one of the deputy adjutant-generals and was commissioned lieutenant-colonel in the army. At Oswego in August, 1760, he was appointed to the command of the Light Infantry battalion and so entered Montreal. In 1762, he commanded a successful expedition sent to expel the French from Newfoundland, and in 1766 became colonel in the army and *aide-de-camp* to the king. On the death of General Bradstreet in 1774, he was appointed Lieutenant-Governor of St. Johns, Newfoundland, and in 1775, Colonel of the 3 2nd Foot; in 1777, Major-General, and in 1779 Lieutenant-General. He died 13th May, 1781, and his son succeeded to the title of Earl of Amherst (Knox; Debrett).

David Kennedy was on the 13th October, 1747, commissioned Captain in the 44th Foot, which regiment made the unfortunate campaign under Braddock in 1755. It was attached to Lord Loudon's expedition in 1757 and formed part of the force under Abercrombie in the unsuccessful expedition against Ticonderoga in 1758. But in 1759 he was attached to Gage's Light Infantry and in the course of the expedition was sent by General Amherst, with a flag of truce, to offer peace to the Indians of St. Francis and was detained by them with his whole party. This insult afterwards brought down severe chastisement on the Indians (Mante's *History of the War*). Captain Kennedy soon after sold out.

★★★★★★

AFTER ORDERS.

Three or four ox carts will be delivered to the New Jersey and first Connecticut Regiment, this evening, and 7 ox carts and a waggon to be delivered to the Royall this evening, that they may be loaded tomorrow at the brake of day. The above regiments are at that time to strick their tents and are to be under the command of Collo. Forster, who will receive his orders from the generall.

★★★★★★

June 19, 1759. The Royal, with the New Jersey Regiment and Connecticut troops marched this morning from Fort Edward to the Seven Mile Post, under the command of Colonel Forster; from thence the Colonel proceeded with the Royal, 55th and New Jersey Regiments, an officer of artillery and two field-pieces, one company of Rangers, and some Indians, towards the lake, and took post about three miles on this side of it. The colonel immediately cleared his ground, threw up an intrenchment, and fortified it with the trees that were felled (Knox, I).

★★★★★

The regiments are to march by the left, the Royall to march along the front of the line, joyning the Jersey Regiment, then both joyning the Connesticut Regiment, the whole to proceed as Collo. Forster will direct. Capt. Brwer and 60 Rangers joyning them as they march from the camp, eight hundred working men for mending the roads tomorrow; half will take their arms, the other half will take tools; the whole to be commanded by two field officers, and repaire the roads to the 4 Mile Post. They are to parade at 5 o'clock in the front of the Massachusetts. Lieut. Rebeier will attend to direct the work. They most take a days provision with them. For this duty Lieut. Collo. Putman and Major Watterbury.

GENERAL ORDERS.

Fort Edward, 19th June, 1759. Parole, Gravesend.

Colo, for the day tomorrow, Colo. Worster; Field officer for the picquit this night, Major Baldwin; tomorrow night, Major Watterbey. The Royal Artillery to deliver 56 bayonets to Colo. Montgomerys Regiment, taking a proper receipt for the same.

GENERAL ORDERS,

20th June, 1759. Parole, Southwark.

Colo, for the day tomorrow. Fitch; Field Officer for ye picquit this night, Lt. Colo. Darby; tomorrow Lieut. Colo. Smedly. The army to be in readiness to march tomorrow morning by day break. The order of march will be given out this evening. Montgomerys and the New Hampshire Reg. will remain here. Colo. Montgomery will receive his orders from ye general. The blockhouses to be relieved this evening at 6 o'clock by the troops in garrison. A waggon for the commanding officers of regiments; one for the staff; one and a half per company for regiments of a 1000; and one waggon per company for regiments of 700. The commanding officer of Gages and Light Infantry, and the captains of Light Infantry to send this afternoon at 2 o'clock to Major Ord, who will furnish them with the bayonets for the carabines, delivered for these corps. Colo. Haviland is to command the grenadiers of the army. A surgeons mate from the hospital to be sent to attend that corps, and a surgeons mate from Montgomerys to attend the Light Infantry.

GENERAL AFTER ORDERS.

Any officer of 6 companys of grenadiers that chuse caribines in room of their fuzees may have them but must leave their fuzees in room of them. A return of them to be given in immediately to Capt.

61

Holmes of the 27th Regiment.

AFTER ORDERS, 20TH JUNE.

Capt Campbell of the Royal Highland Grenediers is apointed Major to the Battalion of Grenediers for the Campaign. Capt. Holmes of the Inniskilling Light Infantry is apointed Major to command the Battalion of Light Infantry formed from ye several corps for ye campaign, and officer of those corps to do the duty of adjutant; a serjeant may do that of quartermaster. Capt. Gladwin, of Brigadier Gages Light Infantry, is apointed Major to the said corps for ye campaign. 2 companys of Montgomerys to march tomorrow morning before day to relieve Capt. Delsell (Dalyell) at the 4 Mile Post; the commanding officer will escort the *batteaux* as far as that post and will receive further orders at 3 o'clock this night.

★★★★★★

James Dalyell was appointed a Lieutenant in the 60th or Royal Americans, on 15th January 1756, and obtained a company in the 2nd Battalion of Royals or 1st Regiment of Foot, on the 13th September, 1760. On the 31st July, 1763, he led a detachment against Pontiac, then encamped beyond the bridge on the creek called Bloody Run, in the vicinity of Detroit. The British Party was obliged to retreat.

"At a little distance," says Parkman, "lay a sergeant of the 55th, helplessly wounded, raising himself on his hands, and gazing with a look of despair after his retiring comrades. The fight caught the eye of Dalyell. That gallant soldier, in the true spirit of heroism, ran out, amid the firing to rescue the wounded man, when a shot struck him and he fell dead. Few observed his fate, and none durst turn back to recover his body" (*Conspiracy of Pontiac.*)

★★★★★★

The army is to march tomorrow, the general to beat half an hour before day break. On the army immediately strike their tents, the assembly to beat half an hour after, on which the right will draw up in the front of the incampments, and to be tould of and ready to march when ordered, the whole in two columns, the Regulars by the left, by half files, the Provencials by the right, two deep, as they have been always accustomed to it. Major Roggers with the Rangers, and Major Gladwin with Gages Light Infantry will form the advanced guard and are to take great precaution in keeping out flanking partys, to the right, as far as Halfway Brook, from there to the lake will have advanced partys and flanking partys, to the left as well as the right.

★★★★★★

Henry Gladwin became a lieutenant in the 48th Regiment of Foot, on 28th August, 1753, and was wounded in the expedition under Braddock in 1755; was promoted to a company in the 80th or Gage's Light Armed Foot, on 25th December, 1757; commissioned Major of that regiment 20th June, 1759; was appointed Major in the Army 13th December, 1760; was next Deputy-Adjutant-General in America, (which post he filled until 1780), and served with great distinction during the war. His gallant defence of Detroit against Pontiac, is familiar to all, in reward for which he was promoted to be Lieut.-Colonel 17th September, 1763; Colonel 29th August, 1777, and Major-General 26th September, 1782 (Army lists). He died at his seat at Stubbing, near Chesterfield, County of Derby, England, on the 22nd of June, 1791 (*Gentleman's Magazine*).

★★★★★★

Those corps will draw up at day break in the road beyond the front of the camp of the left of the Light Infantry. The detachment apresent under Major Gladwin's command will joyn their corps at day break, the Light Infantry of regiments need not strike their tents till the army is near marched by. The Grenadiers will march by the left and halt on the road in the rear of Gages, till Forbess and the Inniskilling regiments joyn them, which two regiments must march in ye front of the first line, the left of the Inniskilling joyning the right of Forbess, till the joyn the Grenadiers. Whiteings will march by the right allong their own front to the front of Worsters. Worsters will follow Whiteings in the same order of march, and Fitches will follow Worsters; the whole marching allong the front of the Rhode Island Regiment which will follow Fitches and march up the hill along the left hand road, till the left of Whiteings is oposite the left of the Grenadiers.

The 2nd Battalion of Rugles will likewise march from the right along their own front, following the rear of the Rhode Island Regiment; when that is past the artillery waggons will follow, then the tents and baggage will follow in the following order: first the generals with his guard, then Brigadier-General Gages, that of the Rangers Light Infantry of Gages, the Grenadiers, Forbess, Inniskilling, Whiteing, Worsters, Fitches, Babcocks, ye 2nd Battalion of Ruggles, the baggage of the Light Infantry.

63

The Light Infantry commanded by Major Holmes will form the rear guard of ye whole. Montgomerys, the New Hampshire Regiment and Williards are not to march, but to remaine under the command of Colo. Montgomery; they will stricke their tents to change their camp as Colo. Montgomery will order them.

★★★★★★

James Holmes was commissioned Captain of the 27th or Inniskilling Regiment 2nd February 1757 and acted as Major of the Light Infantry through the expedition. He accompanied this division under Haviland into Montreal in 1760 and continued with his regiment until 1771 when his name is dropped from the *Army List.*

★★★★★★

The general expects that the flanking plattoons will be ready to turn out at a moment's warning; that the whole army have their arms ready loaded, and that the men are at all times ready to receive the enemy. On all halts, the column on the right will face to the right, the column on the left to the left, and in case any attack should happen, the left column shall not face a man to ye right or offer to fire a shot under pain of the severest punishment. When the regiments are drawn up on the ground, the Regulars will wheel their platoons to ye left, and ye Provincials to the right, then as they were, that the officers and men may know the platoons they belong to before they march of. Every platoon is to be attentive to the officer commanding it. The officers attention must be intirely to his platoon, and obeying the orders of their superiors.

And the general expects that though the officers have fuzees, none of them will be so inconsiderate as to amuse themselves at the enemy, by which they will inumberably neglect the much more esential part of the service, the care of their platoons, and he obsolutely forbids the officers firing unless on a imergent occasion. Whatever post an officer may be sent to take, the general expects that he will first visit the ground round him, and post his centenals as he judges best, and to make it impossible for the enemy to surprise him. Centenals must not be out of sight or hearing of the guard, or each other.

The officer will throw loggs or strengthen his post by the best means he can, so that the enemy shall not force it, as the general never intends to take any post that shall be abandoned but shall be defended and sustained on all occasions. Only he himself on some extraordinary account shall give particular orders to the contrary to the officer who commands the post.

Lake George, 22nd June, 1759. Parole, Richmond.

Field Officer for the picquit this night, Lieut. Colo. Saltonstal; for tomorrow night, Lieut. Colo. Spencer. The commanding officers of regiments to inspect the mens arms and amunition this day. A guard of one subaltern and 30 men, to be posted on the right of the rear of the camp where the ould fort stood, who will suffer nobody to pass but partys with arms. A guard of captain 2 subs, and 50 men to be posted on the left of the rear of the camp; the colo, of the day to post these guards. At 12 o'clock Lieut. Spencer, ingineer, will attend the Colo, and see what is to be done for their immediate defence. The regiments to make their necessary houses in the front of their incampments.

AFTER ORDERS.

For working partys will be given out at 6 this evening. The regiments incamped nearest the wells to clean them out immediately, and post centrys over them. The Provencial Regiments to furnish 2 captains, 8 subs, and 250 men, non-commissioned officers included, for the service of the artillery, who will also serve as a guard for the artillery when no other is ordered. They shall obey all orders they receive from Major Ord.

★★★★★★

Thomas Ord was appointed Captain in the Royal Artillery on 1st March, 1746. He was an excellent officer, and stood high in the Duke of Cumberland's esteem, by whom he was selected to command the artillery in Braddock's Expedition. Landing in Newfoundland, he hastened to New York, and arrived in Philadelphia 7th June, 1755, whence he proceeded to the Seat of War accompanied by 13 non-commissioned officers (Sargent's *Expedition of Braddock*). In 1759 he was Major and commanded the artillery in the present expedition; was promoted to be Lieutenant-Colonel 21st November same year and accompanied Amherst from Oswego to Montreal in 1760. In 1762, he commanded the artillery in the expedition against Martinico; in 1771 became Colonel Commandant of the 4th Battalion of the Royal Artillery serving in America and died in 1777. He had a tract of land in the town of Newcomb, Essex County, N. Y. (*Army Lists*; Burr's Map of Essex County; Knox, I, II; Mante).

★★★★★★

The Provencial Regiments now here to send their proportions this evening, at 2 o'clock, and send tents in proportion to ye numbers they give. The Grand Parade in the centre of the line. The regiments are desired to keep all their empty provision casks in charge of their quarter guard, as they will be very usefull in the service of the artillery and other public works. An evening gun will be fired.

AFTER GENERAL ORDERS.

Major Roggers is on all detachments to take rank as major according to the date of his comission as such, next after majors who have the Kings Comission, or one from his Majesties commander in chief. Lieut. Colo. Robison will mark the ground for the market, in the rear of late Forbess; it is to be under the same regulations as ordered at Fort Edward. The commanding officers are desired to warn all their men who goe into the watter, that they goe in between the two wharffs, the other parts being full of holes and dangers.

The army to receive one days fresh beef tomorrow; it will begin to be issued at 5 in the morning, every corps receiving at a quarter of an hour distance of time after another; first Gages Light Infantry, and following. Rangers, Light Infantry of Regiments, Grenadiers, Rugles, Inniskilling, Royal Highlanders, late Forbess, Worsters, Fitches, Artillery, Whiteing, Babcocks, the Light Infantry of Regiments and Grenadiers; on specifying their receipts, the number of portions, nameing of what regiments. The flower for this days provision shall be issued as soon as it comes up, which they apply for. This compleats the Regulars to ye 26th, ye Provincials to ye 27th, inclusively. If the Royal Highlanders is not compleated till that time, they will doe it. The commanding officers of corps may send their men for greens, but they must go only a small distance from the camp, and never without a covering party. No soldier except with a party or on command is to goe beyond the outposts of the camp.

Camp at Lake George, 23rd June, 1759. Parole, Shrewsbury.

Colo, of the day tomorrow, Ruggles; Field Officer of the picquit this night, Lieut, Colo. Spencer; tomorrow, Lieut. Colo. Putman. All men absent from roll-calling at retreat beating to be reported to the colo, of the day. All the extraordinarys in the Grenediers. Gages and Light Infantry, to be reported to the commander in Chief; Rangers to the Colo, of day. Generals Guard tomorrow, late Forbses.

★★★★★★

Joseph Spencer was born in East Haddam, Conn., in the year

1714, where he was Judge of Probate in 1753; joined the Northern Army in 1758 as Major under Colonel Whiting and as Lieutenant-Colonel in the two following campaigns, where he acquired the reputation of a brave and good officer. He was elected member of the Council in 1766 and was appointed Brigadier-General in the Continental Army in 1775, and Major-General in August, 1776, which post he resigned in 1778. In 1779 he was elected Representative to Congress, and in 1780, was again elected into the Council and was annually re-elected to that body until his death, which occurred at East Haddam in Jan., 1789. Without the advantages of a regular and public education, he acquired that general knowledge and that acquaintance with business which enabled him to discharge happily and usefully the various duties to which he was called, and he at last died, as might be expected, with strong and joyful expectations of a blessed immortality (Field's *Middlesex Co., Conn.*; Farmer and Moore's Coll., III).

★★★★★★

AFTER ORDERS.

One captain 3 subs, non-commissioned officers in proportion, with 100 men of Gages Regiment to be posted tomorrow to serve the communication between Colonel Forsters post and the outposts of the camp. The captain, one sub. and 50 men will post themselves in the centre, one sub. and 25 men half way between the captain and Colo. Forsters post, the other sub. halfway between him and the outposts of the camp, 2 officers and 40 Rangers to march under the captain of Gages, which he will dispose of as he thinks proper; the whole to take a days provision with them, and march at 5 in the morning, and remain till the evening, as carriages will be passing the whole day. The Light Infantry Company of the Royal and Inniskilling to march tomorrow morning at day break.

One sub. and 30 of Gages and 2 officers of the Rangers are to joyn this detachment, the whole to goe in their waistcoats, to take one days provision with them. 390 working men to parade tomorrow at 5 o'clock on the road near the Royal Artillery; working hours from 5 to eleven, and from 3 to seven. When any of the regiments send for greens, in the sight of the camp, and beyond the outposts, they must never send a less party than a serj. and 12 men with arms. All out guards are to stop less partys then that. The general court martial, of which General Limon is President, to meet at his tent tomorrow morning.

Lake George, 24th June, 1759. Parole, Dorset.

Colo, of the day tomorrow, Colo. Whiteing; Field Officer for ye picquit, Lieut. Colo. Putman; for tomorrow. Major Graham. Return of the number of carpenters in every regiment, and a return of the number of real sailors in the Provencials, only both to be given in at orderly time this evening. The officers employed in the several works are not to demand more men than is sufficient to carry on the works. It is expected that every man will doe a good days work; that the men may not be fatigued unesscesarlily in asking more men then what is wanted. Care of the *batteaux* and whaleboats to be given in charge to Capt. Loreing. Everybody concerned to obey him in everything relating to them.

Two orderly drummers to beat ye Pioniers March every morning at 5 o'clock, upon the hill in the rear of Fitches; the retreat at eleven; the Pioniers March again at 3 in the afternoon, and the Retreat at 7. The time to be given by Colo. Montresor, upon which all the men will turn out, or goe home. Two companys of Light Infantry to march early tomorrow morning, one to cover a working party of one lieut, and 40 Light Infantry, which goes to cut spruce. When that business is over they are to take a turn round the hill, and then return to camp. Lieut. Avery, of Colo. Fitches Regiment will attend this party to show them where the spruce is. The other company to be ready to attend Capt. Loreing when he shall call for them. An officer and 6 Rangers is to go with each of these companys. And officer and 30 men to mount tomorrow at 5 o'clock for ye protection of the *batteaux*. Lieut. Brame is to erect a post for this guard, for which he will take a party of 30 men and march of with the guard.

★★★★★★

Diedrich Brehm was a native of Germany. He received a commission of Lieutenant in the 2nd Battalion of the 60th or Royal American Regiment, 21st Feb., 1756. In the present expedition he acted as Assistant Engineer. On 12th September, 1760, four days after the capitulation of Montreal, he was ordered to accompany Major Rogers to Detroit. On arriving near that town, he was sent forward with a letter to the French *commandant* requiring the surrender of the post, which was given up on the 29th November following. Brehm went thence, 'tis supposed, to Michilimakinac. He obtained a company in the same regiment 16th Nov., 1774, and, became Major in the Army 19th March, 1783 (*Army Lists*; Mante; Lanman's *Michigan*).

A corporal and 6 men for the Provision Guard, When the whether is very hot, the arms are not to be left out, but put in the bell tents. General Gages picquit and Rangers to furnish tomorrow the same escort on the road for waggons, as ordered yesterday, and to be posted in the same manner. All bedsteads found in camp to be collected at the several quarter guards for the use of the sick. The effects of late Lieut. Watts of late Forbess Regiment to be sold by auction at the head of the collours of said regiment. (William Watts was commissioned a Lieutenant in 17th Foot, 2nd February, 1757, and died in the course of this campaign.)

Lake George, 25th June, 1759. Parole, Portsmouth.

Colo, of the day tomorrow, Colo. Worster; Field Officer for ye picquit this night, Major Graham; tomorrow night, Major Baillie. The 3 eldest companys of Grenadiers, the 3 eldest companys of Light Infantry under Major Holmes, 200 Rangers and Indians under Major Roggers, the whole under the command of Colo. Haviland, to be ready to march when dark. They will assemble in the front of ye Grenadiers half an hour after gun firing. Colo. Haviland will receive his orders from the general. The Grenadiers to march in their waistcoats, and as light as possible, but are to carry their blankets and one days provision. The Generals Guard tomorrow the Inniskilling Regt.

The detachments of Grenadiers and Light Infantry under the command of Colo. Haviland ordered to parade this evening, are to assemble tomorrow morning, at the front of the Grand Parade, two hours before day light. The quartermasters of regiments to deliver in to Colo. Robison at 8 o'clock this evening, returns of what quantities of spruce they want, that it may be delivered out as soon as it is ready. 200 working men for the inginiers tomorrow, and a working party of an officer and 25 men, Brig. General Gages Regiment to furnish the same escort on the road for the tomorrow waggons as this day, but to be posted in two divisions, as there will be 50 men on the communication from Colo. Forsters post.

Lake George, 26th June, 1759. Parole, Edinburgh.

Colo, of the day tomorrow, Colo. Fitch; Field Officer of the picquit this night, Major Baldwin; tomorrow night, Major — . Colo. Schuyler's Regiment to receive one days fresh provisions tomorrow at 5 o'clock. The Regulars to receive 7 days provisions tomorrow at 5 o'clock; first Gages, and following Light Infantry, Grenadiers, Forbess

Royal Highlanders, Inniskilling, Royal Artillery, at the same distance of time as ordered June 22nd. The quartermaster of each corps to give in a return this evening at 5 o'clock to Mr. Willson, of the quaintity each regiment draws for. An officer and 40 men to mount on the farthest post on the right in the rear of the camp, to cover the *batteaux*. A serj. and 12 men to mount where the ould fort stood. A serj. 2 corporals and 12 men for the Provision Guard. Brig. Gages Regiment to furnish the same escort on the road for the carriages, as this day to be joyned by an officer and 41 Rangers. The Regiments to receive their provisions in the same order as mentioned this day in orders, but that in an hours distance one from another.

Lake George, 27th June, 1759. Parole, Dublin.

Colo, of the day tomorrow, Colo. Babcock; for the picquit this night, Major Baldwin; tomorrow night, Major Watterbury.

★★★★★★

Henry Babcock, eldest brother of he the Rev. Luke B., was born in 1736, entered Yale College at the age of twelve, and took his degree when sixteen years old. At the age of eighteen he was captain of an independent company of infantry, and at nineteen marched to Albany, thence to Lake George, where he formed part of the Force under Colonel Williams, which was defeated by Baron Dieskau. He was promoted to the rank of major in the following year; at the age of twenty-one was lieutenant-colonel, and in 1758 Colonel of the Rhode Island Regiment, when he marched 500 men with the army against Ticonderoga, where had 100 men killed and wounded. He himself received a musket ball in the knee.

He was afterwards at the capture of the same fort by Gen. Amherst. In 1761, he went to England, where he spent a year, and soon after his return married and settled at Stonington, Conn., and commenced the practice of the law. When the Revolution broke out, he joined the Whig Party, and in 1776 was appointed by the Legislature Commander of the Forces at Newport. He was a man of fine person, accomplished manners, commanding voice, and an eloquent speaker (Updike).

★★★★★★

The Provencials to receive provisions tomorrow for 7 days to the 4th of July inclusive, beginning by Babcocks Regiment at 5, followed by Whiteings at 6, Fitches 7, Worsters 8, Jerseys 9, Ruggles 10. Ruggles and New Jersey Regiments to be under arms tomorrow morning. At 5 o'clock the Jersey Regiment to march and joyn Ruggles; these regiments to fire 3 rounds by platoons. The Colo, for the day will fix on the ground, somewhere to the front of Ruggles. The deputy adjutant-general will attend and give directions. The Provencial Regiments are always to have their officers posted to their own companys; their compys to be subdivided, each makeing two platoons; the supernumerary officers are to be posted in the rear.

Two companys of Light Infantry to be in readiness to march in the night if ordered: 50 working men to parade with the working partys this afternoon to clean the ground for the General Hospital. Generals Guard tomorrow, Royal Highlanders; 2 companies of Grenediers with 2 companys of Light Infantry ordered this morning with as many Rangers and Indians as Major Roggers can furnish, under the command of Capt, Johnson, the whole commanded by Major Campbell, to march tomorrow two hours before daybreak, by the same route Colo. Haviland took: which post Captain Johnson will show, and to remain there whilst the boats are fishing. They are to take one days provision, and to go as light as possible, as they are not only a covering party to ye boats, but to attack any body of the enemy they may find.

One boat will be allowed each battalion in camp, one artillery, one Rangers, one Light Infantry, one Grenediers. The general will have an officer in each *batteau*. Captain Stark will have a red flag in his *batteau*, and every *batteau* must be near enough to call each other, and ready to follow Capt. Stark immediately, as he knows where the covering party is posted, and will row in at a proper time. The fishermen will take their arms Captain Lorring will deliver, and great care must be taken they are not to much crowded. Captain Stark will receive his orders when the whole is to return from Major Campbell. Every *battoe* to be returned to the same place that it is taken from, and to be well fastened. Brigadier Gages Regiment are to furnish the same escort for carriages on the road as this day, and to be joyned by an officer and 40 Rangers.

Lake George, 28th June, 1759. Parole, Dartford.

Colo, of the day, Colo. Grant; Field Officer for the picquit this night, Major Watterbury; tomorrow night Major Durgby. The detachment under the command of Major Campbell to march tomorrow as ordered for this day, and the *batteaux* will be delivered as ordered yesterday. Whiteings and Worsters Regiments to be under arms tomorrow at 5 o'clock; to march to the same ground, fire 3 rounds in the same manner as ordered to the Massachusetts and New Jersey Regiments. Any man that have not yet joyned their corps must be reported when they come up, that the whole may fire ball. When the Rangers and Indians draw provisions, each company must make a return of their effectives present, signed by the commanding officer of the company, and Major Roggers will sign for the whole.

And it is a standing order that they are always to receive provision two days before it is dew, that there may be a sufficiency in camp to supply scouting parties. It is a standing order that when 3 guns are fired in camp, all out parties and every soldier is immediately to repair to camp, but this does not extend to fixt posts. The army to receive one days fresh provision tomorrow, beginning with Babcocks, who will receive at 5 o'clock, Whiteing half an hour after; Royal Artillery at 6, Fitches half an hour after; Worsters at 7, Jerseys half an hour after; late Forbess at 8, Royal Highlanders half an hour after; Inniskilling at 9, Rugles half an hour after; Grenediers 10. Light Infantry half an hour after; Rangers 11, Gages half an hour after.

AFTER ORDERS.

The General Court Martial, of which General Limon was Presedent, is desolved. John Caine, soldier in Brig. Gages Regiment found guilty of desertion laid to his charge, is to receive 1000 lashes on his bare back with the cat-and-nine-tails, by the drummers of the regiment. Serjt. John Hunly and Corpl John Innes of late Brig. Forbess Regiment is found not guilty of the crime laid to their charge, and therefore acquited and released. Brigadier Gages Regt. to furnish the same escort for the carriages tomorrow morning as this day, and to be joyned by an officer and 40 Rangers; 250 men to parade tomorrow morning at the useual time.

Lake George, 29th June, 1759. Parole, Colchester.

Colo, of the day tomorrow, Colo. Schuyler; Field Officer for the picquit this night, Maj. Durgey; tomorrow night, Lieut. Colo. Darby. Fitches Regiment to be out tomorrow at 5 to fire 3 rounds in the same manner as has been ordered for the regiment that has already fired. Whiteings Regiment to be ready to march tomorrow morning by day break. Waggon or team for tents and baggage will be delivered this evening by aplying to Colo. Bradstreet. The general will send his orders to Colo. Whiteing this night. The sick of that regiment will be left in the Reg. Hospital. The four battalions that have fired 3 rounds each to compleat their amunition immediately. The general expects that all the Provencial Regiments that have fired, that they will upon all occasions practise their men in going through their motions, that they may more ready when they come on more actual service. The companys of Rangers and Indians incamped are to be under arms tomorrow morning at 5 o'clock, to be inspected by Brigadier Gage.

★★★★★★

Thomas Gage was the second son of the 1st, and father of the 3rd, Viscount Gage of Castlebar, in the County of Mayo, Ireland. In 1755 he accompanied the expedition under General Braddock, against Fort Duquesne, as Lieutenant-Colonel of the 44th Regiment, and commanded the vanguard in the fatal engagement of the 9th July, when he was slightly wounded. After the battle he carried the general off the field (Entick, I). In May, 1758, he was appointed Colonel of the 80th Regiment, and Brig. General (Knox's *Journal*, I), and on the 8th December following married Margaret, daughter of Peter Kemble, Esq., President of the Council of New Jersey (Debrett).

In 1759 he accompanied the expedition under General Amherst, and led the 2nd Column against Fort Ticonderoga, which, however, had been abandoned by the French before the arrival of the English troops. On learning the death of General Prideaux, General Amherst dispatched Brigadier Gage on the 28th July to take command of that division of the army, but Fort Niagara had already been reduced by Sir William Johnson (Knox, I; Entick, IV). On the 11th July, of the following year, he departed from Oswego with the army to Montreal, of which city he was appointed Governor, after its capitulation. He was promoted in May, 1761, to the rank of Major-General, and in March following became Colonel of the 22nd Regiment of Foot.

At the departure of General Amherst for England in 1763, Major-General Gage succeeded him as Commander-in-Chief of his Majesty's Forces in North America. He rose to be Lieutenant-General in 1770, and resided in New York until May, 1774, when he removed to Boston, on being appointed Governor of Massachusetts. He was a suitable instrument for executing the purposes of a tyrannical ministry and Parliament. Several regiments soon followed him, and he began to repair the fortifications upon Boston Neck. The powder in the arsenal in Charlestown was seized; detachments were sent out to take possession of the stores in Salem and Concord and the Battle of Lexington became the Signal of War.

In May, 1775, the Provincial Congress declared Gage to be an inveterate enemy of the country, disqualified from serving the colony as governor and unworthy of obedience. From this time the exercise of his functions was confined to Boston. In June he issued a proclamation, offering pardon to all the rebels excepting Samuel Adams and John Hancock, and proclaimed martial law; but the affair of Breed's Hill, a few days afterwards, proved to him that he had mistaken the character of the Americans.

In October he embarked for England and was succeeded in the command by Sir William Howe. His conduct towards the inhabitants of Boston in promising them liberty to leave the town on the delivery of their arms, and then detaining many of them, has been reprobated for its treachery (Allen). In 1782 he was appointed Colonel of the17th Light Dragoons and rose to the rank of General of the Army in the following month of November. General Gage died in England on the 2nd April, 1787 (*Gentleman's Magazine*). His widow survived him until the 9th Feb., 1824, when she Died, aged 90 years (Debrett).

★★★★★★

The officers commanding companys will returns ready, agreeable to the form that will be sent them by the major of brigade. A reward of 100 guineas with his pardon to any person who shall discover the authors or any concerned in writeing the enormous letter to Lieut. Colo. Darby, of late Forbess Regiment. Brigadier Gages Light Infantry and Rangers to furnish the same escort for the road tomorrow as useual. The Rangers are not to march till after the Review. Colo. Whiteing is to post an officer and 30 men where the detachment from Colo. Forster used to be left. Every regiment to provide themselves with scoops sufficient to bail the *batteaux* when they receive them; the camp not to be alarmed at cannon fireing, as the artillery will exercise tomorrow morning. The Generals Guard tomorrow, the Massachusetts.

Lake George, 30th June. Parole, St. Albans.
Colo, of the day tomorrow, Colo. Lymon; Field Officer for the picquit this night, Lieut. Colo. Darby; tomorrow night, Lieut. Colo. Smedly. The commanding officers of all the Regular regiments in camp

with Lieut. Colo. Eyre, are to attend Brig. General Gage at 5 o'clock this evening. The guns at the Halfway Brook are to be scaled tomorrow morning at 8 o'clock. The army is not to be alarmed at their fireing. 200 workmen and 100 masons to parrade tomorrow morning at the useual hour, to work for the ingineer.

Lake George, 1st July, 1759. Parole, Amboy.

Colo, of the day tomorrow, Colo. Rugles; Field Officer for ye picquit this night, Lieut. Colo, Semdly; tomorrow night, Lieut. Colo. Hunt.

★★★★★★

Samuel Hunt commanded a company in 1755 in Johnson's Campaign at Lake George and was an active military officer in the French and Revolutionary Wars. He settled in Charlestown N. H., in 1759, and in August, 1775, was appointed a Member of a Committee of safety for said town. In May, 1778, he was chosen to represent Charlestown, at a Convention to be held at Concord on the 10th of the following June, and on the 13th September, 1779, he was again chosen to represent the said town agreeably to the request of the selectmen of Portsmouth, at a Convention to be holden at Concord the 22nd of the same Month. On the 13th of November, 1780, he was chosen to join a Convention of Committees from the several towns in Sullivan County, to be holden at Walpole on the 15th of the month; on the 8th December, 1780, was appointed to represent Charlestown, in a Convention there to be holden on the third Tuesday of January, 1781, and was appointed Sheriff of the County, under the new Constitution in 1784. He filled that office till his death in 1799 (N. H. Hist. Coll., IV).

★★★★★★

The men's accounts to be made out and cleard to ye 24th of June. The commanding officers of regiments haveing been asembled to take into consideration the most convenient method of paying the troops, as also weekly stoppages to be made, to enable the captains to provide a necessary supply of shirts, shoes, &c., for their companys. The general directs the payment to be made in the following manner: a serj. 6, a corporal 4s. a drummer 4, a private man 3 shillings per week, New York currency, 8 shillings being equel to a dollar at 4s 8d sterling. The mens accompts are hereafter to be made up, signd and cleard, every two months. 205 working men to parade tomorrow morning at ye useual hour, to work for the ingineers; an uncomissiond officer from each regiment with one from Ruggles constantly to attend the ingineers and receive their dirrections. Generals Guard tomorrow, the Jersey Regiment.

Lake George, 2nd July, 1759. Parole, Brunswick.

Colo, of the day tomorrow, Colo. Worster; Field Officer for the picquit this night, Lieut. Colo. Hunt; tomorrow, Lieut. Colo. Saltenstall.

★★★★★★

David Wooster was born in Stratford, Conn., in 1711, and graduated at Yale College in 1718. On the breaking out of the Spanish War in 1739, he was appointed Captain of an armed vessel fitted out by the colony for the protection of the coast, and in 1745 served as Captain in Col, Burr's Regiment at the Siege of Louisburg, on which occasion he was taken prisoner and sent to France. When released, he passed over to England, and was rewarded with a commission of Captain in Sir William Pepperell's Regiment, and went on half pay in 1748, when that regiment was broke. On the renewal of the war with France in 1755, he was appointed Colonel of the 3rd Connecticut Regiment, in which capacity he served in 1758, 1759 and 1760; and when peace was concluded, returned to private life.

He received half-pay as captain in Pepperell's Regiment until 1774, when his name was stricken off the roll. In the following year he was elected Brigadier General in the Continental Army, and served in Canada in the unfortunate campaign of 1775-6. He soon after resigned his commission and was appointed first Major-General of the Connecticut Militia, when he directed his attention to securing that State against the enemy. Whilst opposing a detachment of British troops sent to destroy the public stores at Danbury, he was mortally wounded on the 27th April, and expired on the 2nd May, 1777, aged 66 years, leaving behind him the character of a brave and good officer, an ardent patriot, and an honest, benevolent and virtuous citizen (Barber's *Conn. Hist. Collections*; *Army Lists*).

★★★★★★

The general sees and does not doubt that the men on all occasions will be very alert in turning out against the enemy, but he cant but disaprove of the men runing out on their own accord, on alarms that may happen, and absolutely forbids it. On any little allarm, the men employed at work are to goe on as if nothing had happened, and not to quit their work till ordered. And all the men not perticularly imployed are immediately to joyn their regiments, and none to turn out till ordered. The regiments to receive one days fresh provision tomorrow, beginning at 5 o'clock, with the Rangers, followed with the Light Infantry half an hour after; Grenadiers, Rugles, Inniskilling, Royal Highlanders, Forbess, Jersey, Worster, Fitches, Babcocks, Gages. A return of the effective numbers of each corps to receive provision to be given in to Lieut. Colo. Robison this afternoon at 5 o'clock. All the regiments that have received spruce beer are to pay for what they have received this day inclusive, to Serj. Airey at the brewery tomorrow morning at 8 o'clock.

Lake George, 3rd July, 1759. Parole, Southhampton.
Colo, for the day, Colo. Fitch; Field Officer for the picquit this night, Lieut. Colo. Saltenstall; tomorrow night, Lieut. Colo. Putman.

★★★★★★

Israel Putnam was born in Salem, Massachusetts, January 7th, 1718. In 1739 he removed to Pomfret, Conn. In 1755 he was appointed Lieutenant of the 6th Company of the 3rd Connecticut Regiment, and was afterwards promoted to be Captain. He rendered much service to the army in the neighbourhood of Crown Point, as may be seen by the reports of his scouting parties in *New York Doc. Hist.* IV. In 1756, while near Ticonderoga, he was repeatedly in the most imminent danger. He escaped in an adventure one night with twelve bullet holes in his blanket. In 1757, the Legislature of Connecticut conferred the commission of Major on Putnam, who served that year under Gen. Webb at Fort Edward and was attached to the army under Abercrombie in 1758.

In August of that year he was sent out with several hundred men to watch the motions of the enemy. Being ambuscaded by a party of equal numbers, a general but irregular action took place. He had discharged his fusee several times, but at length it missed fire while its muzzle was presented to the breast of a savage, who, with his lifted hatchet and a tremendous war-whoop, compelled him to surrender, and then bound him to a tree. At night he was stript, and a fire kindled to roast him alive; but a French officer saved him. The next day he arrived at Ticonderoga, and thence he was carried a prisoner to Montreal. He was soon after exchanged through the ingenuity of his fellow prisoner, Colonel Schuyler, and joined the army under Amherst, as Lieutenant-Colonel in the 4th Connecticut Regiment. In 1760 he accompanied the army from Oswego to Montreal. In 1762, commanded his regiment in the attack on Havana. In 1763 he rose to the rank of colonel, and accompanied an expedition against the Western Indians, after which he returned to his farm.

In 1770, he went to the Mississippi River to select some lands, but returned soon after, and was ploughing in his field in 1775, when he heard the news of the Battle of Lexington. He immediately unyoked his team, left his plough on the spot, and without changing his clothes set off for Cambridge. In the Battle of Bunker's Hill, he exhibited his usual intrepidity. When the army was organised by Gen. Washington at Cambridge, Putnam, who had been elected major-general in June, 1775, was appointed to command the Reserve. In August, 1776, he was stationed at Brooklyn, on Long Island. After the defeat of our army he went to New York and was very serviceable in the city and neighbourhood.

In October or November, he was sent to Philadelphia to fortify that City; in January, 1777, was directed to take post at Princeton, where he continued until the following Spring, when he was appointed to the command of a separate army in the Highlands of New York. After the loss of Fort Montgomery, the commander-in-chief determined to build another fortification, and he directed Putman to fix. upon the site. To him belongs the praise of having chosen West Point. The campaign of 1779, which was principally spent in strengthening the works at this place, finished the military career of Putnam. A paralytic affection impaired the activity of his body, and he passed the remainder of his days in retirement, retaining his relish for enjoyment, his strength of memory, and all the faculties of his mind. He died at Brooklyn, Conn., May 29, 1790, aged 72.

★★★★★★

Generals Guard tomorrow Worsters. The regiment to send all their empty barrels under the care of a serj. to Colo. Montresor and give in a return to the major of brigade of the number sent. Montgomerys, Williards and the New Hampshire Regiments to send in a return of their masons tomorrow morning to the major of brigade. These regiments will be supplyd with spruce beer, by sending their quarter-matters to Colo. Robison. Every regiment that has iron crows or sledge hammers, are immediately to send them to Serj. Grant, at the artillery; 350 workmen to parade tomorrow morning at the useual hour to work for the inginiers.

Lake George, 4th July, 1759. Parole, Chichester

For the day tomorrow, Colo. Grant; Field Officers for ye picquit this night, Regulars Lieut. Colo. Darby, Provencials Lieut. Colo. Gaugh, (Goffe); tomorrow night Maj. Campbell, Lieut. Colo. Smedly, Maj. Whiteing.

★★★★★★

John Goffe was born in 1701, probably in Boston and settled at the Mouth of the Cohos Brook, about three miles below the City of Manchester, N. H., at what is called Moor's Village, and in early life was designated as "Hunter John." He moved subsequently to Bedford, Hillsboro County, where he built some mills, and in 1746 was captain of a company of militia and did duty on the frontier. He was elected Moderator in 1750, and in 1755 commanded one of the companies of the New Hampshire Regiment sent to reinforce General Johnson at Lake George. On the project of an expedition against Crown Point in 1757, New Hampshire raised a regiment part of which under Lieut. Col. Goffe rendezvoused at Charlestown on the Connecticut River, thence marched to Albany and afterwards were sent to Fort William Henry to reinforce Col. Munro.

In the subsequent massacre 80 of Goffe's men were either killed or taken by the Indians. In Amherst's Campaign he was second to Colonel Lovewell, and in 1760 commanded 800 Provincials raised also in New Hampshire, who instead of rendezvousing at Albany cut a road through the woods from Charlestown to Crown Point, and proceeded down Lake Champlain under Colonel Haviland, with whom they entered Montreal.

As a specimen of the military dress and discipline of the time, the following order is inserted. it is copied from Adjutant Hobart's record, and is dated Litchfield, May 25, 1760:

Colonel Goffe requires the officers to be answerable that the men's shirts are changed twice every week at least; that such as have hair that will admit of it must have

79

it constantly tyed; they must be obliged to comb their heads and wash their hands every morning, and as it is observed that numbers of men accustom themselves to wear woollen nightcaps in the day time, he allows them hats; they are ordered for the future not to be seen in the day time with anything besides their hats on their heads, as the above mentioned custom of wearing nightcaps must be detrimental to their health and cleanliness; the men's hats to be all cocked, or cut uniformly as Colonel Goffe pleases to direct. (Fox's *Hist. of Dunstable*).

In 1768, he was Colonel of the 9th New Hampshire Regiment, and was one of the Patentees of Amherst and represented that town and Bedford, which were classed together, from 1767 to 1775. From 1771 to 1776, be was Judge of Probate, and when the Revolution broke out, warmly sided with his country. He died October 20, 1781, and has left his name to Goffestown, N. H. His son, Major John Goffe, served in the War of Independence (Belknap, III; *N. H. Hist. Coll.,* I.,V.; Farmer and Moore's *Collections,* III; Woodbury's *History of Bedford*).

★★★★★★

If the regiments that marched in yesterday want provisions, they will receive, ye Regulars to ye 5th, ye Provincials to the 6th, inclusively, which is the time the regiments in camp are provided to, including the fresh provisions that have been received. A field officer of the Regular Regiment for their picquits, and a lieut. colo, and major of the Provencials for the picquits of the Provencial troops. The advanced guard on the west side is to consist of one captain, 2 subs., 2 serjts., 2 corpus and 30 men. The post beyond the Old Fort to consist of one serj. one corporal and 12 men. Colo. Williard and Colo. Lymon to send their quaintity of men to the artillery in the same manner as ordered on the 22nd of June to Maj. Ord.

At 2 o'clock this day these two regiments are carefully to examine into their amunition and see that their arms are in good order. They are to be out tomorrow morning at 5 o'clock to fire 3 rounds by platoons in the same manner as the other Provencial Regiments have done; the major of brigade will give them all orders relative thereto, and the deputy adj. general will attend and show them the place where they will fire. The camp not to be allarmd at fireing here nor at the 4 Mile Post, where they will fire at the same hour. Gages Light Infantry and Rangers will furnish an escort as usual between the camp and Col. Forsters post. That post furnishes no men tomorrow, and the captan will despose of his detachment accordingly. The regiments will give in a return of their miners tomorrow morning at orderly time to the major of brigade; also of the bricklayers. The masons that have been returned from Montgomerys, New Hampshire and Williards Regiments to attend Colo. Montresor tomorrow morning at 5 o'clock. 350 men for the ingineers, and 2 covering partys, as this day. A corporal and 4 men to mount at the ingineers incampment,

Lake George, 5th July, 1759. Parole, Hampstead.

Collo. of the day tomorrow Collo Montgomery; Field Officers for the picquitts this night, Regulars, Major Campbell; tomorrow night, Major Gordon; Provencialls, this night, Lieut. Collo. Smedley and Major Whitting; tomorrow night, Lieut. Collo. Hunt, Major Baldwin. A generall court martiall to set tomorrow morning at the Presidents tent at 8 o'clock for the tryall of a man suspected of robbery. Collo. Ruggles President, Major Graham and Major Waterbury, late Forbes 2 capt. Innilkilling 2 capt. Royall Highlanders 1, Montgomerys 1, Ruggles one, Williards one, Skylers one, and Limmons one captains members.

The Regular Regiments will receive three days fresh provision to the 8th inclusive, beginning at 5 in the morning with Gages, followed at half an hour distance between each, late Forbess, Montgomerys, Royal Highlanders, Inniskilling, Grenadiers, Light Infantry, Rangers. If the weather should be warm, the men most dress all the provisions, that it may not be spoiled. The Generals Guard tomorrow, Fitches. 350 men to work for the engineers tomorrow and two covering parties as this day. Six miners of Williards Regiment and one of Babcocks to attend the engineers tomorrow morning at 5 o'clock.

The regiments will make a return of their brick makers to the major of brigade tomorrow at orderly time. Gages Regiment and Rangers to furnish a detachment on the road as usuall. The bridges will be repaired and coverd with earth. Ens. Rivett will direct this work. Lieut. George Burton is appointed to act as judge-advocate to the court martial. Two companys of Grenadiers to be readie in an hour to cover a large Provinciall working party; they are to continue at work till noon.

Lake George, 6th July, 1759. Parole, Newtown.

Collo. of the day tomorrow, Collo. Schuyler; Field Officers for the picquits this night, Regulars Major Gordon; tomorrow night Lieut. Collo. Darby, Provincials this night, Lieut. Collo. Hunt, Major Baldwin; tomorrow night, Lieut. Collo. Saltenstall and Major Baldwin.

★★★★★★

John Darby was commissioned Major of the 17th Regiment 21st September 1756 and served in 1758 at the Siege of Louisbourg. He was promoted to be Lieutenant-Colonel 14th May, 1759, and after going through this campaign commanded the battalion of Grenadiers and Light Infantry in Colonel Haviland's division of the invading army in 1760. He was afterwards Adjutant-General in the expedition against Martinico in 1762 and became Colonel in the Army in 1772. The regiment was again ordered to America in 1775, in October of which year he left the army (*Army Lists*; Knox, I, II; Beatson's *Naval and Military Mem.*, III).

★★★★★★

The Provincial Regiments to receive three days fresh provision tomorrow, which completes them to the 9th inclusively, beginning with Ruggles at 5 o'clock, followed at half an hours intervall by Williard, Lyman, Schuyler, Worcesters, Fitches and Babcocks. They will send in returns at 5 this evening to Commissary Wilson of their effectives that draw provisions. The commanding officers of regiments will enspect into their companys having a sufficient number of scoups for belling the *batteaux*, and the general expects that every regiment will have every thing prepared for crossing the lake, whenever the order is given.

The commanding officers who been on the parties in the *Batteaux* Service, are to send in this day the number and names of the men who are entitled to payment for the same, as ordered the 23rd May, to Brigade Major Moniepenny at 4 this afternoon, that the men may be paid for the same tomorrow. 400 men under the command of Major Dougrie to be out tomorrow at 5 o'clock and return at 12. Gages Regiment and Rangers to furnish posts on the road as usuall. 400 working men for the engineers, with 2 covering parties, as this day; the engineers to blow the mines tomorrow morning after Revallie; the camp not to be alarmd.

Lake George, 7th July, 1759. Parole, Nestroy.

Collo. of the day tomorrow, Collo. Lyman; Field Officers for the picquits this night Regulars Lieut. Collo. Darby, Provincials Lieut. Collo. Saltenstall, Maj. Williard; for tomorrow night, Regulars Major Campbell, Provincials Lieut. Collo. Putman, Major Douglais. The post in the front of Fitches Regiment to be occupied by a serj. and 12 men of the Regulars, which are to be sent from the pickets every evening at gunn fireing, and will come off half an hour after Revallie beating. The order releating to ox teams in stead of waggons is recalled, and all suttlers who have passes are permitted to use what waggons, carts or horses they find most convenient for transporting refreshments to the army. The officers commanding at the several posts have orders to let all waggons pass accordingly, the prohibitation of rum and spiritous liquors always remaining in full force. Generals Guard tomorrow, Rhode Islanders. 400 Men to parade at usuall time tomorrow morning for the engineers and two covering partys as usual. 400 ax-men under the command of Major Dowgrie to be out at 5 o'clock and return at 12. All straggling cattle whatever from the different posts will be drove tomorrow to Fort Edward; if any people have lost cattle they will take this opportunity to look for them, as this is the last search that will be made.

Lake George, 8th July, 1759. Parole, Richmond.

Collo, of the day tomorrow, Collo. Worcester; Field Officers for the picquitts this night, Regulars Major Campbell, Provincialls Lieut. Collo. Putman, Major Douglass; tomorrow night Major Gordon, Lieut. Collo. Miller, Major Whitting. The Provinciall Regiments to be under arms tomorrow morning at 5 o'clock. Collo. Townshend will begin on the right, and Lieut. Collo. Amherst on the left, and see they are told off in the menner that has been directed in the generall orders; that their may be no mistake; and that they understand thoroughly what is meant by the front rank and rear platoons; this is not to hinder their furnishing such men for work as may be ordered.

The Regulars to receive 4 days provision tomorrow, beginning at 5 o'clock with the Light Infantry of Regiments, followed by the Grenadiers, Inniskilling, Royal Highlanders, Montgomerys late Forbes, Royall Artillery, Gages. It is repeated that the Rangers always receive 2 days beforehand, and for four days and three days alternatly; thes four days provisions compleats the Regulars to the 12 inclusively; the Regulars to give all the workingmen tomorrow except the masons. Babcocks Regiment to be out tomorrow at 5 o'clock to fire 3 rounds by platoons.

Any man of the other Provinciall Regiments that have not fired to be out at the same time with proper officirs, and will likewise fire three rounds, drawn up on the left of Babcocks. All the other

Provincial Regiments will be out at 6 o'clock, and Collo. Babcocks after fireing will joyn them in order to practise what was given out in this morning orders. 400 working men for the use of the engineers tomorrow the Royall Highlanders to take the General Guard tomorrow half an hour after 4, that Babcocks Guard may joyn the regiment, Babcocks will take the Guard after the field day is over. The Grenadiers and brigade of Royall and late Forbes, are during the campaign to be drawn up two deep on all services; this makes no alteration in the posting of officers, or the telling off the battalions in grand divisions, sub divisions and platoons, or in the front and flank, and rear and flank platoons.

When a battalion is told off in platoons on the parade, the whole battalion is to be three deep, the two centre platoons close, and an interval! of half the front of a platoon left between each platoon from the one on the right of the centre to the platoon on the right of the battalion; the same is to be observed from the platoon on the left of the centre to the platoon on the left of the battalion. The commanding officer will then order the officers commanding platoons to form them two deep, which they will do by dividing the rear rank, those on the right of the colours, facing to the right, and those on the left facing to the left, and halting when in the intervalls the first half forms on the right of the front rank, of each platoon on the right of the colours, and on the left of each rank on the left of the colours; the second half forms in the like manner on the right and left of the 2nd Rank.

If there is an odd man the officer takes what man he chuses as his second. This method is always to be practised, that every officer commanding a platoon may have the men of the third rank opposite to him, that in case the service require it, the whole battalion could be formed three deep in an instant, by the officers of the platoons forming the rear rank as they were, which is never to be done unless the officer commanding the battalion orders it. The men to be acquainted that this is ordered, as the enemy has very few regular troops to oppose us; and that no yelling of Indians or fire of Canadians can possibly brake their rank, if the men are silent, attentive and obedient to their officers, who will led them to the enemy, and their silence will terrific the enemy more then any huzzeaing or noise they can make; which the generall absolutely forbids, and their attention and obedience to the officers who command platoons will ensure success to his Majestys arms.

The General Court Martial, of which Collo. Ruggles was President, is desolved. The general has approved of the sentence of the above General Court Martial. George Dougherty of the Inniskilling Regiment, accused of suspicion of braking open a trunk, is judged not guilty of the crime laid to his charge, and therefore aquited. William Harper, soldier in General Gages Light Infantry, accused of thieft, is found guilty of the crime laid to his charge, and is to receive 400 lashes with a catt-and-nine-tails, John Cotter, soldier in General Gages Light Infantry, accused of desertion is found guilty of the crime laid to his charge, and is to receive 1000 lashes with (cat) and nine tails.

Lake George, 9th July, 1759, Parole, Cashell.

Collo. of the day tomorrow, Collo. —; Field Officers for the picquitts this night, Regulars; Provincials, Lieut. Collo. Miller, Major Whitting; tomorrow night, Major Graham, Lieut. Collo. Gooff, and Major Baldwin. The Provincial Regiments to receive four days provision tomorrow, beginning at 5 o'clock by Babcocks, following Fitch, Worcesters, Schuyler, Williard, Lovell, Ruggles. This compleats them to the 13 inclusive. The Grenadiers to relieve all the out guards of the camp, which are not regimentall at 5 o'clock this evening. The major of brigade to send the details to Collo. Haviland immediately. The Regular Regiments of the line will be readie formed at the head of their encampment between 4 and 5 o'clock tomorrow morning; if a fine day, the men will be in their waistcoats, with their arms and ammunition.

Commanding officers of battalions will have their orders sent them by the generall. Collo. Grant to be on horseback. No soldiers to stir out of camp except those ordered on particular dutys, and no man to go from this to Fort Edward wards untill above regiments return to camp, and none to be permitted to stir from ther posts or the communication tomorrow, untill permission is sent. The Rangers and Indians most be observant of this order, for if they are straggling in the woods, they will be shot. The Generals Guard tomorrow late Forbess. The camp not to be alarmed at any fireing they may hear tomorrow morning from the regiment that are ordered out. 400 working men from the Provincials to attend the engineers tomorrow morning at 5 o'clock and 2 covering partys as usuall. 1 serjt. and 12 men from the Provincialls picquit to cover the oxen tomorrow at nine o'clock and remain till 3 o'clock. Eighteen men from the Provincials to parade every evening at 6 o'clock, to assist the teamsters in cutting grass for the oxen. At night, a serjt. of the Provincials to be fixed upon to look after the teams, and be imployed in that service only.

Lake George, 10th July, 1759. Parole, Flatebosh.

Collo. of the day tomorrow Collo. Babcock; Field Officers of the picquitts this night, Regulars Major Grahams, Lieut. Collo. Goff, Major Baldwin. The Regular Regiments to compleat their ammunition immediately. The court martial of the line of which Capt. James Murray was President; Abram Ashton captain of waggoners, tryed for stealing his Majestys arms and working tools, is found guilty and is sentenced to receive 400 lashies. William Rose, George Waggoner, John Stods, Markives Richard, John Mitchell, John Frederick, Peter Lenan, Hermanes Conreck, John Trice, Peter Miller, tryed for the same is found guilty, but as their crimes did not appear so notorious, is sentenced to receive 300 lashes. George Suple, Danack Esar, and the three negroes are not found guilty and are therefore acquitted.

******

James Murray was the second son of Lord George Murray and grandson of the 1st Duke of Atholl, was commissioned Captain in the 42nd Highlanders, 20th July, 1757; was wounded in the attack on Ticonderoga in 1758 and was again wounded in the expedition against Martinico in 1762. He exchanged into the 3rd Regiment of Foot Guards, in which he became Captain with the rank of Lieutenant-Colonel in the army, 3rd November, 1 769, and was appointed Governor of Upnor, in 1775. His uncle, the 2nd Duke of Atholl, having been authorised to raise a regiment, which was called the 77th or Atholl Highlanders, the command of it was given to Colonel Murray 25th December, 1777.

This regiment remained in Ireland during the war, at the conclusion of which, having received orders for the East Indies, it mutinied and was disbanded. Colonel Murray became Governor of Fort William in 1780, Major-General in 1782, and in the following year was appointed Colonel of the 78th or Seaforth's Highlanders, the number of which was changed in 1786 to the 72nd (*Army Lists*; Browne's *Highl. Clans*, IV). He was not engaged in any active service after leaving the 42nd and died unmarried in March, 1794 (Debrett).

******

The generall approves of the above sentences and orders that the prisoners, Abram Ashton, captain of the waggoners, to receive 36 lashes with the cat-and-nine-tails at the head of the 4 Regular Regiments, and the 7 Provinciall Regiments in camp, beginning with the 17th and ending with Schuylers, and that he be turnd out of camp and deemd unworthie of serving in the army again. The general is pleased to pardon William Ross, George Waggoner, Peter Lenan, Markives Richard, John Mitchell, John Fredrick, John Stodes, Hermanus Conrick, John Trice and Peter Millir, but orders that they be marchd round the camp and see the punishment of Abram Ashton, and they are all to be marchd back to Saratoga, from thence to bring the tools that were stoln back to camp.

One serjt. and 16 Regulars to receive the prisoners from the provost guard, who are to go round and see the punishment inflicted; after which the serjt. will deliver the prisoners to the provost guard. Whittings Regiment to receive provisions tomorrow to the 13th inclusive, at five o'clock; the Indians to receive 2 days provisions tomorrow at 6 o'clock, for their effective numbers; hereafter they are to receive every two days for 2 days. 400 working men to attend the engeniers and 2 covering parties as usuall; ten carpenters to be furnished by the Provincials for the engeniers tomorrow; the Regular Regiments to settle their accompts with Mr. Naiper Doctor General of the hospitall, to the 24th June inclusive.

Lake George, 11th July, 1759. Parole C.

Collo. of the day tomorrow Collo, Lovell; Field Officers of the picquits this night, Regulars Lieut. Collo. Darby, Provincialls Lieut. Collo. Smedly, Major Waterbury; tomorrow night Major Campbell, Lieut. Collo. Hunt, Major Moor. A serjt. and 12 men of each regiment of the line except the 1st Battalion of Ruggless and New Jersey Regiments, to be sent to the water-side at 3 o'clock this evening where Collo. Bradstreet will order an officer to shew them the kind of stones they most gett to moor the *batteaux*, which they most get off the side of the lake and not take any that are within the encampment; they most bring them in the *batteaux* to the shore side; the regiments to receive their *batteaux* at 4 o'clock this evening by applying to Capt. Loaren.

Collo. Bradstreet will show in what manner they are to be moored; and they are to be drawn up Forbess on the left next the Capt's Post on the east side the Lake; Rugles 2nd Battalion on the right on this side the Capt's Post on the west side the lake, Montgomerys the right of Forbess, then Royal Highlanders, Inniskilling; room to be left for Predeaux and the Royal; Williard upon the left of Ruggles, then New

Jersey, New Hampshire, Babcock, Whitting, Fitch, Worcester and Lymans. A whale boat will be allowed to each regiment for the commanding officer which may be received at the same time and moored with the *batteaux*, those of the Regulars on the left, those the Provincials on the right of their *batteaux*. 35 *batteaux* will be delivered to each of the regiments of the Royall, Royall Highlanders and Montgomerys and 26 to Forbess, Inniskilling and Predeaux 2nd Battalion Ruggles, Williards, Lovell, Babcock, Whitting, Fitch, Worcester and Lymman.

Oars and whatever else belonging to the *batteaux* will be delivered at the same time, and each regiment will keep a guard of a corporall and 6 men for the care of the *batteaux*, &c., and they will receive their *batteaux* in the same order as the regiments are given out. Each *batteaux* will carry 12 barrells of flour or nine of pork when ordered to load, and it is supposed will have about 20 men or a few more besides in each *batoe*. If the above number should not agree, commanding officers will apply accordingly and make application for what they shall want for their suttler.

The whole army to receive 3 days fresh provisions tomorrow, beginning by Gages at 5 o'clock following Royall Artillery, Forbes, Montgomerys, Royall Highlanders, Inniskilling, Grenadiers, Light Infantry, Rangers, Whittings, Ruggles, Williards, Lovell, Schuyler, Worcester, Fitch, Babcock. This compleats the Regulars to the 15th and the Provincials to the 16th inclusily. If the weather is hot the men will dress their provisions immediately that it may not spoile. A detachment of a 120 men to be commanded by a major to be made from the Provincialls, as a guard for the posts and protection of the workmen that are to be left here. Major Dowgrie for this command, he will receive particular orders from the generall.

★★★★★★

Dowgrie—this name is spelled so variously in the MS. that it is not easy to determine to whom it belonged. Robert Durkee of Norwich, Conn., was a famous partisan who served with Putnam in 1755, 6, and shared many of his hair breadth 'scapes through the French War. He subsequently moved to the Connecticut Settlement in the Valley of the Wyoming, Penn., and after doing good Service in the Revolutionary Struggle, was killed in the memorable Battle of Wyoming 3rd July, 1778 (Sparks' *Am. Biography*, VII; Chap man's *Hist. of Wyoming*; Stone's *Brant*, I).

★★★★★★

Officers and non-commissioned officers will be left in proportion to their number and a tent for every six men. This detachment will encamp tomorrow morning at 5 o'clock on the ground. Collo. Montrezore will direct the arms for the above men to be inspected and to see they are in good order and their ammunition compleated. Captain Turnie of Ruggle Regiment, and Captain Hearbey of Lymans are appointed to act as Major of Brigade to the Provinciall troops and are to be obeyd as shuch.

Captain John Campbell of the Royall Highlanders is appointed Major in late Forbes and is to be obeyed as such. The regiments to receive their *batteaux* tomorrow morning at 5 o'clock in the same manner as ordered this day. Some recruits will fire ball tomorrow morning at 5 o'clock, the camp not to be alarmed; 400 working men and two covering parties for the engenier as usual. 100 men of Whittings to load shot &c. on board the sloop tomorrow, a non-comisssiond officer will be sent to conduct: them. Eighty working men to be employed by Captain Louing to be sent at 5 o'clock. Generals Guard tomorrow Inniskilling.

Lake George, 12th July, 1759. Parole, Fairfeild.

Collo. for tomorrow Collo. Williard; for the picquits this night, Regulars Major Allexander Campbell, Provincialls Lieut. Collo, Hunt, Major Moor; tomorrow night, Regulars Major Gordon, Provincials Lieut. Collo. Saltenstall, Major Williard.

★★★★★★

Alexander Campbell was appointed Major of the Montgomery Highlanders, then the 62nd, 7th January, 1757, on the organisation of that regiment; made the campaign under Brigadier Forbes in 1758, and under Amherst in 1759; was promoted to be Lieutenant-Colonel of the 95th, 22nd March, 1761, and went on half-pay in 1763; was appointed Lieutenant-Governor of Fort George, Scotland, in 1774, and filled that post until 1778. His regiment was called into service again in 1780, and he returned to half pay in 1783; he became Colonel in the Army in Nov., 1790; Maj. General in Oct., 1794; Lieut. General in January, 1801and died in 1804 (*Army Lists*).

★★★★★★

The guard on the boats must moor them more within shore every evening in shuch a manner as Collo, Bradstreet will direct, and every commanding officer of a regiment will take care to put water in them, or to have them to hold in water every day that they may not be leakie when load. The artificers of the Royall Radow and the Rangers employed at Fort Edward by Collo. Eyre and those employed on the works here, will be paid by Collo. Montrezure (Montresor) according to the order of the 21st May, and up to Saturday the 7th July inclusive.

★★★★★★

James Montresor became Director of Engineers and Lieutenant-Colonel in the British Army 4th January, 1758, in which year he was at the head of the Engineer Department in the expedition against Ticonderoga under Abercrombie. He drew the plan of Fort Stanwix and the surrounding country in the Summer of the same year (*N.Y. Doc. Hist.*, 8vo.). He was Chief Engineer also to Amherst's Expedition and superintended the construction of Fort George, at the head of Lake George, in July, 1759 (Knox's *Journal*, 1). He obtained in 1771 a grant of 10,000 acres of land at the forks of the Pagkatagkan, or Otter, Creek in the present town of Panton, Vt., and in May, 1772, became Colonel in the Army. He died in the month of December, 1775 (*Army Lists ;N.Y. Land Papers*),

★★★★★★

The commanding officers of regiments will have a list sent them of what artificers each corps is to leave here continued; they will leave their arms, ammunition and tents aggreeable to the order given to the detachment under Major Dougrie and will encamp tomorrow morning at Revallie beating as Collo. Montrezure will direct. No evening gunn will be fired this evening, the drummers to take the Retreat from Forbess. The regiments to give in immediately to Mr. Russell at the engeniers encampment all the hammers belonging to the engineers that has not yet been given in.

A General Court Martiall of the Regulars to be held tomorrow morning at 6 o'clock, Collo. Grant President, Collo, Darby, Major John Campbell, Forbess 3 captains, Inniskilling 2, Royall Train 2, Montgomerys 3. Lieut. George Burton Judge Advocate. Major Ord to try some carces's this evening at 9 o'clock, the camp not to be alarmed, as it will tend very much for the good of his Majestys Service, that the works going on here should be carried on with as much expedition as possible that the army may be able to proceed. The work men are at present to work from 5 to 12 and from 2 to 7. Every regiment to march and number their own *batteaux*. 400 working men and 2 covering as usual. 40 men for fatigue to be at work at 5 o'clock to assist Capt. Loaring,

Lake George, 13th July, 1759. Parole, Newhaven.

Collo, of the day tomorrow Collo. Grant; Field Officers for the picquit, Regulars Major Gordon; Provincialls, Lieut. Collo. Saltenstall, Major Williard; tomorrow night, Major Graham, Lieut Collo. Putman, Major Douglass. Generals Guard tomorrow, Royall Highlanders. Richard Stubbs, Soldier in the Inniskilling Regiment, sentenced to suffer death for desertion, to be executed today at twelve o'clock, the picquits of the line to form at the head of the encampment of their regiments at 11 o'clock, the whole under the command of the field officer of the picquitts; the collo. of the day to command the whole when formed. Williards, Ruggles, New Hampshire, Babcocks, Fitches, will march by the left, and proceed by the right of the Grenadiers, and draw up in the front of their quarter guard; the Royall Highlanders, Montgomerys, Forbess, will march to the front, closing in to the Royall Highlanders picquitt, which will joyn the left of Ruggles, in the front of the quarter guard of the Grenadiers; the New Jersey Regiment will march by the right, joyning the left of Forbess; a platoon of the Inniskilling for the execution of the prisoner, who will be marched by the provost and guard to the left of the Jersey Regiment, and so along the front to the right picquitts, where the platoon of Blakeneys will be formed.

The General Court Martiall, of which Collo. Grant was Presedent, is dissolved, Collo. Ruggles to send a serjt. and 12 men to prepear stones and receive *batteaux* for his first battalion, which will be delivered to them at 12 o'clock; which Collo. Lyman will order one of the Connecticut battalions to do the same for his regiment. The Regulars will receive a proportion of flower for 5 days, immediately, beginning with Forbess, Montgomerys, Royal Highlanders, Inniskilling, Gages, Grenadiers, Light Infantry, Rangers, which they are to get baked tomorrow and keept.

The Provincials are to receive the same tomorrow morning at 5 o'clock, beginning with Williard, Ruggles, New Hampshire, Rhode Island, Fitch, Whitting, Worcester, Schuyler, which they will also have baked immediately and not made use of. Fifty more *batteaux* will be delivered to Major Oard for the use of the artillery, and two more to each regiment for the use of their suttlers. If the commanding officers of regiments or artillery have any *batteaux* that they think insufficient, they will immediately apply and have them exchanged. 450 working men and two covering partys as usuall for the engeniers.

Lake George, 14th July, 1759. Parole, Guilford.

Collo, for the day tomorrow, Collo. Montgomery; Field Officers for the picquits this night, Regulars, Major Grahams; Provincialls, Lieut. Collo. Putman, Major Douglass; tomorrow night, Major John Campbell, Lieut. Collo. Miller, Major Whitting. The regiments to pay tomorrow in the afternoon, in the same manner as they did last time, for what spruce beer they have received since that payment. The Rangers and Indians are to fire off their pieces tomorrow morning at 5 o'clock in the front of the encampment, at marks. They will afterwards put their arms in the best order they can. It is repeated to the men are on no account to touch their five days bread they were ordered to keep.

The surgeons of the severall regiments to meet Docter Monroa at the General Hospitall this afternoon at 4 o'clock, who will diredt what proportion of medicens &c. each of them are to furnish for the Light Infantry, which are immediately to be given to the surgeon that takes care of that corps. Ruggles Battalion and Lymans Regiment as well as the detachment that marched in with them, are to be out tomorrow at 5 o'clock to fire 2 rounds in the same manner as the other regiments have done. Collo. Townshend to attend them. The general has observed that several arms of both those regiments and the detachment are much out of repair.

The regiments will send a return to Major Moor of the number of men not. under arms on that account, and they are to repair shuch arms immediately, and when repaired they are to be out to fire. The above two regiments, after fireing, will receive a proportion of flower for 5 days bread, which they are to receive and keep in the same manner as the rest of the army, and are to receive provisions to compleat them to the 16th, inclusive, to which time all the rest of the Provincials are victualled. 430 working men and 2 covering parties for the engineers.

Lake George, 15th July, 1759. Parole, Croydon.

For the day tomorrow, Collo. Schuyler; Field Officers for the picquits this night, Regulars, Major Campbell; Provincialls, Collo. Miller, Major Whitting; tomorrow night, Lieut. Colo. Darby, Lieut. Collo. Pysan, Major Bell; Generals Guard tomorrow, Montgomerys. The Regular Regiments to receive 3 days provision tomorrow begining at 5 o'clock, with Light Infantry of Regiments, and following Grenadiers,

Inniskilling, Royall Highlanders Forbess, Montgomerys, Royall Artillery, Gages. The battalions of Ruggles and Lymans and the detachment that marched into camp this last night, will send this evening at 5 o'clock to Mr. Wilson, Commissary, a return of the effective number that marched in, and they will receive tomorrow morning at 5 o'clock three days fresh provisions, beginning by Ruggles, and following Lymmons, and if detachments of regimentys, the regiments that have baked bread for five days most now expended, that it may not be spoiled, and they will continue to bake the flower they receive, that they may have always five days bread beforehand when the army embarks.

The Rangers and Provincials Regiments that fired this day are to compleat their ammunition, apply to Major Ord of the Artillery. As shells and shot may have been left by the enemy or may be fired from the enemy durring the campaign, will be of use in finding back to them again, the following prices shall be allowed to those who shall pick them up and deliver them to the commanding officer at the Artillery Park, for a 13 inch shell one doller; 10 inch shell a half doller; an 8 inch shell a quarter dollar; large shot shall be paid at 2 pence each, and smaller at 1 penny each. All arms taken from the enemy are to be taken to the head quarters. The men who takes shuch arms will be allowed 5 shillings for every good repairable firelock.

1 capt. 2 subs, 3 serjts. and 60 volunterrs of the Inniskilling Regiment to parade at the head of their regiment half an hour after 9 o'clock this night, with their arms and ammunition, their cloaths on, and to carry their blankets. To take spruce beer with them, and one days bread. They will march down to the waterside, where they will joyn a detachment of the Light Infantry and follow shuch orders as they shall receive from Collo. Townshend.

★★★★★★

Roger Townshend, fourth son of Charles Viscount Townshend, was commissioned lieutenant-colonel 1st Feb., 1758, and served as adjutant-general in the expedition against Louisbourg, and deputy adjutant-general in this campaign with rank of colonel. He was killed in the trenches before Ticonderoga by a cannon ball on the 25th July, 1759, and his remains were transmitted to Albany for interment (Knox, I). His spirit and military knowledge justly entitled him to the esteem of every soldier; and accordingly, the loss of him was universally lamented (Mante).

★★★★★★

The detachment of Montgomerys that marched into camp this

day, to receive fresh provisions tomorrow for 3 days, at the same time that Ruggles do. The quarter-master will send to Commissary Wilson this evening, the effective numbers of the detachment. This detachment, as likewise the recovered men of the Provincialls marched into camp this day are to fire two rounds of ball this day at 6 o'clock, where the Provincials fired. The adjutant of Montgomerys to attend the whole and divide them into small platoons.

The picquits of the 2 battalions of Ruggles, Williards, New Hampshire, and Babcocks, are to parade tomorrow morning at Revallie beating at the head of their camp. They will march to the right, and joyn Babcocks. From thence they will be marchd by Collo. Miller field officer of the picketts to a post on the west side of the lake, where he will be conducted by an officer of the Rangers and will be joyned by a 150 Rangers. The generall will send further orders to the Lieut. Collo. The men to take one days provision, marching with their coats and blankets. 450 working men and 2 covering parties for the engeniers tomorrow; 100 working men for the artillery, 40 for Capt. Loring, 200 for Lieut. Collo. Putman to finish his garden, to take what tools he directs.

Lake George, 16th July, 1759. Parole, Northwalk.

For the day tomorrow Collo. Lyman, for the picquitts this night, Regulars, Lieut. Collo. Darby; Provincialls, Lieut. Paysan, Major Baldwin; tomorrow night, Major Alexander Campbell, Lieut. Collo. Goff, Major Waterbury. The regiments of brigade, the Royall and Forbes and the Provincials Regiments, will each send an officer and 20 men with arms and a party of their *batteaux*; that when they are loaded that none of the provisions may be spoiled those partys to be sent out immediately in *batteaux* to go to the water side, the west side of the lake. But none must attemp to pass the post the five picquits is marched to. Commanding officers of battalions to attend Brigadier General Gage at 12 o'clock this day.

The Provincials to receive 3 days provisions tomorrow at 5 o'clock, beginning with Babcocks, following Fitches, Worcester, Schuyler, Lovell, Williard, Ruggles, Whitting; they will send a return of their effective numbers to the commissary this evening, and will be observant of the order of yesterday concerning the bread. Capt. Loreing will give whale boats this evening to Gages and the Light Infantry that wants. The two companys of Grenadiers next for duty to parade tomorrow morning at 5 o'clock at their own encampment; they will be joyned by an officer and forty Rangers to each companie, and march from thence as a covering party to 500 Provincials; for the above duty the 27 and 42nd Companys of Grenadiers. Commanding officers of Regular Regiments and the corp of Light Infantry and Grenadiers do send in a return without delay of the arms and bayonets wanting to compleat. Eight of the Provincial Regiments are to give 13 men each, and two of the Provincial Regiments 14 men for the Ranging Service; the men to be told they will be paid for it the difference of that between the Provincial pay and that of the Rangers.

Commanding officers of those battalions to turn out all volunteers willing to serve in the Rangers tomorrow morning at 10 o'clock. Major Rogers will attend and chuse the number each regiment is to turn out of shuch voluntiers. A General Court Martial of the line to set tomorrow morning at 8 o'clock, at the Presidents tent, to try two men of late Forbess. Collo. Whitting, President; Lieut. Collo. Putman, Major Alex. Campbell, five captains from the Regulars, five from the Provincials, Lieut. George Burton Judge Advocate. 450 working men, and two covering parties as usual, for the engineers; 20 men for fatigue for Loreing; 100 working men for Major Ord as usual; 500 Provincials to parade tomorrow morning at 5 o'clock with axes, in the front of the Grenadiers; Major Williard to command this party, Lieut. Gray will attend.

Lake George, 17th July, 1759. Parole, Philadelphia.

For the day tomorrow Collo. Ruggles; Field Officers for the picquits this night, Regulars, Major Gordon; Provincials, Lieut. Collo, Goff, Major Waterbury; tomorrow night, Major Graham, Lieut. Collo. Smedley, Major Moor.

******

John Moor is supposed to have belonged to Londonderry, N. H. Two officers of the name served one as a captain and another a lieutenant, at the Siege of Louisbourg in 1745. Captain John Moor raised a Company in Londonderry in 1756, which was drafted into the New Hampshire Regiment (Fanner and Moore's *N. H. Collections*, III; Parker's *Hist. of Londonderry*). Some of the family emigrated afterwards to Cherry Valley, N. Y.

******

Collo. Ruggles Regiment to receive musketts to compleat to their numbers, and they are likewise to change 14 returned defective; for which they will apply to the commanding officer of the artillery. All the men that have joyned the Provincials since the men have been out to fire, are to assemble tomorrow morning at 5 o'clock on the ground the Provincials used to fire. They are to fire two rounds at marks; the brigade majors turn to attend and see them fire. Their ammunition afterwards most be compleated. The whale boats to be marked by the corps they are given to in the same manner as the *batteaux*. The Grenadiers to receive theirs as soon as the whale boats are readie, for which they will apply to Capt. Loaring; the Rangers will receive theirs after the Grenadiers.

All the whale boats to be kept in the creek or will otherwise be subject to be spoiled. The proportion of whale boats and *batteaux* are, for Rangers, 43 whale boats, one *batteaux*; Gages Regiment, flat bottom boat, 41 whale boats, 4 *batteaux*; Light Infantry of Regiments 43 whale boats and five *batteaux*; Grenadiers 43 whale boats and five *batteaux*. The suttlers most provide men for the *batteaux* allowed them, as the general will not permit the men of the regiments to do it. The Regular Regiments will receive firelocks and bayonets as by their returns, tomorrow morning at 5 o'clock, at the Artillery Park. 500 men with axes, 100 with billhooks, under the command of Major Williard, and conducted by Lieut. Gray, are to take their tools tomorrow at Revallie beating, at the artillery, and march directly.

A covering party will be ordered; this party most be out at Revallie, and they will return to camp at one o'clock; if they are not, they shall be out all day. 400 working men and two covering partys for the engeniers as usuall. Forty men on fatigue for Captain Loring; 200 men for the artillery. Gages Regiment to be out tomorrow morning to discharge their pieces at 5 o'clock.

Lake George, 18th July, 1759. Parole, Halfmoon.

For the day tomorrow, Collo. Worcester; Field Officers for the picquits this night, Regulars, Major Graham; Provincials, Lieut. Collo. Smedley; tomorrow night, Major John Campbell, Lieut. Collo. Hunt, Major Slap. The Regular Regiments to receive three days fresh provisions tomorrow at 5 o'clock, beginning by Gages, following Royal Artillery, late Forbess, Montgomerys. Royal Highlanders, Inniskilling, Grenadiers, Light Infantry of regiments. This compleats them to 21st inclusively. The Provincial Regiments to send in a return to the major of brigade this day of arms, ammunition, or anything else that may be wanted to compleat them. As it is supposed the men that have joyned the several regiments may not have every compleat as fast as others comes up, the commanding officers will immediately have them reviewed, and report to the major of brigade without delay every thing that may be wanted.

Every man is to have a good flint in his firelock, and a spare flint in his pockett, which the officers most take care is not wanted. They will receive them by applying to Major Ord, Commanding Officer of the Artillery. A *batteaux* pr brigade will be allowed to the surgeons of the Regulars, and one *batteaux* to the surgeons of the 5 Provinciall Battalions of Ruggles, Williard, New Hampshire, Babcock, and to those of Schuyler, Worster, Fitch, Whitting, and Lymmons. Those *batteaux* must be received from Captain Loring, and kept by the eldest regiment of each.

All the regiments to return their tools to the artillery, and take up their receipts, at 4 o'clock this afternoon, and each Provincial Regiment will send a return to Brigade Major Moniepenny this evening, of the number of axes or any other tools that may belong to their regiments. If the regiments who have had companys lately joyned them, since the order for *batteaux*, should want more then have been ordered, they will apply accordingly. The men that have chose to serve with the Rangers to joyn them this afternoon at 5 o'clock and follow shuch orders as they shall receive from Major Roggers. They are not to take their tents, but live in hutts, in the same manner as the Rangers do.

They most take the provisions which they have for tomorrow inclusive, and they will afterwards draw their provisions with the Rangers and are not to be returned in the provision returns of their respective regiments. Thomas Burk, waggoner, tryed by a court martiall of the line for abusing and offering to strick his officer at Halfway Brook, is found guilty of the crime laid to his charge and sentenced to receive four hundred lashes. The general approves of the above sentence, and orders that the said Thomas Burk is marched tomorrow morning at 5 o'clock by the provost guard, regiment to regiment and that he receives 30 lashes at each of the 4 Regular Regiments, begining at Forbess and so on to the right, that he also receives 30 lashes each at the head of 8 Provincial Regiments, and 40 at the head of Schuylers. He is afterward to be marched back to the provost and remaine there till further orders.

A detachment of 600 Pioneers with axes, under the command of Major Williard, and conducted by Lieut. Gray to parade tomorrow at Revallie beating at the artillery, where they will receive axes; they will set out at the same hour as this day, that they may finish their work in time.

★★★★★★

James Gray was taken from the half-pay list and appointed Lieutenant in the 42nd Royal Highlanders 30th January, 1756, during the entire of which year the regiment was quartered in Albany. His name is omitted in the *Army List* of 1765 (Stewart's *Highlanders*).

★★★★★★

A covering partie will be appointed. 200 working men for the artillery at the usual time; 450 working men for the engineers; 30 working men for Capt. Loreing.

Lake George, 19th July, 1759. Parole, Sopass.

Collo. for the day tomorrow, Collo. Fitch; Field Officers for the picquitts this (night), Regulars, Major John Campbell; Provincials, Lieut. Collo, Hunt; tomorrow night, Lieut. Collo. Darby, Lieut. Collo. Saltenstall, Major Hawks. Generals Guard tomorrow. Second Battalion Ruggles. The Provincials to receive 3 days provisions tomorrow, beginning at 5 o'clock by Whittings, and following Ruggles, Williard, Lovells, Schuyler, Worcester, Fitch, and Babcock; this compleats the Provincials to the 22nd inclusively. The battalions of Ruggles, Williard, Lovell and Babcock will exchange their deffective arms, and receive their ammunition and flints and bayonetts this day at 12 o'clock, by applying to Major Ord, Commanding Officer of the Artillery, according to the return sent in by those battalions this day.

The General Court Martial of which Collo. Whitting was President, is dissolved. The general has approved of the following sentences of the above court martial. Tunass Douglass of Collo. Ruggles Regiment, tryed for desertion, is found guilty and sentenced to receive 1000 lashes; Thos. Bayley, of late Forbess, tryed for robbery, and being a notorious offender, is found guilty and sentenced to suffer death. John Williams Elias Lodwick, of Collo. Ruggles first battalion, tryed for robbery, is acquitted; Capt. Hasgell, of Collo. Babcocks Regiment, accused of disobedience of orders, is adjudged not guilty of the crime laid to his charge, and is therefore acquitted.

The regiments of Schuyler, Whitting, Worcester, Limen, and Fitch, will receive their arms, &c., agreeable to the return they gave in, by applying to Major Ord tomorrow morning. The picquitts of the line to be out tomorrow morning at 7 o'clock, and will march to the front of the Grenadiers, drawing up in the same manner as the last day they were out for the execution of Thos. Baylie, of late Forbess Regiment, at the head of the picquitts. He will be marched by the provost, in the like manner as the last creminall; the collo. of the day will attend; a platoon of late Forbess will be drawn up in the centre for the execution.

Ten *batteaux* will be delivered to Collo, Lymons Regiment, on applying to Capt. Loreing. A general court martial to set tomorrow of the Regulars, at 6 o'clock, at the Presidents tent, Collo, Montgomery President, Lieut. Collo. Darby, Major Graham, the Royal Highland Regiment, Montgomerys Guages one captain each, late Forbess 2 capts., Inniskilling one, Grenadiers 2, Light Infantry two capts., for that duty. Lieut. George Burton of the Royall, Deputy Judge Advocate. 45 working men for the engineers and two covering partys as usuall. 200 working men for the artillery tomorrow morning at 5 o'clock, 30 working men for Captain Loreing.

The regiments to load their *batteaux* tomorrow morning, beginning at 5 o'clock in the following manner, agreeable to the order of the eleventh instant, Forbess flower, Montgomerys pork, Royall Highlanders flower, Inniskilling pork, Predeaux flower, Royall pork, Ruggles and Williards must follow the Royall Highlanders and Inniskilling Regiments, and are to load Ruggles pork, Williards flower, Lovells pork, Babcocks flower, Whittings pork, Fitches flower, Worcesters pork, Limans flower; two regiments to load at a time, one flower one pork, and to be allowed an hour for loading, and when loaded to return to their stations and the *batteaux* to be taken care off as usuall. If any *batteaux* are found out to be leaky they most be changed or repaired before night.

Mr. Wilson will attend, and that each regiment loads a proper quantity; and the quartermasters of each regiment to give him a receipt for the provisions they receive. The Connecticut boats now on the beech before the provisions to be movd to the east shore beyond Forbess, and remaine till the last, when they will load in their station. The whole army Regulars and Provincials to receive flower this day, to compleat them with bread to the twenty-fifth inclusively, by which they are to get baked immediately, beginning with Gages at 5 o'clock, and following Rangers, Whiting, Light Infantry, Grenadiers, Ruggles, Williards, Inniskilling, Royall Highlanders, Montgomerys, Forbess, Schuylers, Worcesters, Limmans, Fitches, Lovells, Babcocks, and the Royall Artillery; a quarter of an hour intervall between each regiment.

Lake George, 20th July, 1759. Parole, Godliman. For the day this day Regulars Collo. Grant, Provincials Collo. Fitch; tomorrow Collo. Forster, (Foster), Collo. Babcock; Field Officers of the picquits this night, Regulars Major Alexander Campbell, Provincials Lieut. Collo. Saltenstall, Major Hawkes; tomorrow night Major Gordon, Lieut. Collo. Ingersall, Major Douglas.

★★★★★★

William Foster was appointed Lieutenant-Colonel of the 1st Royals 24th December, 1755 and served at the Siege of Louisbourg in 1758; after making this campaign, he was left in command of Crown Point in August, 1760, on Colonel Haviland's departure for Montreal. He became colonel in the army in February, 1762 and is dropped in the *Army List* July, 1768 (*Army List*; Knox).

★★★★★★

On landing the Collo. Grant to take the command of late Forbess Brigade, and Colonel Forster the brigade of the Royall. All artificiers that have been imployed by Collo. Montrezure are now to joyn their regiments and are to be paid by Collo. Montrezure this afternoon.

ORDERS FOR THE ARMY PASSING THE LAKE.

The advanced guard is to consist of Gages Light Infantry with the flat bottomed boat, in the front of the centere, their whale boats drawing up abreast covering the heads of the columns from right to left; the army to row in 4 collumns, the right and first collumn to consist of Rangers, Light Infantry of Regiments, Grenadiers, Williards, and Ruggles. Second Battalion to be drawn up and row the boats 2 deep; the commanding officers in a whale boat on the left of the battalions, the front rank in the boats on the right, the rear rank in the boats on the left as the whole of this collumn marches and embarks by the left, on which order they will land.

When this collumn lands Collo. Brodstreet will send men to take care of all the whale boats, the Rangers, Light Infantry, and Grenadiers are to leave only what are absolutely necessarie to take care of their tents, baggage and *batteaux*. The 2nd collumn to consist of the 2 brigades of Regulars, marching and embarking by the left, beginning by late Forbess, their front rank in the boats on the right and rear rank in the boats on the left, rowing two boats abreast; the 3 collumn is to consist of all the boats of artillery, the radow ahead followed by the rafts, all the carpenters, the boats with the tools, Schuylers Regiment, and Ruggles 1st Battaleon with artillery stores and embarking from the right, rowing two boats abreast, their front rank in the boats on the left and the rear rank on the right; the commanding officers in whale boats on the left of the battalion, the left of Ruggles will be followed by the boats belonging to the quartermasters, then ingeniers. surgeons, hospital, commissarys and suttlers and large boats with provisions, floats with horses.

The 4th and left collumn is to consist of Lyman, Worcester, Fitch, Babcock and Lovell. They are to march and embark by the right, rowing two *batteaux* abreast; the front rank on the right and rear on the left; the commanding officers in a whale boat on the right of the battalion, Whittings will form the rear, covering the rear of the four collumns from right to left, their right to the 4th collumn their rear rank to the collumns and front ranks to the *Halifax* sloop; the *Halifax* sloop will cruze close to the rear of the whole. All the battalions except Whittings are to leave nether more nor less than one serjeant pr regiment and one man pr company for the care of the *batteaux*, tents, and baggage, and one officer per brigade of the Regulars on for the five regiments of Provincials on the left, and one for the four on the right; the officers, serjeants, and men to be fixed on and their names returned to the major of brigade; Rangers and Light Infantry of regiments and Grenadiers to be commanded by Collo. Haveland, Lieut. Bryhen to attend Collo. Haveland. Williards 2nd Battalion and Ruggles commanded by Collo. Ruggles, Lieut. Gray to attend Collo. Ruggles.

The 2 last battalions to receive 50 axes each, by applying to Mr. Russle, which with those already they have, may do for what work may be required of them. The 2nd collumn will be commanded by Brig. General Gage; Collo. Schuyler will command the two regiments of the 3rd column, which will have each 100 axes allowed to them by applying to Mr. Russle, that they may be readie to clear the roads the moment they are ordered to land. Lieut. Rose will attend Collo. Schuyler. The collumn on the left will be commanded by Collo. Lyman, and will be readie to land on the west side, or where ordered. The collumns to row at the same hight; the boats to keep dear of each others oars; signals to be made on board me *Invincable* radow or the *Halifax* sloop.

A smal Union flag for majors of brigade and adjutants to come for orders; a reed flagg is for sailing or rowing; when struck is for halting; when the reed flage is taken down, which is the signall every boat most then dress in its proper place immediately.

A blue flage is for the right collumn to land; when repeated, for Gages Light Infantry and 2nd collumn to land; if repeated a third time, for the left collumn to land. The artillery will land after the 2nd collumn. Whittings Regiment to have the guard on the *batteaux*; Collo. Broadstreet will make such despositions for them as he thinks best. A twelve pounder on the left of the Rangers, an eighteen pounder on the right of Lymans. The greatest care most be taken of arms and ammunition.

The men to land in their waist coats, and go as light as possible, carrying only their blanketts and provisions. No hurrie, no huzzaing on any account whatever, and no man to fire without orders from his officer. The officers appointed to commands will receive particular orders from the generall, in whatever suituation the regiments may be in when landed and night comes on; no motions are to be made in the night. Each regiment will secure his own ground. Fireing in the night most be avoided.

The enemy most be received with fixed bayonets, and the regiments not to quite their ground, even if the enemy could brake through; the regiments are never to go up in heaps but keep their ranks on all occasions. Silence amongst the men most absblutely be keept; no password to be regearded; no orders to be obyed but shuch are delivered or sent in writting by deputy adjutants general or *aids de camp*, major brigade, deputy quartermaster general or engineers. No man is to go back when landed to fetch provisions, tents, or any thing else, till there is a generall order for it.

They most expect to ly a night or two on their arms. All the empty provision barrells to be sent to Collo. Montrezure. Barrells belonging to the brewerie to be sent there. Eight barrells of spruce beer to be delivered to each regimnt this evening, and one barrell to each company of Grenadiers and Light Infantry, a proportion to the artillery; this most be taken in the whale boats and *batteaux*; the regiments to pay Serjeant Airey this afternoon for their beer, or their quartermasters to give their notes for what is due. Every thing to be put on board this day, that the regiment may be readie to strick their (tents) in the night, or when orderd, that the whole may embark as soon as possible. The men most row in turns; there most be no pressing any where; the whole will move gentley that the men may not be fatigued. Those that are not employed in rowing must go to sleep, that they may be alert and fit for service when landed.

AFTER ORDERS.

Mr. Stewart, Surgeons Mate of the Hospital, is to attend the Light Infantry of regiments; Mr. Peebles, Surgeons Mate of Collo. Montgomerys is to return and do duty with the reigment. The Generall to beat at two o'clock tomorrow morning, the troop at half an hour after, and march at 3 or as soon as daylight will permit, beginning by the Rangers, followed by the Light Infantry of regiments, Grenadiers, Williards and Ruggles 2nd Battalion who all march by ye left, and will pass over the right hand bridge going down to the lake and embarking as ordered. The regiments of Lyman, Worcester, Fitch, Babcock, Lovell (Lovewell) and Whitting will march by the right, following each other in that order, and eroding the bridge on the left hand, embark as ordered.

★★★★★★

Zacheus Lovewell, brother of John Lovewell the famous Indian Fighter who was killed at the Battle of Pigwaket, was born at Dunstable, N. H., 24th July, 1701. On the death of Colonel Blanchard in April, 1758, he succeeded to the command of the New Hampshire Regiment. On 23rd July, 1759, he was ordered to join the army at Niagara under Brigadier-General Prideaux and returned home after the peace. He died 12th April, 1772, in the 72nd year of his age (Fox's *Hist. of Dunstable*; Knox's *Journal*).

★★★★★★

The two brigades of Regulars will follow, the first collumn marching by the left and embarking as ordered. Gages Light Infantry forms the rear of all, and when the whole is near embarked, will embark like wise, and move up in the front of their station. The men to carry their tents when they march down to embark; the regiments to send a man immediately to each *batteaux* that is loaded; no man to fire out of the *batteaux* on any account. It being represented that some of the suttlers of the regiment have not people sufficient to row their boats, the comanding officers of regiments are permited to give leave to some men to help them; but great care most be taken that all land with their regiments, and those *batteaux* will accordingly remaine in the rear of each regiment. All guards to come off at beating the Generall.

Camp near Ticonderoga, 22nd July, 1759. Parole, Boston.

Collo. of the day for this day, Regulars Collo. Forster; Provincials, Collo. Babcock; for tomorrow. Regulars Collo. Montgomery; Provincials, Collo. Lovell: for the picquit this night, Regulars Major Gordon; Provincials Lieut. Collo. Ingersoll, Major Douglass; tomorrow night, Major Graham, Lieut. Collo. Putman, Major Whitting.

★★★★★★

John Whiting, eldest son of Charles Whiting and Elizabeth Bradford, granddaughter of Governor Bradford of Plymouth Colony, was born August 3, 1719, and married a Miss Cogswell. He removed to Rhode Island and was appointed major, and in September, 1759, lieutenant-colonel of the regiment of that Colony. He died in New London December 17, 1770 (Goodwin's *Genealogical Notes*).

★★★★★★

The regiments to remain on the ground they are now on, each regiment advance their picquitt and secure their front by throwing up loggs in the best manner they can. The regiments that are nearest the water may send as many men as are necessarie to fetch the boats of their companies. The regiments of Schuyler and first battalion of Ruggles, Worcester, Fitch, and Lovells to joyn Royall; the second battalion Ruggles and Williards to remaine as posted; Limons to joyn the corps on the hill, and Babcocks to remaine with that corps under the command of Collo. Haviland. The regiments to be readie to march when ordered. The generall court martial of which Collo. Montgomery was President, is disolved. The Generals Guard this night, Schuylers.

Camp before Ticonderoga, 23rd July, 1759. Parole, Cumberland. Collo. of the day tomorrow. Regulars Collo. Grant; Provincialls, Collo, Schuyler: Field Officers of the picquits this night, Regulars Major Graham; Provincialls Lieut. Collo. Putman, Major Whitting: for tomorrow night, Major West, Lieut. Collo. Pysan, Major Waterbury.

★★★★★★

George Augustus West, youngest son of the 1st Earl of Delaware, was born in the year 1733, and on the 7th November, 1755, was commissioned a captain in the 55th Regiment, which came to America in 1757, and served in the expedition against Ticonderoga in 1758, on which occasion its Colonel, Lord Viscount Howe was killed; thus, the regiment lost two commanding officers within little more than a year, Colonel Perry, his Lordship's predecessor, having died on the passage to this country in June, 1757. Major Proby having been also killed at Ticonderoga, was succeeded by Captain West, who, after the present campaign, exchanged into the 1st Foot Guards with the rank of Lieutenant-Colonel in the Army, 6th Nov., 1759; married Mary, daughter of the Earl of Stamford, in 1764; was appointed Colonel in the Army and *Aid-de-Camp* to the King 25th June, 1766; Colonel of the 58th Foot 18th October, 1775, and died, without issue, in February, 1776 (*Army Lists*; Beatson's *Polit. Index,* II; Debrett).

★★★★★★

The regiments to march and encamp as soon as the ground is marked. The Regulars, who are to defend the Brest works, most immediately raise a bankuet in the front of the sentre of each regiment with loggs and earth, so that the picquits of each regiment can stand upon it and defend the brestwork without pulling any of the brestwork down, as it covers the camp from the shott. The men may boil their pots as soon as they will. A camp will be marked out for Lymons, Worcesters, and Fitches, in the wood; they will face outwards, and advance their picquitts to the front, that no straggling Indians may pick up their people. As Fitches regiment has by mistake not received the provisions as were ordered, they must send to the Landing Place for three days provisions.

Camp at Ticonderoga, 24th July, 1759 Parole, New York.

Collo. of the day tomorrow, Regulars Collo. Forster; Provincialls, Collo. Fitch: Field Officers for the picquitts this night, Regulars Major West, Provincialls Lieut. Colo. Paysan; tomorrow night Major John Campbell and Major Waterbury.

★★★★★★

John Campbell of Strachur, in the Highlands of Scotland, entered the army in June, 1745, as Lieutenant of Loudon's Highlanders; served through the Scotch Rebellion; made the Campaign in Flanders, 1747, and was promoted to a company on the 1st October of that year. At the peace of 1748, he went on half-pay and so remained until the 9th April, 1756, when he was appointed. to the 42nd Highlanders previous to the embarkation of that regiment for America (Brown, IV). He was wounded in the attack on Ticonderoga in 1758 and was appointed by General Amherst Major of the 17th Foot on the 11th July, 1759; was promoted to be Lieutenant-Colonel in the Army 1st February, 1762 and commanded his regiment in the expedition that year against Martinico and Havana.

On the 1st May, 1773, he became Lieutenant-Colonel of the 57th or West Middlesex Foot; returned to America in 1776 with his regiment at the breaking out of the Revolution; was appointed Maj. General 19th February, 1779, Colonel of his regiment 2nd November, 1780, and commanded the British Forces in West Florida, where after a gallant though ineffectual defence he was obliged to surrender Pensacola to the Spaniards 10th May, 1781. He became Lieutenant-General 28th September, 1787; General in the Army 26th January, 1797 and died in the fore part of 1806 (Stewart's *Sketches of the Highlanders*, I, II; Knox *Journal*, I, II; Beatson's *Naval and Mil. Mem.*, V, VI; *Army Lists*).

★★★★★★

The commanding officers of each of the Regular Regiments will chuse an intilligent serjeant that they judge will answre for assisting the engineers as overseers; they will give in their names to the major of brigade and order the serjeants immediately to attend Lieut. Collo. Eyre. The Rangers to be furnished with what ammunition they may want to compleat them, by applying to Major Ord. Houses of office to be made in the rear of the camp, and wells to be dug for each regiment, that the men may gett water as easie as possible. When working parties are ordered into the trenches, they most take their arms with them; when they work to the right they most lodge their arms to the right, and when they work to the left they most lodge their arms to the left.

A return to be given in by every corps of all accidents that have happened on the 22nd, 23rd and 24th, to the adjutant-generall at orderly time tomorrow, and for the future a daily report to be made to the adjutant general at orderly time. If any officers have letters to send by the New York post, they will send them to head quarters this evening. Serjeant Murray of the Royall Highland Regt. is appointed to oversee people making fasciens, and to keep an accompt of the number made. Adjutant of the day tomorrow, late Forbess. (William Howard was appointed Adjutant of the 17th Foot, 12th December, 1746, and became Captain 22nd November, 1756. He left the army in the latter part of 1767—*Army Lists*).

The picquits of the line to be out tonight in the same manner as last night, except the pickett of Montgomerys, which will be as ordered. The drums of all the regiments to beat the Retreat without waiting for the drums of the Inniskilling, taking it from the Royall. The First Brigade to send tomorrow for three days provisions at Revallie beating; they will receive but two days bisquett in leu of flower, and three days pork, which compleats them of all species to the 28 inclusive. Schuylers, Lymans, Worcesters, Fitches, two battalions of Ruggles, will receive 4 days provisions, after it is issued out to the Regulars, and bisquitt instead of flower, which compleats them to the 27th inclusive.

As Collo. Babcocks Regiment is ordered to the Landing Place, the four battallions of Schuyler, Lyman, Fitch, Worcester, will furnish a guard of 200 men, to be commanded by a field officer, who will take post half way betwixt the camp and sawmill, which guard is to be relieved daily by the said four regiments.

Camp at Ticonderoga, 25th July, 1759. Parole, Kensingtone.

Collo. for the day, Collo. Montgomery; for tomorrow, Regulars Collo. Grant, Provincials Collo, Schuyler; Field Officers for the picquitts this night, Major John Campbell, Provincials Major Waterbury; tomorrow night, Major Allexander Campbell, Lieut. Collo. Smedlie. The generall can be but surprised that shuch brave and good troops should be subject to be alarmed in the night, and that any of the men should fire after the orders he has given, without being ordered by their officer to do it, by which they wounded and killed their comerads, and they not obeying the orders of receiving the enemy in the night with fixt bayonetts will cost more men then all the force the enemy can bring against us, and he hopes no further alarms of this sort will happn.

The piquitt of the Royall to be relieved by a picquitt of Forbess this day at 12 o'clock, and to be under the command of Major West, the field officer of the picquitt. The battalion of the Royall to mount in the trenches at Retreat beating, at which time the picquitts will return to camp. Six companys will mount on the right, three on the left, and one in the centre; the whole will march by the right; they will leave their colours and a guard in camp; the Inniskilling Regiment to furnish a guard of 50 men on the right where the picquit of the Royal was posted. The Light Infantry and Grenadiers to send immediately to the Landing Place, to receive three days provision, 2 days bisquitt in lieu of flower, which compleat them to the 28 inclusive. Whittings, Williards, Babcocks Regiments will receive four days provisions tomorrow, and bisquitt in lieu of flower, which compleats them to the 29 inclusive. The Generall Hospital is by Worsters Regiment, near the

107

road coming into camp, where any wounded men may be sent to. Adjutant for the day tomorrow, Inniskilling.

★★★★★★

William Moore entered the 27th Regiment as Ensign and was appointed Adjutant 21st Sept., 1756; Lieutenant 7th March, 1762; Captain-Lieutenant in the 57th, 12th September, 1764; Captain in the Army 25th May, 1772, and in the 45th Foot 14th May, 1774. His name is dropped from *the Army List* of 1776.

★★★★★★

Sixty of Major Rogers Rangers will march with the commanding officer to the trenches this night, and will be employed at a proper time to alarm the enemy by firing into their covered way, and keeping their attention from the workmen, The commanding officer who marches out to the trenches will acquaint the officer who releives him of the different post and of every thing is material for him to know. Gages Regiment to receive this day two days provisions, bisquit in lieu of flower, and three days pork, which compleats them with the rest of the army.

The following carpenters, John Greenhold, Robert Everott, John Cox, and James Craig, John Mills of the Inniskilling Regiment, James Frazer, George McDougall, James Frazer, John McColme, John Robison, James Cumming, and James McDonald, of the Royal Highlanders, and James Cross of late Forbess, to be at the Sawmills tomorrow at 5 o'clock, and if Captain Loreing should not be there they will receive their directions from Brigadier Ruggles. As it may be necessarie to have a countersign by which the men in the trenches may know each other in the night; the countersign is this night, *Boston*. The Royall Highland Regiment to draw tomorrow earlie two days bisquitt, and two days pork, bisquitt in lieu of flower, which compleats them to the 2Sth inclusive.

Ticonderoga, 26th July, 1759. Parole, Springfield.

Collo. for the day tomorrow, Collo. Forster; Provincials, Collo. Lyman; Field Officers for the picquitts this night, Regulars Major Alexander Campbell, Provincials Lieut. Collo. Smedlie; tomorrow night, Major Hamilton, Lieut. Collo. Hunt; Adjutant for the day tomorrow, Royal Highlanders.

★★★★★★

Alexander Donaldson received a commission as Ensign in the 42nd in October, 1758; was appointed Adjutant 20th March,

1759, and Lieutenant 8th May, 1 760. On the 31st March, 1770, he obtained the command of a company and on the 19th December, 1777, was appointed Major of the 76th, or the Macdonald Highlanders, a new corps then raised for service in America, but his state of health not permitting him to embark with the regiment, he sold out to Major Needham, afterwards Lord Killmorey, 10th August, 1780 (Stewart's *Sketches of the Highlanders*, I, II; *Army Lists*).

******

Late Forbess Regiment to mount the trenches this night. The regiment will march in by the right; three companys to the trenches on the right and five to the trenches on the left. Brigadier Gages will give one captain 2 subalterns and 100 men for the centre. The regiment that mounts the trenches will leave only a quarter guard sufficient for the care of the camp. The 4 Connecticut Regiments to add to their numbers with the artillery to replace the New Hampshire Regiment, one sub. one serj. and 30 private, Massachusetts one sub.one serj. and 20 private, Rhode Island one serj. and 10 private, to joyn the artillery tomorrow morning at 5 o'clock.

The Royall Artillery to compleat their provisions to the 28 inclusive, being the same day the Regulars Regiments are compleatd. As there has been some Indians fireing in the rear this day, the generall depends on the regiments not being alarmd if they should hear some fireing in the rear. The countersign for this night is *London*. The regiments will not set fire to any of the wood in the rear of the camp, except what they immediately use to boil their potts, which most be separate from the rest. The generall will send dispatches to England this day; any officers that have letters to send will give them in earlie tomorrow to Mr. Appie.

Ticonderoga, 27th July, 1759. Parole, King George.
Collo. for the day tomorrow. Regulars Collo. Montgomery, Provincials Collo. Lyman; Field Officers for the picquits this night, Regulars Allex. Campbell, Provincials Lieut. Collo. Hunt; tomorrow night Major Graham, Lieut. Collo. Puttman; Adjutant of the day tomorrow, Predeauxes.

******

William Winepress was commissioned a Lieutenant in the 55th Foot 29th August, 17519 and appointed Adjutant of the Regiment 13th March, 1756. He obtained a company on 9th June,

1762, and continued in the regiment until 1775, when 'twas again ordered to America (*Army List*).

★★★★★★

The quartermasters and camp colour men of the brigades of Regulars to assemble at the front of Predeaux to attend Lieut. Robison to mark out the camp. As soon as the working parties of Provincialls arraive, the approaches and batteries to be immediately levelld. The regiments will have orders when they are to remove their camp; the arms and ammunition to be carefully inspected into; the Rangers must compleat their ammunition, sending a report to the major of brigade of the number of rounds they want; 130 men of Montgomerys lately come up to be compleated to 36 rounds. The commanding officer of the artillery to send a report immediately of what guns he fired on the fort.

The 2 brigades of Regulars to encamp this night within the lines; on a ruffle the regiments to strick their tents; the brigade on the left will march in by twos by the left, thro the sally port, to the front of Montgomerys; the brigade on the right in the like manner will march by the right thro the sally port by the front of Predeaux, and will pass the front of the Second Brigade; the regiments to mount only one serjant and 8 men to keep one centry one the lines; the picquitts as usuall; an evening gunn to fire the first ruffle, on the parties from the fort returning to camp; to take the beatings from right and left. The regiments encamped in the rear of the sally ports are to let no man out or in but those whose business may call them.

The Rangers, Light Infantry and Grenadiers, Lymans and Worcesters Regiments will interly destroy the road they have made in their front, by laying loggs across and cutting some trees if necessarie, so as to make it impassible from Lake Shamplaine to the road leading from the saw mills to the fort, that the brush may grow up and no appearance of a road may remaine; they will begin to this earlie tomorrow morning or this evening, and finish it as soon as they can. When the great road is all stoped up as ordered, the beforementiond corps will all march to the roads thro the woods, and draw up in the front of the lines from whence the quartermasters and campcolourmen will attend Lieut. Collo. Robison, who will mark out their camp. Major Roggers will send a company of Rangers tomorrow morning with all the boats to the fort. The companies ported on the lake side from Collo. Haviland's corps will joyn their corps at Revallie beating, after which Major Roggers will put trees across the foot path that has been

110

made by the lake side.

Major Roggers will receive his orders from the generall; all tools these corps may have with them must be collected and great care taken that they leave non behind them, and bring them to the front of the lines. Lieut. Collo. Robison will mark out a park for the artillery; Major Ord will send this night for the two 12 pounders that are at Major Roggers camp. The Royall will hall in the 12 pounder that is on the right in the front of the lines, when they get to their ground, and that ammunition that is with it, and Montgomerys will do the same by the 12 pounder that is on their left, when they get to their new ground.

Ticonderoga, 28th July, 1759. Parole, Ticonderoga.

Collo. of the day tomorrow. Regulars Collo. Grant; Provincialls, Collo. Schuyler; Field Officers for the picquitts this night, Regulars Major Grahams, Provincials Lieut. Collo. Putman; tomorrow night Major West, Major Slap: Adjutant for the day tomorrow, Montgomerys.

★★★★★★

John Campbell of Melford, Scotland, was commissioned Lieutenant in the 62nd, afterwards the 77th, or first Highland Battalion, 30th July, 1757, and proceeded immediately to Halifax; made the Campaign against Fort Duquesne in 1758; was appointed Adjutant of the Regiment 11th July, 1759; Captain 26th July, 1760; exchanged into the 27th Inniskillings 25th March, 1762, and continued in that regiment until the Summer of 1770, after which time his name is dropped from the *Army Lists*.

★★★★★★

The Rangers will be posted beyond the saw mills on the right, as orderd to Major Roggers; the Light Infantry of regiments to encamp on the ground where Collo. Worcesters Regiment is at present encamped on the road on the right leading to the saw mills; the Grenadiers will encamp at the entrance of the wood leading from the fort to the saw mill, where Worcesters Regiment was at first encamped. The commanding officers of each of those corps will report all extraordinarys to the generall; 30 men of the Light Infantry of regiments, and 30 men of the Grenadiers, with 2 subalterns to go immediately to the hospitall without arms, to carry the wounded to the saw mills. An officer and 20 men of the Light Infantry with arms to go with them and escort the party back.

Collo. Whitting will apply to Collo. Bradstreet for *batteaux* and will send a sufficient number to row them to Fort George; 2 mates of the hospittal to go with them; the hoipitall will then change there ground and move to the rear of Forbess. The 2 brigades of Regulars are to give an officer and 30 men as a guard in the fort: a serjeant and 12 men to the advanced works by the waterside; a serjt. and 12 on the right of the fort near the lake side; a serj. and 12 for the garden; a sub. and 30 on the right of the lines by the lake side, where the Grenadiers were posted; a serjt. and 12 halfway between that and the right of the Royall: a corporal and 6 at the enterance at the bottom of the hill between the Royall and serjeants post.

The guards in the fort will take care that nothing of boards, iron, or any utensils whatever, are taken away by stragglers, as they will be of service to the repaires of the fort, and sick of the hospitall. Schuylers, Worcester, Fitch, Limans Regiments, are to give no guards only what may be necessarie for the camp, and those regiments must furnish what workingmen may be wanted for repairing the fort with the utmost expedition. The Regulars to receive tomorrow 4 days provision, beginning half an hour after Revallie beating by the Royall, Predeaux, Inniskilling, Royall Highlanders, Montgomerys, Forbess, Grenadiers, Light Infantry, Gages, which compleats them to the 1st of August, inclusive. Divine Service tomorrow at 11 o'clock, to return thanks for the success of his Majesty's arms, Forbes Regiment to face to the right and joyn the Royall Brigade, and with that brigade are to have the service done by the chaplin of the Royall. The other regiments will attend by their own chaplain.

★★★★★★

Rev. William Halliburton was appointed Chaplain of the Royals 22nd May, 1747 and continued to fill that Office until 27th March, 1765.

Rev. James Moore was Chaplain of the 17th; Henry Bayly of the 27th; James Stewart of the 42nd; Charles Paulett of the 55th; Harry Munro, afterwards Rector of St. Peter's, Albany, of the 77th Highlanders. We have no means of ascertaining the names of the chaplains of the Provincial Regiments.

★★★★★★

The Grand Parade for the Regulars in the rear of the Royall. The quarter guards of the 2nd Brigades are to furnish centrys in the lines during the night; the picquits not to be out; the men will receive their provisions tomorrow at the saw mills; the regiments may bake their bread at the ovens in the fort by applying to Lieut. Collo. Robison who will allot what ovens the different regiments are to have. A general court martiall of the line to be held at the Presidents tent at 8 o'clock tomorrow morning. Collo. Grant President, Major Allexander Campbell, Major Hamilton, Captains, Royall one, Forbess one, Inniskilling two, Royall Highlanders two, Predeaux one, Montgomerys 3; totall ten; Lieut Geo. Burton of the Royall Deputy Judge Advocate. For the day tomorrow, Collo. Forster.

Ticonderoga, 29th July, 1759. Parole, Gage.

Collo. for the day tomorrow, Collo. Montgomery; Provincialls, Collo. Lyman; Field Officers for the picquitts this night, Regulars Major West, Provincials Major Slap; tomorrow night Major John Campbell, Major Douglass; Adjutant for the day tomorrow, Royall. (Henry Balfour). The Provincialls to receive 4 days provision tomorrow, beginning at Revallie beating by Schuylers, Fitch, Worcester, Lyman, Ruggles, 2 battalions, Williards, Babcock, Whitting. Lieut. Collo. Eyre will make a disposition for the different imploys of the work to be carried on by the 4 Provincial Regiments in repairing the fort, which his Majestys Service requires should be done in the utmost expedition.

Each regiment will immediately send a return to the major of brigade of the numbers of carpenters, masons and lime burners they have. Collo. Schuyler is to have the superattendancie of the work under the direction of Lieut. Collo. Eyre; and Collo. Schuyler will appoint shuch field officers and other officers to observe it as he judges best for carrying on the service. The commanding officers of corps will take all opportunitys of having their men out at exercise. Montgomerys recruits to be out and fire tomorrow at 6 o'clock. The troops on the communication not to be alarmd. The General Hospital in the rear of Forbess.

The ovens to be given for the use of the troops in the following manner: No. 1 on the right to the Royall and Predeaux; No. 2 to the Inniskilling and Royall Highlanders; No. 3 to Montgomerys and Forbess; No. 5 the Grenadier and Light Infantry; No. 6 General Gages Royall Artillery, Engineers and Workmen; No. 7 Lymans, Worcesters; No. 8 Schuylers and Fitch. No bakers but shuch as those corps imploy to bake in any of those ovens. Each corps of the army will send immediately to Mr. Russle at the Park of Artillery the entrenching tools

113

now in their possession, reserving shuch as are absolutely necessary for cleaning their encampment. The Royall Highland Regiment to strick their tents and march inmiediately to the Landing Place, and they will send their tents and baggage in *batteaux*. The Provincialls are to receive 4 days fresh provisions tomorrow, each regiment will send a return of their effective numbers to Commissary Wilson this night.

Ticonderoga, 30th July, 1759. Parole, Windsor.

Collo. of the day tomorrow. Regulars Collo. Forster; Provincialls, Collo. Worcester; Field Officers for the picquits this night, Regulars Major John Campbell, Provincials Major Douglass; tomorrow night Lieut. Collo. Darby, Major Water Burry; Adjutant of the day tomorrow, late Forbess. The regiments and corps to keep 4 days bread baked beforehand, and that that quantity may be always when the troops embark, and they will apply to Mr. Wilson the commissary for shuch a proportion of flower, which will be allowed when the provisions are afterwards received. It is forbid to make use of whale boats unless particular orders, as they will be rendered unfit for service.

The corps who have had any arms spoiled by the shot or shells from the enemy, to give them in to the artillery and they shall receive others in their room and send a report to the major of brigade what they exchange. Any firelocks that have been a great while loaded most be drawn. They may blow some powder out of them at 6 o'clock tomorrow morning, and then all the arms to be put in thorough good order. Montgomerys additional men to fire at a mark in the swamp on the right at 6 o'clock tomorrow morning.

Ticonderoga, 31st July, 1759. Parole, Marlborough.

Collo. of the day tomorrow. Regulars Collo. Montgomery, Provincials Collo. Schuyler; Field Officers for the picquitts this night, Regulars Major Darby, Provincials Major Waterbury; Adjutant of the day tomorrow, Inniskilling. Captain Skeene (Skene) of the Inniskilling Regiment is appointed Major of Brigade.

★★★★★★

Philip Skene was the grandson of John Skene, of Halyards, in Fifeshire, Scotland, and a descendant of the famous William Wallace. He entered the army in 1739, in which year he served in the expedition against Portobello, and in 1741 was at the taking of Carthagena. He fought in the celebrated Battle of Fontenoy in 1745, and in Culloden the following year, and in 1747 was present at the Battle of Laffeldt, under the Duke of Cumberland (*Gentleman's Magazine,* LXXX, 672). He came to America in 1756, and on the 2nd of February, 1757, was promoted to a company in the 27th or Inniskillen Regiment of Foot, which formed part of the force under Lord Loudon's command that year; was next engaged under Lord Howe at the unfortunate attack on Ticonderoga in July, 1758, on which occasion he was wounded, and was appointed, on the 31st July, 1759, Major of Brigade by General Amherst; in October following was left in charge of Crown Point, the works of which he had orders to strengthen.

His position at Crown Point made him familiar with the surrounding country, and encouraged by General Amherst, he projected a settlement at Wood Creek and South Bay, at the Head of Lake Champlain, and in the prosecution of that design, soon after settled about thirty families there; in 1762 he was ordered on the expedition against Martinico and Havana and was one of the first to enter the breach on the storming of Moro Castle. On his return to New York, in 1763, he renewed his efforts to complete his settlement at Wood Creek; went to England; obtained a Royal Order for a considerable tract of land at that place, for which a patent was granted, March, 1765, and it was formed into a township under the name of Skenesborough (*New York Land Papers*, XVII; *Book of Patents*, XIV, 56).

His regiment having been ordered to Ireland, Major Skene exchanged into the 10th Foot in May, 1768, so as to remain in America; but he did not continue long in the army, for he sold out in December of the following year (*Army Lists*), and in 1770 established his residence at Skenesborough, now Whitehall, Washington County.

Here he erected forges for smelting iron, mills for sawing timber, and opened a road to Salem and Bennington, which was afterwards known as Skene's Road (Fitch, in *Transactions of New York State Agricultural Society*, VIII, 967). His plans were interrupted by the Revolution. In June, 1775, he was arrested at Philadelphia and brought to New York and thence taken to Hartford, He was allowed to reside on parole at Middletown, Connecticut; but in May of the following year, on refusing to renew his parole, was committed to prison.

He was finally exchanged in October, 1776, when he was conveyed to the City of New York, whence he failed in the beginning of 1777 for England (4 *American Archives*, VI; 5 *American Archives*, II, III). He Volunteered to accompany Burgoyne the same year, and in August was ordered to attend Lieut. Colonel Baume in his secret expedition, which met a disastrous defeat at Bennington, at the hands of General Stark, on the 16th of that month (Burgoyne's *Expedition*, App. xxxvi-xxxix). In this campaign Colonel Skene had his horse twice shot under him and was afterwards taken prisoner with Burgoyne's army. In 1779, he was attainted and his property confiscated by the legislature of New York.

After the war Colonel Skene, 'tis said, came to this country during Governor Clinton's administration and tried to recover his property, but not succeeding, went back to England where he lived in retirement and died on the 9th October, 1810, at an advanced age, at Addersy Lodge, near Stoke Goldington, Bucks. In the obituary notice he is styled: "formerly Lieutenant-Governor of Crown Point and Ticonderoga, and Surveyor of his Majesty's Woods and Forests bordering on Lake Champlain." (*Gentleman's Magazine*).

★★★★★★

Ticonderoga, 1st August, 1759. Parole, Carolina.

Collo. of the day tomorrow, Collo. Forster; Provincials Collo. Lyman; Field Officers for the piquitts this night, Regulars Lieut. Collo. Darby, Provincials Lieut Collo. Paysan; tomorrow night, Lieut, Collo. Smedly; Adjutant of the day tomorrow Predeaux.

As a number of shoes are come up, intended for the use of the army, and will be delivered to them at the prime cost in England, which three shillings and six pence per pair. The regiments may receive in the following manner and proportion, or as many of that proportion as they like to take by applying to Mr. Tucker, agent to Mr. Kilby at the Landing Place.

Royall	384	Grenadiers	288
Forbes	276	Light Infantry	288
Inniskilling	276	Gages	276
Royal Highlands	366	Royal Artillery	056
Predeaux	276		——
Montgomerys	514		3000

The quartermasters must pay for them at the above rate, and each corps may immediately send and receive the numbers they want, each corps to send an officer and a partie with arms to escort the people and keep proper order. A corporall and 6 men to mount on the provisions near the fort, and a corporall and 6 on the brewerie, the Rangers Light Infantry of regiments, Grenadiers and Gages to send to the saw mills and receive the whale boats in the same proportion as ordered at the lake. Mr. Glen will deliver them to them and will shew them where they are to be keept, namely, the right of the Rangers, extending toward an Officers Post by the lake side, as that the left of Gages may joyn the pickitts by the artillery. The two brigades of Regulars to send to the saw mills and receive the *batteaux* in the same proportion as orderd at the lake.

Mr. Glen will deliver them to them, and they will extend from right to left as fronting the camp, the Royall to the right and Forbes to the left. Each commanding officer will have a whale boat, and the same guards must be keep under the same order as at the lake. *Batteaux* for the suttlers shall be hereafter ordered. Gages Light Infantry will receive the English boat; another that carrys a three pounder, and seven whale boats that are at the Artillery Park, so that they will take no more from the Sawmill then their compliment to those boats; the Royall to send and bring down from the saw mills all the provisions now their and land them.

The general court martial of which Collo. Grant was President is disolved. The generall approves of the following sentence of said court martiall; that Capt. Russle, of late Forbeis Regiment is to make the following submission to Lieut. Collo. Darby on the parade before the officers of the regiment.

Sir, I am sorry that I have been guilty of desrespectfull behavour to you as my commanding officer, and therefore ask your pardon.

Captain Howard found not guilty of the crime laid to his charge and is honourably acquitted. Ens. Carden (Garden) is found not guilty of the crime laid to his charge and is honourably acquited.

★★★★★★

Christopher Russell was commissioned Captain in the 17th Foot, 1st June, 1750, and seems to have left the service soon after the above difficulty, as his name is not found in the *Army Lists* subsequent to this date.

John Garden entered the 17th Regiment as Ensign, 24th July, 1759, only seven days before he was court-martialled; he was promoted to a lieutenancy in April, 1762; exchanged into the 15th Foot in August, 1767, and remained in the service until 1771, when his name is dropped from the *Army List.*

★★★★★★

Thos. Badley, soldier in the 17th Regiment, acused of thieft, is found guilty and is sentenced to receive 1500 lashes with a cat and nine tailes. William Read of Gages Light Infantry acused of insolence and threatning language is found guilty and sentenced to receive 500 lashes with a catt and nine tails. Samuel White of Gages Light Infantry acused of insolent behavor, is found guilty and sentenced to be reduced to the ranks. Samuel Merryman of Collo. Ruggles Regiment, accused of shooting a man of the Royal, is adjudjed to have done his duty and is therefore acquited. Thomas Reid and John Rees of late Brigadier Forbess Regiment accused of mutiny; Thomas Reid is found guilty of the crime laid to his charge and is therefore sentenced to suffer death; but in consideration of Serjeant Hartford striking John Reid two or three times without provication, John Rees is sentenced to receive 500 lashes with a catt of nine tails.

The Regular Corps to receive provisions tomorrow beginning at day brake by Forbes and followed by Montgomerys, Royall Highlanders, Inniskilling, Predeaux, Royall, Gages, Light Infantry; they will receive for 4 days, and each man will have 2 pints pease; the provisions is to be immediately drest, as the men will carry it with them: this compleats the Regulars to the 5th inclusive. Babcocks and Williards to be readie to march when ordered; they will immediately receive four days provision and 2 pints of pease per man, which they will dress immediately; and this compleats them to the 6th inclusively. Capt. Reid is appointed Major to the Royall Highland Regiment.

Ticonderoga, 2nd August, 1759. Parole, Schenectady.

Collo of the day tomorrow. Regulars Collo. Montgomery, Provincials Collo, Worster; Field Officers for the picquits this night, Regulars Major Hamilton, Provincials Lieut. Collo. Smedlie; tomorrow night, Major Gordon, Lieut. Collo. Putman: Adjutant of the day tomorrow, Montgomerys.

★★★★★★

Frederick Hamilton was appointed Major of the 2nd Battalion of the 1st Royals, 7th March, 1757. He served at the Siege of Louisbourg in 1758, and in the Campaign against the Cherokees in 1760; was appointed Lieut. Colonel by Brevet, 11th October, 1761, and retired from the Army 24th Nov. 1766. (*Army List* of 1767, p. 166.)

★★★★★★

The Rangers, Light Infantry, Granediers, Gages, will take their whale boats to the Saw Mill River, and put them immediately to the neast places to their encampment, provided they do not stop the passage of any boats going down, and that the boats will be safe: these corps are desired to take no more whale boats then what are absolutely necessarie to carry their numbers. The Royall and Forbes will load their *batteaux* with provision that are on the beech; the major of brigade will send the proportion each is to take; the corps to have the same quantity of *batteaux* for their suttler, *viz.* 2 for the regiment as was allowed coming to Ticonderoga. If the *batteaux* are loaded as are expected, the regiments will embark this night, so that every thing most be readie, but none of the guards relieved till ordered.

The regiments immediately to send a return to the major of brigade of what number of *batoes* they want to compleat them, and most have parties weating at the sawmill to receive them. So soon as they come Mr Napier, Director of the Hospitall will send for two *batteaux*, and the commissarys are to have one *batteaux*; Mr Wilson and Tucker will either proceed or send two of their commissarys forward. The regiments to cutt as many boughs immediately as are necessarie to put in the bottom of their *batteaux* for the security of provisions. As the army is under orders of marching for the reduction of all Kenedy, the general is willing to give an opportunity to the following persons under sentence of a court martiall, *viz.* Thomas Badley, Thomas Reid, John Rees of late Forbess, Corporall White and William Reid of Brigadier Generall Gages to wipe off their crimes by their future good behaviour, and they are hereby pardoned.

Williards Regiment to remaine at the Landing Place; Ruggles 2nd Battallion and Schuylers Regiment are to receive provisions immediately to compleat them to the 6th inclusively and to be readie to march when ordered. If Ruggles 2nd Battalion should have any men working with Capt. Loran, that are absolutely necessary, they must be left with him. The sawers and carpenters furnished by the Regulars to Capt. Loran, are to remaine with him so long, as he absolutely wants them. Collo. Fitch is to leave Serjeant Hide with the masons of his regiment who are at present at work with him; for the repair of the works here he will likewise leave Ensign Waterman and Lieut. Bishop, Lieut. Collo. Pysan, Major Slap, Capt. Parsons and Lieut. Sumnar of

General Lymans Regiment and Capt. Holdby of Worcesters are appointed to have the care and inspection of the workmen imployd in the repairs of the fort.

★★★★★★

Lieutenant Hezekiah Sumner, was the son of William Sumner of Middletown, Conn, and was born about the year 1732. He was Lieutenant of Rangers at first, and afterwards, of the 1st Connecticut Regiment He moved into Berkshire Co., Mass. and died about the year 1802. Lieut. Sumner married Abigail Frary, who died 13th May, 1772, aged 90 (*N. E. Genealogical Register*, VIII, IX).

Captain Parsons. The *N. E. Gen. Reg.*, I, mentions Moses Parsons, who died at the Havanna, in 1762. This is probably the officer whose name occurs in the text; he belonged to the regiment of General Lyman, who commanded the Provincials at the siege of that place

★★★★★★

The Provincials to receive 4 days provisions tomorrow, begining at Revalie beating by Whittings, following 1st Battalion Ruggles, Lymans, Worcesters, Fitches. Each man is to receive 2 pints of pease; this compleats them to the sixth inclusively. As Schuylers and Fitches are to be readie to march on the first notice, Lymans and Worcesters will furnish all the workingmen for the fort except those left per order. Fitches will boyle their provision in the same manner as ordered to the other regiments. Collo. Lymman will have the Command of the troops left here and will have particular orders from the generall. Lieut. Brian is to remaine here to direst the works, in which Capt. Whelock will assist, and Lieut. Gray remaine as overseer.

Ticonderoga, 3rd August, 1759. Parole, Louisburgh.

Collo. for the day tomorrow Collo. Forster, Provincialls Collo. Fitch; Field Officers for the picquitts this night, Regulars Major Gordon, Provincials Lieut. Collo. Hunt; tomorrow night, Major West; Lieut. Collo. Putman; Adjutant of the day tomorrow Royall. George Edwards a deserter of the 17th Regiment is to suffer death. The picquits of the line to assemble immediately in the front of Montgomerys; the commanding officer of Forbes (Lieut. Colo. Darby) will order that regiment to errect a gallos immediately on the battery in front of Montgomerys, where the prisoner George Edwards is to be hanged in his French coat, with a libble on his breast, *Hanged for Deserting to the French*. He is to be hanging all day and at the Retreat beating he is to be buiried very deep under the gallos, and his French coat with him. This to be put in execution instantly, and if the provost martiall does not find an hangman, the commanding officer of the picquitts will order that provost martiall does it himselfe. Limans and Worcesters Regiments are to change their camp; the quartermatters and camp colourmen to attend Lieut. Collo. Robison, who will mark out the ground for them.

The regiments to take care that all the *batteaux* are tight caulked; calkers are ordered down to repaire those that are lakie. The Generall to beat tomorrow morning at 2 o'clock; Assembly half an hour after, and the regiments will send their tents and baggage to their *batteaux* as soon as possible, that the whole may be embarked at day brake and readie to move off. Gages Light Infantry will cover the front of the collumns in the same manner as Lake George, dividing their boats with the three pounders to the right and left; they will as soon as embarked draw up opposite to the post where Major Roggers was encamped, and remaine till the collumns joyn. The Rangers, Light Infantry of Regiments, and Grenadiers march by the right and form the collumn of the left.

The 2nd Brigades of Regulars will march by the right and form the collumn the left of the centre. The artillery will form the collumn on the right of the centre. Schuylers with Fitches Regiments will march by the left and are to man the artillery boats. A raft will lead that collumn from whence the same signals will be given as on the lake, for failing and landing, and the collumn will be followed by the boats of the quartermasters, ingeneers, generalls and staff, baggage, hospital, commissarys and suttlers boats with the tools will immediately follow the rafts of the collum of artillery. Babcocks and Ruggles 2nd battalion will form the collumn on the right, and will march by the left and embark in the morning as soon as they can receive their boats and will bring with them any provision that are at the sawmills.

All the collumns are to have their boats two deep; those that march by the right have their front rank to the left, and those that march by the left, their front rank to the right. A boat with a 24 pounder is to be on the right of the left collumn, the other boat with the 24 pounder on the left of the right collumn, and a 12 pounder between the two centre collumns. Collo. Ruggles commands the collumn on the right; Collo. Haviland the collumn on the left; Collo. Schuyler the collumn on the right of the centre; Collo. Grant the collumn on the left of the centre.

The men will disembark with their coats on unless it is ordered to the conterarie. Provincial battalions that remain here will receive their provisions alternitly for four days on those days it becomes due. Collo. Whitting and Lieut. Collo. Ingersoll will report all extraordinarys to Collo. Lyman at the fort; commanding officers of the detachment of Montgomerys will mount the following guards from his detachment: an officer and 24 men at the fort; a serjeant and 10 men in the fort by the waterside; a corporall and 6 men on the garden, and will obey shuch orders as he shall receive from Collo. Lyman. All guards from the regiments ordered to march tomorrow, are to joyn their regiments at the beating of the Generall.

GENERAL ORDERS.

Camp at Crown Point, 4th August, 1759. Parole, Virginia.

Collo. for the day tomorrow Collo. Montgomery; Field Officers for the picquitts this night Major West; tomorrow night Major John Campbell; Adjutant of the day tomorrow Forbess. The quartermasters and campcolourmen to assemble immediately at the fort. Lieut. Collo. Robison will mark the camp as soon as the regiments are on the ground. Each corps to send for their tents, and officer to see that the boats are properly placed and a guard to be left on them. A place will be fixed for the provisions to land at; 150 paces will be allowed to each regiment to encamp on, and they will have 16 rowes in stead of eight, without closing their tents too near.

No soldier must be allowed to straggle without the guards of the camp; if they go for wood a serjeants guard must go and cover them; they are always to be upon their guard, as it is not impossible but there may be some lurking Indians. Quarter guards to face outwards. Major Roggers to send a sufficient party of men with an officer to take 3 *batteaux* tomorrow morning very earlie to Ticonderoga; to apply to Serjeant Airy who will load them with spruce beer which they are immediately to bring to camp here; a serjeant and 12 men to mount guard in the front; to place sentrys at the gate and let no bodie to go in till further orders. This guard is also to remain at the outside of the gate.

Crown Point, 5th August, 1759. Parole, Lancaster.

Collo. of the day tomorrow. Regulars Collo. Grant, Provincials Collo. Fitch; Field Officers for the picquitts this night, Regulars Major John Campbell, Provincials Maj. Douglass; tomorrow night Maj. Reid, Lieut. Colo. Hunt; Adjutant for the day tomorrow Inniskilling

(William Moore). Communications to be made in the intervalls of the regiments from the Royall to Forbess; the Royall will then clear half way to the left of the Light Infantry, and Forbes half way to where Schuyler is encamped. Gages Light Infantry, Grenadiers Light Infantry, will open their communications a little in front of there intervalls, so that there may be an untrupted communication in the whole circle wide enough for three men to march in abreast, in case of any attack upon the Light Infantry and Grenadiers they are to maintain their ground and shall be supported, the regiments to receive three days provision in pork tomorrow at Revallie beating beginning by Gages, following Grenadiers, Royall, Predeaux, Inniskilling, Royall Highlanders, Montgomerys, Forbess.

They are to receive for three days at the magazine in the fort, this complets them to the eight inclusively, the regiments to send a return of what bakers they left at Ticonderoga to Major of Brigade Moniepenny, and those who have left none to send their bakers to him that they may be immediately sent back, where they will receive flower for seven days, bake it and bring it back to camp. John Sutherland of the 55th, Chaser and Lee of the 27th and a Grenadier of Montgomerys, that were imployed in the garden, to be sent back with the bakers and follow such directions as they will receive from Lieut. Gray of the Highlanders at Ticonderoga; the camp not to be alarmed at Major Roggers fireing on the other side of the lake; the regiments must take the greatest care of their *batteaux*; the comanding officer of each corps is permitted to send two *batteaux* out a fishing for the corps, an officer or a careful serjeant must be always with them; they must never go more than halfway over to the opposite side, and never more than a mile from camp.

The Light Infantry, Grenadiers and Gages Rangers must make their houses of office in the front, the two brigades may make theirs by the lake side if they can, if not in the rear. Commanding officers of corps are desired to send in to the major of brigade this night a very exact return of the carpenters, masons, lime burners and colmakers that they have in their respective corps. If any regiments have any broad-axes they will likewise make a report of it to the major brigade; as there is a field of pease found they shall be divided amongst the army and the corps are to send tomorrow two men per company with arms, a serjeant per regiment and an officer per brigade; each corps and the artillery taking two *batteaux* and assembling in the front of the fort at 5 in the morning; Gages Light Infantry sends a captain two subalterns and a partie of men in the English boat and the other boat with the three-pounder to cover the *batteaux*, Lieut. Willamoze to shew where the pease are and Major of Brigade Skeene will proportion out the quantity each regiment is to take, taking care that they pluck them and to take none but what is fit to be gathered and that they do not spoil them in gathering them; they are then to return altogether to camp and the pease most be equallie divided amongst the messes.

★★★★★★

Charles Willyamoz was appointed Lieutenant in the 80th Light Infantry, 29th December, 1757, and on the disbanding of the regiment in 1763, went on half-pay where he remained until 1799, when his name is dropped from the *Army List*.

★★★★★★

Crown Point, 6th August, 1759. Parole, New Jersey.

Collo, of the day tomorrow Regulars Collo. Forster, Provincials Collo. Babcock; Field Officers for the picquits this night, Regulars Major Reed, Provincials Lieut. Collo. Hunt; tomorrow night, Lieut. Collo. Darby, Lieut. Collo. Saltenstall; Adjutant of the day tomorrow Royall Highlanders. As twenty-four barrells of spruce is come to the fort the corps may send for it immediately in the following proportion, Royall, Royall Highlanders and Montgomerys three barrells each; late Forbes, Inniskilling, Predeaux two barrells each; Light Infantry, Grenadiers and Gages two each. Major Roggers to send a party of men with an officer to take two *batteaux* immediately to Ticonderoga to apply to Serjeant Airy for spruce beer, which they are to load with and bring to camp here without the loss of time.

The Provincials to receive three days provisions tomorrow, beginning with Ruggles at 5 o'clock and following Schuyler, Fitch and Babcock; this compleats them to the 9th inclusively; the three ovens in the fort to be for their use to bake their bread, orders are given to all suttlers to be permitted to bring over the cattle from Fort George to Ticonderoga and as a road will be finished this day from Ticonderoga to this place the regiments will acquaint their suttlers accordingly that they may bring any cattle to camp.

Lieut. Moncrieff is appointed *aid-de-camp* to the generall during the absence of Captain Priscot (Prescott).

★★★★★★

Thomas Moncrieffe, brother of Mr. M., afterwards Lord Mayor of Dublin, began his military career in Flanders under General Cornwallis, from whom he received his first commission about the year 1745. He obtained a lieutenancy on the 20th of Sept., 1754, in Shirley's or the 50th Foot, with which regiment he was taken prisoner at Oswego in 1756. He joined the 1st Royals in 1757; was appointed *aide-de-camp* to Brigadier Monckton, Lieut. Governor of Nova Scotia, in 1758; in 1759 accompanied the expedition under General Prideaux against Niagara, and on the 28th of July of that year was sent by Sir William Johnson with the news of the surrender of that fort to General Amherst, whose *aide-de-camp* he was immediately appointed; in February, 1760, obtained a company in the 55th and accompanied that corps into Montreal.

He returned to Ireland in 1764, but in 1768 exchanged into the 59th and came back to America with that regiment in which he continued until 1774, when he received the appointment of Brigade-Major from General Gage, whom he accompanied to Boston. He returned to the province of New York the following year with the Royal Army and was taken prisoner at the Battle of Brooklyn, though shortly after released. His residence after this was at Flatbush where 'twas again his luck to fall into the hands of the Americans, a party of whom from Middletown, N. J., seized and carried him in June, 1778, to Princeton. He was soon after exchanged.

Major Moncrieffe was married three times: 1st, at Halifax, to Margaret, daughter of Captain Heron of the 40th Regiment; 2nd, in Oct., 1764, to Mary Livingston of New York; this lady dying in 1774, he married, 3rd, Helena, daughter of Andrew Barclay and Helena Roosevelt of New York. He continued after the peace of 1783 to reside in New York, where he died suddenly, by the bursting of a blood vessel on Friday the 9th of December, 1791.

On the following Sunday evening his remains were followed to the grave by a large concourse of people, eight of the principal gentlemen of New York acting as pall-bearers, and he was interred in Trinity Churchyard, in the same tomb with Colonel Maitland, uncle to Lord Lauderdale. (*Army Lists*; N.Y. *Doc. Hist.*, 8vo, I; *Memoirs of Mrs. Coghlan*; Knox, II; *N. Y. Journal and Patriotic Register*, Dec. 14, 1791; Onderdonk's Kings Co.; Strong's *Flatbush*; Holgate's *American Geneal*).

Robert Prescott obtained a company in the 15th Regiment of Foot on 22nd January, 1755, and served in the expedition against Rochefort in 1757, against Louisbourg in 1798; acted as *aid-de-camp* to Amherst in 1759, and afterwards joined the army under Wolfe. On the 22nd March, 1761, he was appointed Major of the 95th Foot, which regiment formed part of the army sent under General Monkton to reduce Martinico; became Lieutenant-Colonel of the 72nd Foot on the 10th November, 1762, and went on half-pay the following year, on the regiment being disbanded.

He remained on half-pay until the breaking out of the troubles in the colonies, when he was appointed Lieutenant-Colonel of the 28th Regiment (8th September, 1775,) and in the following Summer was quartered on Staten Island and was present at the battle of the 1st of August, 1776 (Beatson, VI). He was also present in the several other engagements which took place that year in Westchester County, and terminated with the storming of Fort Washington in November, after which he passed the Winter at Brunswick, N. J. In 1777, he was attached to the expedition against Philadelphia; was appointed Colonel by Brevet 29th August and was in the Battle of Brandywine 11th September of the same year.

In 1778 he was appointed 1st Brigadier General in the expedition under Grant against the French West India Possessions and remained about a year in that quarter, and on the 13th October, 1780, was promoted to the Colonelcy of the 94th; became Major-General 19th October, 1781 and returned to half-pay on the disbanding of his regiment at the peace of 1783. On the 6th July, 1789, he was appointed Colonel of his former regiment, the 28th, and Lieutenant-General 12th October, 1793. On the 12th July, 1796, he succeeded Lord Dorchester in the Government of Lower Canada, which he administered until 31st July, 1799, when he was recalled in consequence of a rupture with the Executive Council. He reached the rank of General in the army on the 1st January, 1798, and died at Rose Green, near Battle, on the 21st December, 1816, aged 89 Years (Beatson's *Naval and Military Memoirs*, III,VI; *Army Lists*; *Gentleman's Mag.*, LXXXVI, 88).

★★★★★★

An officer from the line and a corporall and fix men from each regiment of the Regulars to assemble immediately in the *batteaux* near the Royall and to proceed this evening to Ticonderoga, from whence they are to bring all the spruce beer and brewing utenfils to camp. All the corps in camp to send a return of what sawers, miners and black smiths they have to Major of Brigade Moniepenny this evening. An officer and 50 Rangers to assemble at Gages Light Infantry at 5 o'clock tomorrow morning; they will take fix *batteaux* and proceed two miles down the lake where they will cut spruce; the officer will take the French prisoner who is on the generals guard who will show him where the spruce is, and a man who can talk Jerman to the interpreter; a party of Gages Light Infantry will go in the English boat to guard the *batteaux*; the officer will deliver the spruce under the care of the sergeants guard at the fort.

The Regulars are to furnish for the engineers 300 men to parade tomorrow at 5 o'clock in the front of the Royall Highlanders, where Lieut. Collo. Eyre will order them to their different works; 200 men of the Provincials to assemble tomorrow morning at five o'clock in the front of the Royall and are to take with them what tools they want from the magazine by the fort. Major Roggers will send one captain 2 subalterns and 60 men as a covering party, with some Indians and an officer who was with them to show the commanding officer of the working party the best wood on the other side of the lake; the covering party must not fire any dropping shots at any game; they are to take as many *batteaux* from the Royall as they want, a days provisions with them, and when they return at night they will deliver the *batteaux* to the guard of the Royall, putting them in the same place they received them.

Crown Point, 7th August, 1759. Parole, Boston.

Collo. of the day tomorrow. Regulars Collo. Montgomery, Provincials Collo. Schuyler: Field Officers of the picquitt this night, Regulars Lieut. Collo. Darby, Provincialls, Lieut. Collo. Saltenstall; tomorrow night, Major Allexander Campbell, Lieut. Collo. Putman; Adjutant of the day tomorrow Predeaux. The Light Infantry to change the firelocks that they received at the train and to take carabines in their room. The generall observes that some people are not obedient to the order of the fifth of August, which permitted 2 *batteaux* per regiment to go a fishing, by which we may lose men, and if any are found disobedient to that order hereafter they shall not be permited a *batteaux* out. The arms of the draughts to be examined and every regiment to compleat them with whatever are wanted.

The Provincials to mount a guard of one serjeant and 12 men in the fort, to put centrys on the ovens and take care that none come there but what have permission; Collo. Robinson will show them what ovens they are to use. A generall court martial of the army to set tomorrow morning at 8 o'clock at the Presidents tent; Collo. Fitch President, Major Gordon, Major Douglass, six Captains from the Regulars and four from the Provincials members; Lieut. George Burton of the Royall Deputy Judge Advocate.

200 working men from the Regulars at five o'clock tomorrow for the engineers, 300 men from the Provincials at the same time; Capt. Pembroke of the Jersey Regiment and 50 men to work this day with him to be of the number who are to finish the works in the rear of the Grenadiers; 100 Light Infantry to throw up a work, beginning at 5 o'clock tomorrow morning, Lieut. Collo. Eyre will trace it out this evening and Capt. Williams will oversee the work. A captain and 60 Rangers to set out tomorrow morning at five o'clock with 6 *batteaux*, Gages Light Infantry will send at the same time the English boat to cover the *batteaux*, and the English boat to stay out till towards evening; the captain of the Rangers will take out the French deserter from the generals guard and must go to the place that the deserter will shew him, at which place the French have supplied them selves with spruce, and they must bring as much spruce to camp as they can.

Corporal Sinclair of the Highlanders and Parceloo of the Inniskilling Regiment with 16 leabrours used to digging to attend Lieut. Gray tomorrow at 5 o'clock; the evening gunn is the signal for the working party to leave of work. The draughts that arraived last night to be in the front of their regiments tomorrow at eleven o'clock, the generall will see them. 4 caulkers are arraived in camp to repair the *batteaux*; they will begin earlie tomorrow with the boats of the Royall and are to go round the line; the commanding officers of corps are desired to give them all the assistance they require.

Crown Point, 8th August, 1759. Parole, Newport.
Collo. of the day tomorrow. Regulars Collo. Grant, Provincialls Collo. Ruggles: Field Officer of the picquitts this night, Regulars Major Hamilton, Provincialls Lieut. Collo. Putman; tomorrow night, Major Campbell and Major Whitting. Adjutant for tomorrow, 77th (John Campbell). The Regulars to receive 4 days provisions tomorrow of pork, beginning at Revallie Beatng by Forbess following Montgomerys, Royall Highlanders, Inniskilling, Predeaux, Royall Light Infantry, Grenadiers, Gages and artillery; this compleats them to the twelth

inclusively. It is concluded they have their bread from Ticonderoga as was ordered, and on the next dilivery they shall receive flower and bake it here, and all the bakers as soon as the seven days bread is readie are to come and joyn their regiments in camp here. Montgomerys, Schuylers, Fitches and Babcocks Regiments are to move their camp this night, if they have time, or tomorrow morning.

The quartermasters and camp colourmen of those regiments to assemble at 3 o'clock this afternoon on the left of Forbess, and Lieut. Collo. Robison will mark out their camp; the quarter-guard of Forbess will remaine on the same grown where they were posted. If it is fine weather about three o'clock all the corps to strick their tents for about an hour. The generall court martiall of which Collo. Fitch was President is desolved; the generall has aproved of the sentence of said court martiall in the tryall of James Watkins, soldier in Collo. Ruggles Regimint, who is sentenced to receive 1000 lashes in the following manner tomorrow morning at 8 o'clock: 250 at the head of Schuylers, and the same number at Fitches, Babcocks and Ruggles; a surgeon to attend the punishment.

A company of Light Infantry and one of Grenadiers, the next for duty, to receive immediately 4 days Provision ordered tomorrow, and they are to assemble tomorrow morning at Revallie beating on the left of the Light Infantry to cross the lake and serve as a covering partie to some workingmen of the Provincialls; the Light Infantry and Grenadiers to take their tents and provision with them; 334 Provincialls to receive 4 days provisions this afternoon which they will take with them; they parade tomorrow morning at Revallie beating in the front of the Royall; the whole to pass over the lake in *batteaux* and to be under the command of Lieut. Collo. Putman; the Provincialls will likewise take their arms and tents with them; two orderly drumers to attend the engineers that the workmen may assemble at beating the Pioners March and leave of on the Retreat beating.

300 workingmen from the Regulars for the engineers tomorrow, 100 for the artillery, 16 carpenters from the Regulars, as many wheel-wrights as can be found; an officer and 40 Rangers to take 6 *batteaux* and to go to the eastern side of the lake to fetch 600 boards from the houses are there; they are to go to Gages Light Infantry at five o'clock in the morning; a serjeant that was out to day will shew them where the houses are and the detachment of Gages Light Infantry will at the same time go out in the English boat to guard the *batteaux*; they will bring the boards to the fort and deliver them to Lieutenant Robison.

Crown Point, 9th August, 1759. Parole, New London.

Collo. for the day tomorrow. Regulars Collo. Forster, Provincials Collo. Fitch: Field Officers for the picquitts this night, Regulars Major Hamilton, Provincials Major Douglass; tomorrow night, Major Gordon, Major Whitting; Adjutant of the day tomorrow Royall. The Provincialls to receive four days provisions tomorrow at 5 o'clock, begining with Ruggles and following Schuyler; Fitch and Babcocks; this compleats them to the 13th inclusively. The regiments will now receive spruce beer regularly and as much as they want by sending to the brewery near the fort any time after 4 o'clock this afternoon; 400 workmen from the Regulars and 200 from the Provincials tomorrow.

The Provincials Regiments may use the large ovens in the fort; they most hereafter serve for bakeing for all the corps here, in the following manner, and the regulars are to receive three days flower for the provisions that will be due to the 15th inclusive, that they may take it on the 11th: The Royall to have one oven, the Grenadiers another from 12 at noon till twelve at night; then Predeaux and Light Infantry to keep the oven 12 hours and deliver them at 12 next day to Blakeneys and the Rangers; the Royall Highlanders follow Blakineys, Montgomerys the Royall Highlanders, Forbess, Montgomerys, and Gages, Forbess, Ruggles takes the ovens from the Rangers, then Schuylers, Fitches and Babcocks; each corps keeping a oven 12 hours and no longer, as each oven is capable of bakeing 900 loaves of 6 pounds in 12 hours; the small ovens is for the artillery and hospitall.

The regiments must carefully bring the empty barrells of spruce beer that they may not be damaged, and no corps will get a supply without returning the barrells they have received. As there are three thousand pair of shoes arraived at Ticonderoga which are for the use of the troops, at 3s and 6d per pair, and are to be deliverd to the regiments in the same manner as by the order of the 31st July, each corps will send a return to Major of Brigade Moniepenny of the number they chuse to take that they may be sent for accordingly.

Crown Point, 10th August, 1759. Parole, Amboy.

Collo. of the day tomorrow. Regulars Collo. Montgomery, Provincials Collo. Babcock: Field Officers for the picquits this night, Regulars Major Gordon, Provincials Major Whitting; tomorrow night, Major West, Lieut. Collo. Hunt; Adjutant of the day tomorrow, late Forbess. Lieut. Symcocks of the Inniskilling Regiment, Ens. Gregor of the Royall Highlanders, and Ens. Hill of Predaux are appointed overseers of the works that are carrying one at the fort.

******

Henry Symcocks was appointed Lieutenant in the 27th or In-niskillen Regiment of Foot 27th April, 1756. His name is not found in the *Army List* of 1765.

John Gregor or Mac Gregor, after having served some time as Ensign, was promoted to a Lieutenancy in the 42nd Highland-ers 28th July, 1760. He went on half-pay in 1763 and was not called again into active service until 27th August, 1775, when he returned to America. On 22nd March, 1780, he obtained a company in the 2nd Battalion, and served through the Ameri-can War. He retired or died in December, 1782.

Lancelot Hill was promoted to be Lieutenant in the 55th on the 17th September, 1760; Captain-Lieutenant 28th May, 1768; Captain 31st August, 1770 and left the regiment in 1773. (*Army Lists*).

******

They will attend Lieut. Collo. Eyre tomorrow morning at 5 o'clock and follow such direction as they shall receive from him. A detachment of 200 Rangers, 100 of Gages Light Infantry and one company of Light Infantry and one of Grenadiers to assemble tomor-row in their whale boats as soon as Revaille is beat in the front of the fort. Gages Light Infantry will be commanded by a captain and 3 subalterns and are to take the two boats with the three-pounders and one boat with a 2 pounder; the whole most take one days provi-sion with them. Majors Roggers will command the Rangers and the whole detachment is to be commanded by Lieut. Collo. Darby, who will receive his orders from the generall. A working party of 800 men tomorrow morning for the fort; Regulars gives 500, Provincials 300, a field officer to attend of the Regulars and comand the working party; for this duty tomorrow, Major Allexander Campbell.

Crown Point, 11th August, 1759. Parole, Albany.

Collo, of the day tomorrow. Regulars Collo. Grant, Provincials Collo. Schuyler; Field Officers for the picquits this night, Regulars Major West, Provincialls Lieut. Collo. Hunt; tomorrow night, Major John Campbell, Lieut. Collo. Saltenstal; field officer for the work to-morrow Major Hamilton; Adjutant of the day tomorrow Inniskill-ing. The following seaman from Collo. Babcocks Regiment to joyn Captain Loran, namely: Nathaniel Armstrong, Franciss Ealand, James

Hevotson, John Kean, John Smith, James Dinnie, Allexander Ginnis and John Hill, who are to assemble immediately at the artillery from whence they shall have a *batteaux* to proceed to Ticonderoga; a serjeant and 4 men of the Regulars shall go with them and return with all the recovered men at the hospittal.

The working party at the fort are to take their brekfast with them in the morning, and they will be allowed time at 9 o'clock to eat it when the drum beats the Retreat, but they are not to go back to their regiments but remain on the ground till the drum beats the Pioneers March, when they are to begin work again. As the bakers of Ruggles Regiment remaine at Ticonderoga that regiment is to receive their flower there and to send for their bread there; any corps in the army that chuses it may do the same on sending a report of it to the brigade major. A report to be sent in to the brigade major at fix o'clock this evening of the number of men in each corps who have been used to quarring of stones. Lieut. Cooke of the Royall is appointed overseer to the building the fort, he will receive his directions from Lieut. Collo. Eyre.

★★★★★★

William Cook was commissioned Lieutenant 25th October, 1755 and joined the Royals 1st January, 1757. His name is not in the *Army List* of 1765. Robert Cooke was also a Lieutenant in the Royals by Commission 18th July, 1758. He is dropped in the *List* of 1767.

★★★★★★

The following quarriers, as per return this evening, namely, ten of the Royall, five of the Royall Highlanders, 2 of Predeaux, ten of Montgomerys and one of Schuylers, to attend Lieut. Collo. Eyre tomorrow morning at the hour of work and are to continue daily to work as quarriers. Majors Rogers may have biskett for the men employed in working at the road by applying to Mr. Wilson, comisary, but he is not to take bisquit for any other but that detachment. 1200 working men for the fort tomorrow, the Regulars gives 800 the Provincials 400; the Provincials as weel as the Regulars must take their brakefast with them as ordered this day.

Crown Point, 12th August, 1759. Parole, Fort George.
Collo. of the day tomorrow. Regulars Collo. Forster, Provincials Collo. Ruggles: Field Officers for the picquits this night, Regulars Major John Campbell, Provincials Lieut. Collo. Saltenstall; tomorrow

night, Major Reid, Major Douglass; Field Officer for the work tomorrow. Major Gordon; Adjutant of the day tomorrow, Royall Highlanders. The quartermasters of the Grenadiers and Light Infantry will immediately draw three days salt provisions for the companies that are on the other side of the lake, and send it over to them; this compleats them to the 15th inclusively. Those companies are to remaine there and cover the men bringing the timber to the lake till further orders. The 334 men cutting timber on the other side of the lake are this day to proceed up the lake for cutting of timber about five miles from the camp on the western side.

Capt. Johnston or Lieut. Holmes will shew them the place. 4 days provision must be received this day for those 334 men, and a quartermaster of the Provincials must take it in a *batteaux* to the place on the western side where they are gone to cutt the timber. Two officers and 50 men to march this morning along the road to the place where the timber is to be cutt, to which Capt. Johnson will direct them, are to remaine there as a covering party for the workmen. Capt. Johnson or Lieut. Holmes to come immediately to Lieut. Collo. Putman that the men may proceed directly to the place where they are to cutt the timber.

The Regulars to receive four days fresh provisions tomorrow, begining at 5 o'clock with the artillery, following Gages, Grenadiers, Light Infantry, Royall, Predeaux, Inniskilling, Royall Highlanders, Montgomerys, Forbess; they will send their returns this day of their numbers to Commissary Wilson; this compleats them to the 16th inclusively. 1400 working men for the fort tomorrow; the Regulars to give 900, the Provincialls 500. The regiments to send for their fresh provisions tomorrow to the front of the left of Forbess.

Crown Point, 13thAugust, 1759. Parole, Sheffield.

Collo. of the day tomorrow, Regulars Collo. Montgomery, Provincials Collo. Fitch; Field Officers for the picquitts this night, Regulars Major Reid, Provincials Major Douglass; tomorrow night, Major Campbell, Lieut. Collo. Hunt; Field Officer for the work tomorrow. Major John Campbell; Adjutant for the day Predeaux.

******

John Reid, son of Alexander Robertson of Straloch, Scotland, was born on the 13th January, 1722. He was educated at the University of Edinburgh and entered the army as a lieutenant in Loudon's Highlanders 8th June, 1745, which regiment was reduced in 1748. He was appointed on the 3rd June, 1752, captain in the 42nd Highlanders, on its augmentation in 1758 he became major. He served under General Amherst in the French War and was wounded in the expedition against Martinico in 1762. In reward for his services he was promoted to a lieutenant-colonelcy the same year. After this, his regiment returned to New York in October and was stationed at Albany until 1763, when 'twas sent to the relief of Fort Pitt, then besieged by the Indians, who were defeated in the well fought Battle of Bushy Run.

In the following Summer, the 42nd again formed part of another expedition under Bouquet against the Muskingum Indians. In 1765, Lieutenant-Colonel Reid commanded all His Majesty's Forces in the district of Fort Pitt, where he was somewhat annoyed by the lawless Frontiersmen (*Pennsylvania Colonial Records*, IX. 269); and in 1766, an officer of the same name is mentioned as *commandant* at Fort Chartres, Illinois (Monette's *Valley of the Mississippi,* I). In 1770, Lieutenant-Colonel Reid went on half-pay of the 87th Highlanders; in the following year he obtained a large tract of land on Otter Creek, in Vermont, from which, however, his tenants were expelled in 1772 by the people of Bennington (*New York Documentary History,* IV).

In 1780, he was appointed Colonel of the 95th Foot, a newly raised regiment, and became major-general in October, 1781, but his regiment was reduced in 1783. He was raised to the rank of a Lieutenant-General 12th of October, 1793; was made Colonel of the 88th or Connaught Rangers, 27th November, 1794; became a general in the army 1st January, 1798, and died at his house in Hay Market, London, 6th February, 1807, aged 85 years. General Reid was esteemed the best gentleman player on the German flute in England and composed several military marches which were still much admired at the time of his death. Whilst Major of the 42nd he set to music the words of *The Garb of Old Gaul*, written by Captain, afterwards Sir Charles, Erskine, a composition that has ever since been a Regimental March. He left a fortune of £50,000 Sterling, subject to the life rent of his daughter, for the purpose of establishing a professorship of music in the University of Edinburgh, and by his will appointed an Annual Concert to be held in the hall of the Professor of Music on the anniversary of his birth day, to commence with several pieces of his own composition; among the first of which is that of *The Garb of Old Gaul* (*Army Lists;* Brown's *Highland Clans,* IV; *Gentleman's Magazine,* LXXVII, 275)

★★★★★★

A generall court martiall of the line to sett tomorrow at 8 o'clock at one of the hospitall tents; Collo. Babcock, President, Major West, Major Whitting; the Regulars to give 4 captains, Grenadiers, Light Infantry Gages, one each, and the Provincial 3 captains for this duty; Lieut. George Burton, Deputy Judge Advocate, for the tryall of two deserters of Gages and shuch other prisoners as may be brought before them; all evidences to attend. As the fort now a building is of the utmost consequence for the future protection and security of his Majesty's most faithfull subjects, who are or may be inhabitants of any part of the country behind this, whom the enemy can now no longer disturb, the generall recommends in the most earnest manner that all officers and soldiers employed in any of the above works will use his utmost endeavours in executing every one his own parte to the best of his power, which cannot fail of finishing this very essential peice of service in due time, and which he hopes will give plenty, peace and quiet to his Majestys subjects for ages to come.

The Provincials to receive 4 days provisions tomorrow, begining at 5 o'clock by Ruggles and following Schuyler, Fitch and Babcock; this compleats them to the 17th inclusively. The 2 officers and 50 Rangers as ordered yesterday to march this towards Ticonderoga, and as remaine as a covering partie to the Provincials cutting timber, the officer commanding the Rangers to obey much directions as he shall receive from Lieut. Colo. Putman, or the officer commanding there. For the works at the fort tomorrow. Regulars 900, Grenadiers 100, Light Infantry, Provincials 500, to digg the sawpitts, an officer and 30 men of the Provincials.

From the artillery, Gages Light Infantry to give a captain 2 subalterns and 60 men in the English boat who must take a days provisions with them to guard some Provincialls who are to cutt hay tomorrow on the eastern the Provincials to take *batteaux* from those belonging to Ruggles Regiment; Major of Brigade Skeene will shew them where to cutt the grass; as they do not receive pork till tomorrow those men are to carry their bread with them for the day, the whole to parade at the front at 5 o'clock and to return at night. The generals guard tomorrow, Ruggels, one serjeant, one corporall and 18 men.

Crown Point, 14th August, 1759. Parole, Newhaven. Collo. of the day tomorrow. Regulars Collo. Grant, Provincials Collo. Schuyler: Field Officers for the picquits this night, Regulars Lieut. Collo. Darby, Provincials Lieut. Collo. Hunt; tomorrow night, Major Allexander Campbell, Lieut. Colo. Saltenstal; Field Officer for the work tomorrow. Major Reid; Adjutant of the day tomorrow, Montgomerys. Major Christie is appointed Deputy Quartermaster-Generall in America, and is to be obyed as shuch

★★★★★★

Gabriel Christie was commissioned Captain in the 48th Foot on the 13th November, 1754 and was in command of the garrison at Albany in the Summer of 1757. He served at the Siege of Louisbourg in 1758 and was appointed Major in the Army 7th April, 1759; Deputy Quartermaster-General in America 14th August following, and entered Canada with the British Army in 1760.

He became Brevet Lieutenant-Colonel 27th January, 1762; Lieutenant-Colonel of the 60th Royal Americans 24th December, 1768, but was put on the unattached list in November, 1769, and so remained until the 14th August, 1773, when he returned his Post of Lieutenant-Colonel of the 2nd Battalion of the 60th. On the 18th September, 1775, he was changed to the 1st Battalion; was appointed Quartermaster-General in Canada 2nd April, 1776; was promoted to be Brevet Colonel 29th April, 1777; Colonel *Commandant* of the 2nd Battalion 14th May, 1778; Major General 19th October, 1781.

On the reduction of the regiment in 1783, Major-General Christie went again on half-pay, where he remained until 1786, when he was reappointed Colonel-*Commandant* of the 2nd Battalion of the 60th. He became Lieut. General 12th October, 1793; and General in the Army 1st January, 1798. General Christie was Proprietor of Isle Aux Noix in the Richelieu River, a little North of Lake Champlain, which he afterwards sold to the Crown; and of several *seigniories* in the vicinity of that island, He died at Montreal in November, 1798 (*Army Lists; Annual Register; Gent. Mag.* Bouchett).

★★★★★★

1500 Working men for the fort tomorrow, the Regulars give 900, Light Infantry 100, Provincials 500. The generall courtmartial of which Collo. Babcock was President is dissolved; the generall approves of the sentence of said courtmartial, and that William Fielden and Patrick Phillips, soldiers in General Gages Regiment being found guilty of the desertion laid to their charge are to receive 1000 lashes each with a catt of nine tails. The provost guard is to march them tomorrow morning at 6 o'clock, first to Gages where they are to receive each 200 lashes, then to the Grenadiers, Light Infantry, Royall, Predeaux, Inniskilling, Montgomerys, Forbess, at the head of each of which corps they are to receive 100 lashes each; the surgeon of Gages to attend. (Joseph Williams was the name of the surgeon of Gage's Light Infantry—*Army List*, 1761). Lieut. Clark of Collo. Fitches Regiment, accused of neglect of duty and also of disposing of provisions is adjudged to be reprimanded by his comanding officer as guilty of the neglect: of duty laid to his charge; with respect to the 2nd part of the charge he is acquited.

Crown Point, 15th August, 1759. Parole, Salem.

Collo. of the day tomorrow, Collo. Forster: Field Officers of the picquitts this night, Regulars Major Allex. Campbell, Provincials Lieut. Collo. Saltenstall; tomorrow night, Major Hamilton, Major Douglass; Field Officer for the works tomorrow, Lieut. Collo. Darbie; Adjutant of the day tomorrow, Royall. The following surgeons mates are to joyn the regiments and serve as mates in room of officers serving as shuch: Mr. Monro to Montgomerys, Mr. Malison to the Royall, Mr. Goldthwat an additional mate in the Royall Highlanders to be put on the establishment of Forbess, Mr. Carter to the Royall Highlanders, Mr. McManes to joyn the Rangers as soon as he arraives. The commanding officer of each corps will make something of a regimental hospitall that may serve to put any sick in who have not desperate cases; it is supposed a small hospitall will be sufficient.

As some of the collonels and severall of the Provinciall officers are employed in carring on the works for the building the fort there will be no collo. of the day of the Provincials till further orders, and the field officers of the picquitts will report to the collo. of the Regulars. The Regulars to receive 3 days flower immediately, begining by the Royall and following Predeaux, Inniskilling, Royall Highlanders, Montgomerys and Forbess, Grenadiers, Gages Light Infantry, Royall Artillery; this compleats them to the 19th inclusively. 1500 working men for the fort tomorrow; the Regulars give 900, Grenadiers 100, and the Provincials 500. An officer and 30 men from the artillery tomorrow morning at 6 o'clock to clean out the houses at the old fort for a generall hospitall.

Crown Point, 16th August, 1759. Parole, Halifax.

Collo. of the day tomorrow, Collo, Montgomery; Field Officers for the picquitts this night, Regulars, Major Hamilton, Provincials Major Whitting; tomorrow night, Lieut. Collo. Darbie, Major Douglass; Field Officer for the works tomorrow. Major Allexander Campbell; Adjutant of the day tomorrow, Forbess. The Regulars to receive 3 days provisions tomorrow, beginning at 5 o'clock by Forbess and following Montgomerys, Royall Highlanders, Inniskilling, Predeaux, Royall Light Infantry, Grenadiers and Gages Royall Artillery; this compleats them to the 19th inclusively. The Provincials may receive 3 days flower this afternoon at 3 o'clock, begining by Ruggles and following Schuylor, Fitch and Babcock; this compleats the Provincials with flower to the twentieth inclusively.

If the Provincials Regiments have any caulkers capable of caulking a new vessle, they will report the same to the major of brigade this afternoon, as calkers are very much wanted. 1500 working men for the fort tomorrow; the Regulars give 900, the Light Infantry 100, Provincials 500. The following sawiers are to attend Lieut. Collo. Eyre tomorrow at 5 o'clock: of the Royall, John Elkins and George Birll; Inniskilling, George Cooke and Robert Nutter; Royall Highlanders Robert Kennedy, John McFarling and Robert Bain; Predeaux, Peter Wright; Montgomerys, Main and Gordon; Grenadiers, John Campbell.

The following masons are likewise to attend Lieut. Collo. Eyre tomorrow morning at 5 o'clock: Royall, William Pringle and John Aird; Royall Highlanders, Dougal McKeaster and John Stewart; Predeaux, John McClean and George Wrightan; Montgomerys, Donald McDougall. The above artificers are to work daily and to follow shuch directions as they shall receive from Lieut. Collo. Eyre.

Crown Point, 17th August, 1759. Parole, Newyork

Collo. of the day tomorrow, Collo. Grant; Field Officers for the picquit this night, Regulars Major Gordon, Provincials Major Whitting; tomorrow night, Major West, Lieut. Collo. Hunt; Field Officer for the work tomorrow. Major Hamilton; Adjutant for the day tomorrow, Inniskilling. The Provincialls to receive three days pork tomorrow, begining at five o'clock by Babcocks and following Fitch, Schuyler and Ruggles. The 29 carpenters of Ruggles first Battalion Williards and Whittings Regiments will receive provisions this evening after work, for three days; this compleats the whole for the 20th inclusively. Four barrells of spruce beer shall be constantly kept at different places in the fort that the men at work may be supplyed when they want it on paying a half-penny per quart; this beer to be sent from the brewerie and none suffered to drink without paying for it. The following masons to attend Lieut. Collo. Eyre tomorrow morning at five o'clock: Royall, William Pringle, James McElwrath,; Royall Highlanders, Angus McDonald and William Milligan; Predeaux, William Kirkland and John Butcher, John McClelland; Gages, Wyllie Wilson, Birn Stirwood. 1600 working men for the fort tomorrow; the Regulars gives 900, Provincials five. Grenadier 100, Light Infantry 100.

As Captain Williams of the Royall has been robbed of some money taken out of a box that was carried out from his tent, if any one can discover any person concerned in the robbery and will discover so as he or they can be convicted, he shall have five guneas reward, and if any person conserned in the said robry should be a soldier and will discover the others he shall be pardoned, and as a further encouragement, on the conviction have his discharge at the end of the campaign if he chuse it 10 Rangers and 15 of Gages, fifteen of the Light Infantry of Regiments to assemble tomorrow at Revallie beating at the left of the Light Infantry; a serjeant to command each of those corps; if a subaltern officer chuse to command each corps the commanding officer may send them; they are to go a hunting on the other side the lake, and obey shuch orders as they shall receive from Major Rogers. A serjeant and ten grenadiers to go over at the same time and remaine as a guard to the boats till Major Roggers returns; the whole to take a days provisions with them. If two officers of the Light Infantry and two of the Grenadiers chuse to go a hunting the commanding officer may permit them.

Crown Point, 18th August, 1759. Parole, Philadelphia.
Collo. of the day tomorrow, Collo. Forster; Field Officers of the picquitts this night, Regulars Major West, Provincialls Lieut. Collo. Hunt; tomorrow night, Major John Campbell, Lieut. Collo. Saltenstall; Field Officer for the works tomorrow. Major Gordon; Adjutant of the day tomorrow, Royall Highlanders. 1600 working men for the fort tomorrow; the Regulars give 900, Provincials 500, Grenadiers 100, Light Infantry 100.

Crown Point, 19th August, 1759. Parole, Charlestown.
Collo. of the day tomorrow, Collo. Montgomery; Field Officers

of the picquits this night, Regulars Major John Campbell, Provincials Lieut. Collo. Saltenstall; tomorrow night, Major Reid, Major Douglass; Field Officer for the works tomorrow. Major West; Adjutant of the day tomorrow, Predeaux. The Regulars to receive 4 days provisions tomorrow, beginning at 5 o'clock with the artillery and following Gages, Grenadiers, Light Infantry, Royall Predeaux, Inniskilling, Royall Highlanders, Montgomerys, Forbess; this compleats them to the 23rd inclusively.

All the regiments may apply for their flower before they receive their pork and in case they want it for baking, taking alternatly 4 days and 3 days. As Ruggles bake their bread at Ticonderoga, Whittings will take the time of the oven alloted for Ruggles. 1600 working men for the fort tomorrow; Regulars give 900, Provincials 500, Grenadiers 100, Light Infantry 100. Gages Light Infantry to send at day brake a serjeant and 12 men to Ticonderoag in 3 *batteaux* with 2 days provisions to bring from thence the generall hospitall and recovered men; the serjeant to receive his orders this night from the brigade major.

Crown Point, 20th August, 1759. Parole, Gaudaloupe.

Collo. of the day tomorrow, Collo. Grant; Field Officers of the picquitts this night, Regulars Major Reid, Provincials Major Douglass; tomorrow night, Lieut. Collo. Darbie, Major Whitting; Field Officer for the work tomorrow. Major John Campbell; Adjutant of the day tomorrow, Montgomerys. The Provincials to receive 4 days provisions tomorrow, beginning at five o'clock by Ruggles and following Whitting, Schuyler, Fitch and Babcock. The 36 carpenters of Ruggles first battalion and Williards Regiment will receive this evening after work 4 days provisions. The men imployed under the command of Lieut. Collo. Putman in the woods, are to receive their provisions this evening and will draw for seven days; this compleats the Provincials to the 24th inclusively, and Lieut, Collo. Putmans Detachment to the 27th inclusively, 1600 working men for the fort tomorrow; the Regulars give 900, Provincials 600, Grenadiers 100, Light Infantry 100.

Crown Point, 21st August, 1759. Parole, Fort Edward.

Collo. of the day tomorrow, Collo. Forster; Field Officers of the picquits this night, Regulars Lieut. Collo. Darby, Provincials Major Whitting; tomorrow night, Allexander Campbell, Lieut. Collo. Hunt; Field Officer for the works tomorrow. Major Reid; Adjutant of the day tomorrow, Royall. 1600 working men for the fort tomorrow; the Regulars give 800, Provincials 600, Grenadiers 100, Light Infantry 100.

Crown Point, 22nd August, 1759. Parole, Oswego.

Collo. of the day tomorrow, Collo. Montgomery; Field Officers for the picquits this night, Regulars Major Allexander Campbell, Provincials Lieut. Collo. Hunt; tomorrow night, Major Hamilton, Lieut. Collo. Saltenstall; Field Officer for the works tomorrow, Lieut. Collo. Hunt; Adjutant of the day tomorrow, late Forbess. A detachment of 600 Men composed of 250 of the Grenadiers, 250 of the Light Infantry of Regiments and one hundred of Gages with officers and none commissioned officers in proportion, to parade tomorrow morning at Revallie beating on the left of the front of Light Infantry, the whole to be commanded by Major Holmes; they are to take 100 *batteaux*, allowing fix to each *batteaux* and to go to Ticonderoga where 50 will load with 20 barrells of flower in each *batteaux* and the other 50 with 16 barrells of pork in each.

The officers and non comissiond officers only will take their arms with them. A detachment of one captain 2 subalterns and 100 men of Gages Light Infantry with their arms to be under the command of Major Holmes and to take the smal boat with the three-pounder and whale boats. Fifty *batteaux* are to be furnished from those that Collo. Whitting brought up, which 50 of the Grenadiers and 50 of the Light Infantry must this afternoon take to where the Light Infantry boats ly; 30 *batteaux* will be taken from the Royall and 20 from Predeaux. Mr. Wilson the comissary to go with Major Holmes.

******

Nathaniel Whiting was graduated at Yale College 1743; married in 1750 Mary, daughter of Captain Roswell Saltonstall of Brandford. Conn., and died April 9, 1771 (Goodwin's *Genealogical Notes*, 336).

******

Crown Point, 23rd August, 1759. Parole, Stanwix.

Collo. of the day tomorrow, Collo. Grant; Field Officers of the picquitts this night, Major Hamilton, Lieut. Collo. Saltenstall; tomorrow night, Major Gordon, Lieut. Collo. Spencer; Field Officer of the works tomorrow. Major Allexander Campbell; Adjutant of the day tomorrow, Inniskilling, The Regulars to receive three days pork tomorrow at 5 o'clock, begining by Forbess following Montgomerys, Royall Highlanders, Innilkilling, Predeaux, Roydl Light Infantry, Grenadiers, Gages and Royall Artillery; this compleats them to the 26th inclusively. 1600 working men for the fort tomorrow; the Regulars give 900, the Provincials 700.

Crown Point, 24th August, 1759. Parole, Springfield. Collo. of the day tomorrow, Collo. Forster; Field Officers of the picquits this night, Regulars Major Gordon, Provincials Lieut. Collo. Spencer; tomorrow night, Major West, Major Douglass; Field Officer for the work tomorrow. Major Hamilton; Adjutant of the day tomorrow, Royall Highlanders, The Provincials to receive three days provisions tomorrow, begining at five o'clock by Babcocks and following Fitch, Schuyler, Whitting and Ruggles. The 26 carpenters of Ruggles first Battalion and Williards Regiment will receive provisions for three days likewise this evening after work; this compleats the Provincials to the 27th inclusively.

Lieut. Collo. Eyre will mark out three forts, the one the left where the windmill was is to be the Grenadier Fort, the one in the centre is to be the Light Infantry Fort, the one on the right is to Gages Light Infantry Fort. Those three corps are to furnish men for building the respective forts. The works of the Grenadier Fort is to be under the care of Major Campbell, the Light Infantry Fort under the care of Major Holmes, Gages Light Infantry under the care of Major Gladwin, the whole under the inspection of Collo. Haviland, Captain Arnott to have the direction of building the fort of Gages Light Infantry,

★★★★★★

Hugh Arnot was taken from the half pay list and appointed a Lieutenant in the 42nd Highlanders, 9th April 1759, at the augmentation of that regiment on its coming to America and was promoted to a Company on the 27th December, 1757. He served in the unfortunate affair of Fort William Henry in 1758, and in 1759 accompanied Amherst as above. On 16th August, 1760, he exchanged into the 46th Foot, in which regiment he continued to serve until 1769, when his name is dropped from the *Army Lists,*

★★★★★★

The Grenadiers to furnish 100 working men to be out this afternoon at 3 o'clock at their fort to follow shuch directions as they shall receive from Lieut. Collo. Eyre; the other two corps to begin tomorrow morning and their number given in at evening orders, and after this day the commanding officer of each of those corps will order as many men as he finds necessary for the works, which the generall recommends to them to have executed with the utmost expedition. Collo. Haviland will report to the generall the numbers imployed each day. 1600 working men for the fort tomorrow; the Regulars give

900, Provincials 700; Grenadiers 100 to work at the Grenadier Fort tomorrow; 100 Light Infantry of Regiments and 100 of Gages Light Infantry at 6 o'clock tomorrow to mark out the ground where their forts are to be built.

Crown Point, 25th August, 1759. Parole, Connecticut.

Collo. of the day tomorrow, Collo. Montgomery; Field Officers of the picquit this night, Regulars Major West, Provincials Major Douglass; tomorrow night, Major John Campbell and Major Whitting; Field Officer of the work tomorrow. Major Gordon; Adjutant of the day tomorrow, Predeaux. Lieut. Robert Blakeney of the Inniskilling Regiment is appointed overseer to the miners and quarriers; he will receive his directions from Lieut. Collo. Eyre.

(Robert Blakeney's commission is dated 27th April, 1756, but his name is dropped in the *Army List* of 1765.) 1600 working men for the fort tomorrow; the Regulars 900, Provincials 700.

Crown Point, 26th Aug., 1759. Parole, Newhampshire.

Collo. of the day tomorrow, Collo. Grant: Field Officers of the picquitts this night, Regulars Major John Campbell, Provincials Major Whitting; tomorrow night, Major Reid, Major Baldwin; Field Officer for the works tomorrow, Major West; Adjutant of the day tomorrow, Montgomerys. Late Forbes Regiment and the part of Montgomerys that did not receive fresh provisions the last day they were issued, to send a return of their numbers to Commissary Wilson this afternoon at 6 o'clock and to receive 4 days provisions tomorrow morning at 5 o'clock begining by the Royall Artillery, Gages Grenadiers, Gages Light Infantry, Royall, Predeaux, Inniskilling, Royall Highlanders, Montgomerys and Forbess; this compleats them to the 30th inclusively.

Crown Point, 27th August, 1759. Parole, Piscataqua.

Collo. of the day tomorrow, Collo. Forster; Field Officers of the picquits this night, Regulars Major Reid, Provincials Major Baldwin; tomorrow night, Lieut. Collo. Darby, Lieut. Collo. Hunt; Field Officer for the works tomorrow. Major John Campbell; Adjutant of the day tomorrow, Royall. The Provincials to receive 4 days pork tomorrow, begining at 5 o'clock by Ruggles and following Whitting, Schuyler, Fitch and Babcock and the 36 carpenters of Ruggles first Battalion and Williards Regiment will receive provisions for 4 days likewise this evening after there work is finished; this compleats the Provincials for the 31st inclusively.

The detachment of Provincials cutting timber under the comand of Lieut. Collo. Putman will send for provisions and receive for 7 days; this will be to the 3rd of September inclusively. As all the tools are now much wanted for the works the regiments must deliver those they have to the place where the tools are kept by the fort, reserving only what they absolutely want. Some beef will be killed for sale tomorrow in the front of Forbess, and as it is now expected that there will be a continued supply of beef and mutton in camp, the markett will be daily keept there.

The following soldiers to attend Lieut. Collo. Eyre tomorrow morning at 5 o'clock and to take their directions from him: the Royall Highlanders, John Fraser, John McElvore, James Bruce, Allexander Sutherland; of Montgomerys, Malcum Reid, Daniel McNeil, Angus McVie, James Mitchell, John McDonald, Gregor McGregor; of Predeaux, George Williams; of Fitches, Josh. Hissard. The 29 draughts that arraived this day are to receive provisions tomorrow, for 3rd's to the 31st inclusively. They are to be subsisted by their regiments. They are drawn into from the 25th June and to have their ammunition compleat to 18 rounds. 1600 working men for the fort tomorrow, the Regulars give 900, the Provincialls 700.

Crown Point, 28th August, 1759. Parole, Annapolis.

Collo. of the day tomorrow, Collo. Montgomery; Field Officers of the picquits this night, Regulars Lieut. Collo, Darby, Provincials Lieut. Collo. Hunt; tomorrow night, Major Allexander Campbell, Lieut, Colo. Saltenstall; Field Officer for the work tomorrow. Major Reid; Adjutant of the day tomorrow, Forbess. 1600 working men for the fort tomorrow, the Regulars give 900, Provincials 700.

Crown Point, 29th August, 1759. Parole, Cape Breton.

Collo, of the day tomorrow, Collo, Grant; Field Officers of the picquits this night, Regulars Major Allexander Campbell, Provincials Lieut. Collo. Saltenstall; tomorrow night, Major Hamilton, Lieut. Collo. Spencer; Field Officer for the works tomorrow, Lieut. Collo. Darby; Adjutant of the day tomorrow, Inniskilling. 1600 working men for the fort tomorrow. Regulars give 900, Provincials 700. The following miners are to attend Lieut. Collo. Eyre tomorrow at 5 o'clock and receive their directions from him: Hocraft and David Roche of the Inniskilling, and Robert Harrice of late Forbess.

Crown Point, 30 August, 1759. Parole, Newfoundland.

For the day tomorrow, Collo. Forster; Field Officers for the picquits this night, Regulars, Major Hamilton; Provincials Lieut. Collo. Spencer; tomorrow night, Major Gordon, Major Douglass; Field Officer for the work tomorrow. Major Allexander Campbell; Adjutant of the day, Royall Highlanders.

Mr. Napier, Director of the Hospitall, to send surgeons to examine into the state and condition of the Provincial Regiments; Brigade Major Monniepenny to give him the numbers each regiment return's sick. Mr. Napier will return to the generall their state and the care that is taken of them. The Regulars to receive 3 days pork tomorrow, begining at 5 o'clock by Forbes and following Montgomerys, Royall Highlanders, Inniskilling, Predeaux, Royall Light Infantry, Grenadiers, Gages and Royall Artillery; this compleats them to the 2nd of September inclusively. 1600 working men for the fort tomorrow, the Regulars give 900, Provincials, 700,

Crown Point, 31st August, 1759. Parole, Kenderhook.

Collo. of the day tomorrow, Collo. Montgomery; Field Officers for the picquitts this night, Regulars Major Gordon, Provincials Major Douglass; tomorrow night, Major West, Major Whitting; Field Officer for the works tomorrow. Major Hamilton; Adjutant of the day tomorrow, Predeaux, The Provincials to receive 34 tomorrow, begining at 5 o'clock by Babcocks, and following Schuyler, Fitch, Whitting and Ruggles; the 36 carpenters of Ruggles first Battalion and Williards Regiment to receive provision for 3 days likewise this evening after their works is finished; this compleats them to the 3rd of September inclusively.

Crown Point, 1st September, 1759. Parole, Niagara.

Collo. of the day tomorrow, Collo. Grant; Field Officers of the picquits this night, Regulars Major West, Provincials Major Whitting; tomorrow night, Major John Campbell, Major Baldwin; Field Officer for the works tomorrow Major Gordon; Adjutant for the day tomorrow, Montgomerys, Captain Baldwin with 26 carpenters of Ruggles Regiment is to encamp with the other carpenters of Williards, &c. He is to receive three days provisions between 12 and 2 this day for 26 men; this compleats them to the third inclusively. One thousand six hundred working men for the fort tomorrow, the Regulars gives 900, the Provincials 700.

As the days are now shortened and that the heat in the middle of the day is not so great at any time to hinder the men from working, the hours of reast are to be half an hour at breakefast and from 12 to

2, that the works may be finished before the bad weather comes on.

Crown Point, 2nd September 1759. Parole, Prince of Wales.

For the day tomorrow, Collo. Forster; Field Officers for the pic-quits this night, Regulars Major John Campbell, Provincialls Major Baldwin; tomorrow night, Major Reid, Lieut. Collo. Hunt; Field Officer for the works tomorrow Major West; Adjutant of the day tomorrow, Royall. The Regulars to receive 4 days provisions tomorrow at 5 o'clock, begining by the Royall Artillery, and following Grenadiers, Light Infantry, Gages, the Royall, Predeaux, Inniskilling, Royall Highlanders, Montgomerys, Forbess; this compleats the Regulars to the 6th inclusively. The army to strick their tents this day at 12 o'clock and to leave them down for two hours. 1600 working men for the fort tomorrow, the Regulars give 900, the Provincials 700. John Stewart of the Royall and James Stevenson of Montgomerys to attend Lieut. Collo, Eyre tomorrow.

Crown Point, 3rd September, 1759. Parole, Lake George.

Collo. of the day tomorrow, Collo. Montgomery; Field Officers of the picquits this night, Regulars Major Reid, Provincials Lieut. Collo. Putman; tomorrow night, Major John Campbell; Field Officer of the works tomorrow, Allexander Campbell; Adjutant of the day tomorrow, Forbess. The Provincials to receive 4 days provisions tomorrow, begining at 5 o'clock by Ruggles and following Whitting, Schuyler, Fitch, and Babcock; the 62 carpenters of Ruggles first Battalion and Williards Regiment to receive 4 days provisions this evening after their work is finished; this compleats the Provincials to the 7th inclusively.

The detachment under the command of Lieut. Collo. Putman to send this night or tomorrow morning to receive provisions for 7 days. John McNeal, grenadier in the Royall Highland Regiment, Saml Sucker, James Doyle and James Kerry of late Forbess, and George Matthews of the Inniskilling, blacksmiths, to attend Lieut. Collo. Eyre this day at 12 o'clock and to follow such directions as they shall receive from him. The Director of the hospital has reported to the generall that the hospitals of the Provincials Regiment are not finished the commanding officers of these corps are desired imediately to have them compleated and that particulare care are taken that the men ly properly defended from the damps by dryed grass and brushwood; that every fair day that the sick can walk are paraded together and marched down to the lake to wash their hands and faces and clean themselves; that they are afterwards keept walking about for an hour or shuch time as their strength will permit, during which time their tents are to be struck and aired.

Crown Point, 4th September 1759. Parole, Prince Edward.

Collo. of the day tomorrow, Collo. Grant; Field Officers of the picquitts this night, Regulars Major Allexander Campbell, Provincials Lieut. Collo, Saltenstall; tomorrow night, Major Hamilton, Collo. Spencer; Field Officer for the works tomorrow, Major Reid; Adjutant of the day tomorrow Inniskilling. If the weather turns out fine and the men go to work this afternoon they most only be allowed an hour to dinner. This day the serjeants and men of Lymans, Worcesters and Fitches Regiments imployed in making fasceins at Ticonderoga will receive what is due them by the quartermaster of said regiments applying to Lieut. Gray for payment. The men of the Royall Highland Regiment, Montgomerys and the Light Infantry who have been imployed in makeing basketts will be paid for the same by the quartermasters mailers applying to Mr. Gray this afternoon after the work is over.

The regiments to receive tomorrow morning two pounds of fresh meat and one pound of rice for the number of men set opposite to the names of each corps, begining at 5 o'clock and following as the regiments are named, which will be turned into rations and stopt out of the delivery of next provisions and the regiments are to apply said fresh beef and rice entirley for the use of the sick; Royall 43, Forbes 37, Inniskilling 26, Royall Highlanders 22, Predeaux 21, Montgomerys 41, Gages 41, Rangers 61, Royall Artillery 14, Schuyler 78, Ruggles 48, Whitting52, Fitch 84, Babcock 55.

Crown Point, 5th Sept., 1759. Parole, Lake Shamplaine.

For the day tomorrow, Collo. Forster; Field Officers for the picquits this night, Regulars Major Hamilton, Provincialls Lieut, Collo. Spencer; tomorrow night, Major Gordon, Major Douglass; Field Officer for the works tomorrow Major Reid; Adjutant of the day tomorrow, Royall Highlanders. The tents of the army to be struck at 12 o'clock for two hours if the weather continues fair. The Grenadiers and Light Infantry of regiments to receive each 60 pounds of beef and 30 pounds of rice by applying to Mr. Wilson, comissary this day, which they will apply for the use of the sick, and this to be deducted when provisions are next issued. 1600 working men for the fort tomorrow; Regulars give 900, Provincials 700.

None of the men of the regiments to take away from the fort any of the hand-barrows, wheel-barrows or any of the tools or timber belonging to the fort, and if any of the barrows are at present in the regiments they must be returned immediately. The following artificers to attend Lieut. Collo. Eyre tomorrow and follow such directions as he will give them: Edward Foster of Predeaux and John Bellows of the Inniskilling, blacksmiths; Robert Lowrie, John Little of the Royall and Allexander Forbes of the Royall Highlanders, masons; John Knight and Robert Fanton of Collo. Fitches, miners; Benjamin Mezes, John Asby, William Ape, Joseph Jobb, Rubin Tunso, John Priam, Daniel Sythes of Collo. Fitches, quarries.

Crown Point, 6th Sept., 1759. Parole, Vinango.

Collo. of the day tomorrow, Collo. Montgomery; Field Officers of the picquits this night, Regulars Major Gordon, Provincials Major Douglass; tomorrow night, Major West, Major Whitting; Field (Officer) for the works tomorrow, Allexander Campbell: Adjutant of the day tomorrow, Predeaux. The Regulars to receive three days provisions tomorrow, they will be supplyed with a proportion of species of all kinds, begining at five o'clock, by Forbes following Montgomerys, Royall Highlanders, Inniskilling, Predeaux, Royall Light Infantry, Grenadiers, Gages and Royall Artillery; this compleats them to the 9th inclusively.

As the provisions the regiments have received for their sick will now be deducted, they will give their receipts for the number of portions they have received exclusive of that deduction. Four serjeants to attend the works daily and to receive their directions from Lieut. Collo. Eyre. The commanding officers will send the serjeants that they judge best qualified for this work to Major of Brigade Moniepenny this evening. 1600 working men for the fort tomorrow; Regulars give 900, the Provincials 700. The 4 serjeants for the works are Serjeant Clark of the Royall Highlanders, Serjeant Hosie of the Royall, Serjeant Anderson and Serjeant McDonald of Montgomerys.

Crown Point, 7th September, 1759. Parole, Brunswick.

For the day tomorrow, Collo. Grant; Field Officers for the picquits this night, Regulars Major West, Provincials Major Whitting; tomorrow night, Major Gordon, Major Baldwin; Field Officer for the work tomorrow Major Hamilton; Adjutant for the day tomorrow, Montgomerys. The Provincials to receive 3 days provisions tomorrow at 5 o'clock, begining by Babcocks and following Fitch, Schuyler, Whitting and Ruggles. The 62 carpenters of Ruggles first Battalion and Williards Regiment to receive three days provisions likewise this evening after their work is finished; this compleats the Provincials of as species to the 10 inclusively.

Crown Point, 8th September, 1759. Parole, Presqueisle.

For the day tomorrow, Collo. Forster; Field Officers for the picquits this night, Regulars Major John Campbell, Provincials Major Baldwin; tomorrow night, Major Reid, Lieut. Collo. Hunt; Field Officer for the works tomorrow. Major Gordon; Adjutant of the day tomorrow, Royall.

Crown Point, 9th September 1759. Parole, Durham.

Collo. of the day tomorrow, Collo. Montgomery; Field Officers for the picquitts this night, Regulars Major Reid, Provincials Lieut. Collo. Hunt; tomorrow night, Major Allexander Campbell, Lieut. Collo. Saltenstall; Field Officer for the works tomorrow. Major West; Adjutant of the day for tomorrow, late Forbess. The Regulars to receive 2 days fresh and 2 days salt provisions tomorrow, begining at 6 o'clock by the Royall Artillery and following Gages Grenadiers, Light Infantry, Royall, Predeaux, Inniskilling, Royall Highlanders, Montgomerys and Forbes; they are to send a return of their numbers this evening at 6 o'clock to Commissary Wilson; this compleats them to the 13th inclusively.

Crown Point, 10th September 1759. Parole, Hartford.

Collo. of the day tomorrow, Collo. Grant; Field Officers of the picquits this night, Regulars Major Allexander Campbell, Provincials Lieut. Collo, Saltenstall; tomorrow night, Major Hamilton, Lieut. Collo. Spencer; Field Officer for the works tomorrow. Major John Campbell; Adjutant of the day tomorrow, Inniskilling. The Provincials to receive 2 days pork tomorrow, begining at 6 o'clock by Ruggles and following Whitting, Schuyler, Fitch and Babcock; this compleats them with pork to the 12 inclusively.

The 62 carpenters of Ruggles first Battalion and Williards Regiment to receive 2 days pork this evening and 2 days fresh meate after their work is finished; this compleats them to the 14th inclusively. The detachment under the command of Lieut. Collo. Putman is likewise to receive this evening or tomorrow morning 2 days fresh provisions and 5 days pork which compleats them to the 17th inclusively. Lieut. Collo. Putman will send an exact list of his numbers to Comissary Wilson that he may provide fresh provisions accordingly.

Crown Point, 11th September 1759. Parole, Baltimore.

For the day tomorrow, Collo. Montgomery; Field Officers of the

149

picquits this night, Regulars Major Hamilton, Provincials Lieut. Collo. Spencer; tomorrow night, Major Gordon, Major Douglass; Field Officer for the work tomorrow. Major Allexander Campbell; Adjutant of the day tomorrow, Royall Highlanders. A generall courtmartiall of the Regulars to sitt tomorrow at the Presidents tent at 8 o'clock; Collo. Forster, President, Major John Campbell, Major Reid, two captains of the Royall, two of Forbess, one of the Inniskilling, one of the Royall Highlanders, 2 of Predeaux, two of Montgomerys, members. Lieut. George Burton, Deputy Judge Advocate, to try all shuch persons as shall be brought before them.

Crown Point, 12th Sept., 1759. Parole, Alexandria.

Collo. of the day tomorrow, Collo. Grant: Field Officers of the picquitts this night, Regulars Major Gordon, Provincials Major Douglass, (this officer belonged to the Jersey Blues, served as a captain at Ticonderoga in 1758, and was wounded in the affair of the 8th of July); tomorrow night, Major West, Major Whitting; Field Officer for the works tomorrow, Major Hamilton; Adjutant of the day tomorrow, Predeaux. The Provincials to receive 2 days fresh provisions tomorrow at 6 o'clock, begining by Ruggles and following Whitting, Schuyler, Fitch and Babcock. They are to send a return of their numbers this afternoon to Comissary Wilson; this compleats them to the 14th inclusively. 1600 working men for the fort tomorrow, the Regulars give 900, Provincials, 700.

The generall courtmartiall of which Collo. Forster was President is disolved. A detachment of 100 grenadiers, 30 of the Light Infantry of regiments, non-commissiond officers in proportion to be commanded by a captain of Grenadiers and 2 subalterns of each corps to parade tomorrow at Revallie beating on the left of the front of the Light Infantry and to take 30 *batteaux* to Ticonderoga where he is to apply to the commisary and load 15 with 30 barrells of flower in each *batteaux*, the other 15 with 16 barrells of pork each; the officers and non-comissioned officers to take their arms only. The captain will go in a whale boat and keep his party clos to the western side of the lake both going and coming back. The Royall Highland Regiment to furnish the *batteaux*, and the captain commanding the party will see them this night that they may be readie to set off at Revallie beating and to return as soon as they are loaded.

Crown Point, 13th September 1759. Parole, Providence.

For the day tomorrow, Collo. Forster; Field Officer of the picquits this night, Major John Campbell, Major Baldwin; tomorrow night, Major West, Major Whitting; Field Officer for the work tomorrow. Major Gordon; Adjutant of the day tomorrow, Montgomerys.

The Regulars to receive three days provisions tomorrow at fix o'clock, begining with Forbes following Montgomerys, Royall Highlanders, Inniskilling, Predeaux, Royall Light Infantry, Grenadiers, Gages, Royall Artillery; this compleats them to the 16 inclusively. 1600 Working men for the fort tomorrow, the Regulars give 900, Provincials 700. A generall courtmartial of the line to set tomorrow at 8 o'clock to try shuch prisoners as shall be brought before them; Collo. Schuyler, President, Major Allexander Campbell, Major Baldwin, five captains of the Regulars and 5 of the Provincials, members; Lieut. George Burton of the Royall, Deputy Judge Advocate. All evidences to attend.

Crown Point, 14th September 1759. Parole, Princess Agusta.

Collo. of the day tomorrow, Collo. Montgomery; Field Officer of the picquits this night, Regulars Major John Campbell, Provincials Lieut. Collo. Saltenstall; tomorrow night Major Reid, Lieut. Collo. Spencer; Field Officer of the work tomorrow. Major West; Adjutant of the day tomorrow, the Royall. The Provincials to receive three days provisions tomorrow, begining at 6 o'clock by Babcocks and following Fitch, Schuyler, Whitting and Ruggles. The 62 carpenters of Ruggles First Battalion and Williards Regiment to receive three days provisions this evening after work is over; this compleats the Provincials to the 17th inclusively. The 15 drawghts arraived this day to be drawn for 4 to each of the regiments of the Royall, Forbess and Predeaux, and three to the Inniskilling; they are to be supplyed by 18 rounds of ammunition each.

The Director of the Hospitall to visit the Regimental Hospitals of the Regulars to see that the men are properly provided with every necestary and report the state he finds them in to the generall. Timothy Fisher is sentenced to receive 1000 lashes for desertion, but the generall in consideration of his age is pleased to remit 500 lashes; he is to receive 500 and then be drummed out of the army as unworthie to serve the King. John White, soldier in Generall Gages Regiment, found guilty of the crime laid to his charge, is to receive 1000 lashes with the catt and nine tails by the regiment. James McMullen, soldier in Brig. Gen. Gages Regiment, accused on suspicion of thieft and is adjudged not guilty, and is therefore acquited.

A detachment of 110 Grenadiers and 70 of the Light Infantry of regiments, non-comissioned officers in proportion, to be commanded by a captain of Light Infantry with 3 subalterns of the Grenadiers and one of the Light Infantry to take 30 *batteaux* tomorrow to Ticonderoga where he will apply and load them according to a list that shall be given him this day; the officers and non-comisioned officers only to carry their arms; the captain will go in a whale boat and a crew from the company he commands with their arms; the *batteaux* to be received this evening at 4 o'clock from Montgomerys Regiment, and brought to the left of the Light Infantry; this party must set off at Revallie beating, shall take two days provisions with them.

In case the wind be conterarie for their coming back, the captain will receive further orders from the generall. The arms of the men of the Provinciall Regiments who have died are to be given in to the artillery and a list of their numbers to be sent to the brigade major. 1600 working men for the fort tomorrow, the Regulars give 900, Provincials, seven hundred.

The generall courtmartial of which Collo. Schuyler was President is disolved. The generall approves of the sentences of said court. Captain Heastens of Collo. Williards Regiment, accused of mutines behavor is found guilty of the crime laid to his charge and is dismised the service with disgrass; the generall orders a pass to be made out for Mr. Hastens to go home or where he chuses, and that he shall not be permited to stay with any part of the army. Lieut. Chick of Collo. Lymans Regiment, accused with not regarding orders, is adjudged by the court not guilty of the crime laid to his charge and thirefore acquited. The following artificers to attend Lieut. Collo. Eyre tomorrow morning and receive their directions from him: Enoch Ball of the Royall, James Cumming of the Inniskilling, blacksmiths; Angus McDonald of the Royall, Miner; Allexander Clark of Montgomerys, Elisha Crocker and Andrew Chaple of Fitches, quarriers, and Jas Mann of Montgomerys, carpenter.

Crown Point, 15th September 1759. Parole, Hampton.

For the day tomorrow, Collo. Grant; Field Officers for the picquits this night, Regulars Major Reid, Lieut. Collo. Spencer; tomorrow night, Major Allexander Campbell, Major Douglass; Field Officers for the works tomorrow Major John Campbell; Adjutant for the day tomorrow, Forbess. 1600 working men for the fort tomorrow, the Regulars give 900, Provincials 700. When the drum beats daily for the work after dinner the regiments to take it immediately on the right and on the left that the men may set out for the fort and that no time may be lost in their assembling to the work.

Crown Point, 16th September 1759. Parole, Sandyhook.

For the day tomorrow, Collo. Forster; Field Officers for the picquits this night, Major Allexander Campbell, Major Douglass; tomorrow night, Major Hamilton, Major Whitting; Field Officer for the works tomorrow. Major Reid; Adjutant of the day Inniskilling. The Regulars to receive two days fresh provisions tomorrow morning, begining at 6 o'clock by the Royall Artillery and following Gages, Light Infantry, Grenadiers, Royall, Predeaux, Inniskilling, Royall Highlanders, Montgomerys and Forbes; this compleats them to the 16th inclusively.

As the regiments of the Regulars and Provincials will for the next 4 days provisions of fresh and salt meat receive of all species as far as the magazine can supply it in equal proportions to the whole, the different corps will set aparte a sufficient quantity of the freshest kind for the use of the sick. The generall warns the regiments that if they do not make a better use of the priviledge which is given them in taking *batteaux* a fishing, and that the *batteaux* are regulated in the manner they have been, he will intirely put a stop to any being taken out. Every corps to return the number of *batteaux* and whale boats they have to the major of brigade and are to mark them with the name or number of the regiment, after which if a *batteaux* is found dirty, the regiment it belongs to will not be suffered to to take any *batteaux* a fishing.

Crown Point, 17th September 1759. Parole, Long Island.

For the day tomorrow, Collo. Montgomery; Field Officers for the picquits this night, Regulars Major Hamilton, Provincials Major Whitting; tomorrow night, Major Gordon, Major Baldwin; Field Officer for the works tomorrow. Major Campbell; Adjutant of the day tomorrow, Royall Highlanders. The 62 carpenters of Ruggles first Battalion and Williards Regiment and the 31 masons under the Command of Lieut. Pickerin to receive 2 days fresh provisions this evening, which compleats them to the 19th inclusively. The detachment under the comand of Lieut. Collo. Putman to receive 2 days fresh provisions and five days pork tomorrow morning, which compleats them to the 24th inclusively.

Collo. Putman to send an exact list of their numbers to Commissary Wilson this evining that the fresh meat may be provided accordingly. The Provincials to receive 2 days fresh provisions tomorrow, begining at 6 o'clock by Ruggles and following Schuyler, Fitch, Whitting and Babcock; this compleats them to the 19 inclusively; they are to send a return of their numbers to Comissary Wilson this evening. The regiments to receive from Mr. Tucker the proportion of English shoes according to the return of the 9th of August; the quartermasters to pay for them when they receive them in the same manner as they did last time.

Crown Point, 18th Sept., 1759. Parole, Cherrevallie.

For the day tomorrow, Collo. Grant: Field Officers for the picquitts this night, Regulars Major Gordon, Provincials Major Baldwin; tomorrow night, Major West, Lieut. Collo. Saltenstall; Field Officer for the works tomorrow, Major Hamilton; Adjutant of the day tomorrow, Predeaux. Capt. Smiths Company to receive four days provisions for their effective numbers to the 21st inclusively. The Regulars to receive 2 days pork tomorrow, begining at 6 o'clock by the Royall Artillery and following Gages, Grenadiers, Light Infantry, Royall, Predeaux, Inniskilling, Royall Highlanders, Montgomerys and Forbess; this compleats them to the 20th inclusively. Barny Wallace and Benjamin Barrett, carpenters of Capt. Smiths Company, to joyn the carpenters under Capt. Baldwin, and William Hancock, mason, to joyn Lieut. Pickerin this evening. The regiments to strick their tents at 12 o'clock that the grownd may be thoroughly dryed and aired. 1600 working men for the fort tomorrow, the Regulars give 900, Provincials 700.

Crown Point, 19th Sept., 1759. Parole, Deerfield.

For the day tomorrow, Collo. Forster; Field Officers for the picquits this night, Regulars Major West, Lieut. Collo. Saltenstall; tomorrow night, Major John Campbell, Lieut. Collo. Spencer; Field Officer for the works tomorrow Major Gordon; Adjutant for the day tomorrow, Montgomerys. The 62 carpenters of Rugles first Battalion and Williards Regimint, the 31 masons under the comand of Lieut. Pickerin to receive two days pork this evening after their work is finished; the Provincials to receive two days pork tomorrow, beginning at 6 o'clock by Ruggles and following Whitting, Schuyler, Fitch and Babcock; this compleats them to the 21st inclusively. The regiments to strick their tents at 12 o'clock that the grownd may be thorowghly dryed and aired.

Crown Point, 20th September 1759. Parole, Northampton.

For the day tomorrow, Collo. Montgomery; Field Officers for

the picquits this night, Regulars Major John Campbell, Lieut Collo. Spencer; tomorrow night, Major Reid, Major Douglass; Field Officer for the works tomorrow. Major West; Adjutant for the day tomorrow, Royall. The Regulars to receive tomorrow 3 days provisions, begining at 6 o'clock by Forbes and following Montgomerys, Royall Highlanders, Inniskilling, Predeaux, Royall, Light Infantry, Grenadiers, Gages and Royall Artillery; this compleats them to the 23rd inclusively.

The corps that have boats are to mark them distinctly on the upper part of the bow of the left side of the boats; it most be either with pitch or tar, or by cutting the boat without damaging it. The boats that are lent most be marked by the corps to whome they belong. The engineers to have as many boats as are required for their works and for the future no boats are to be lent without an order from the deputy quartermaster generall, and then a receipt are to be taken for them. The quartermaster to report tomorrow the difficencies of deffects of all the boats of their respective corps to Lieut. Collo. Robison, and to report to him the state of the whole every Saturday morning. Mr. Vanvighter to pick up all the straggling boats and put them under the care of Gages *Batteaux* Guard. Lieut. Collo. Robison will order the boats to be removed in shuch manner as he thinks best that they may not be dammaged by the weather.

Crown Point, 21st September 1759. Parole, Deleware.

For the day tomorrow, Collo. Grant; Field Officers for the picquits this night, Major Reid, Major Douglass; tomorrow night, Major Allexander Campbell, Major Whitting; Field Officer for the works tomorrow. Major John Campbell; Adjutant of the day tomorrow, Forbess. The 62 carpenters of Rugles first Battalion and Williards Regiment, and 27 men of Capt. Smiths companie under the direction of Capt. Baldwin, and the 31 masons under the command of Lieut, Pickerin to receive three days pork this evening after their work is finished. The Provincial Regiments to receive three days pork tomorrow, begining at 6 o'clock by Babcocks and following Fitch, Schuyler, Whitting and Ruggles.

Capt. Smith will receive tomorrow at 10 o'clock three days provisions for the remainder of his companie; this compleats the Provincials to the 24th inclusively. The tents of the army to be struck and aired at 12 o'clock. An officer, serjeant, corporall and 30 men from the Grenadiers and Light Infantry to parade tomorrow at day brake on the left of the Light Infantry and to proceed to Ticonderoga in five of their own whale boats which they are to load with shuch stores as Mr. Dice

155

shall deliver to them, and to return directly to this camp; Mr. Dice will go with the party. The officers and non-comissioned officers will carry their arms.

Crown Point, 22nd September 1759, Parole, Windsor.

For the day tomorrow, Collo. Forster; Field Officers for the picquits this night, Regulars Major Allexander Campbell, Major Whitting; tomorrow night, Major Hamilton, Major Baldwin; Field Officer for the works tomorrow. Major John Campbell; Adjutant of the day tomorrow, Inniskilling.

Crown Point, 23rd September 1759 Parole, Saybrook.

For the day tomorrow, Collo. Montgomery; Field Officers for the picquits this night, Major Hamilton, Major Baldwin; tomorrow night, Major Gordon, Lieut. Collo. Saltenstall; Field Officer for the works tomorrow. Major Allexander Campbell: Adjutant of the day tomorrow, Royall Highlanders. A detachment of one 100 Grenadiers and 80 of the Light Infantry to be commanded by a captain and 2 subalterns of the Grenadiers and two sub of Light Infantry, to take 30 *batteaux* this night at gunn fireing and proceed to Ticonderoga, where the captain will apply and load them according to a list that will be given him this day; the officers and non-comissiond officers only to carry their arms; the captain will keep his party close together, and as soon as loaded will return with the whole and see the casks put into the magazine and the boats returned where received, Lieut. Collo. Robison will give an order for the *batteaux*; the captain will take a whale boat and crew with arms from his own companie and will carry a days bread for the detachment.

The Regulars to receive 2 days fresh and 2 days salt provisions tomorrow, begining at 6 o'clock by the Royall Artillery and following Gages, Grenadiers, Light Infantry, Royall, Predeaux, Inniskilling, Royall Highlanders, Montgomerys and Forbess; this compleats them to the 27th inclusively. 1600 working men for the fort tomorrow; the Regulars give nine hundred. Provincials 700.

Crown Point, 24th Sept., 1759. Parole, Scorticock.

For the day tomorrow, Collo. Grant: Field Officers for the picquitts this night, Major Gordon, Lieut. Collo. Saltenstall; tomorrow night, Major West, Lieut. Collo. Spencer; Field Officer for the works tomorrow. Major Hamilton; Adjutant of the day tomorrow, Predeaux. The 62 carpenters of Ruggles first Battalion and Williards Regiment and the 27 Men of Capt. Smiths companie under the direction of Major

Baldwin, the 31 masons under the command of Lieut. Pickerin to receive this afternoon after their work is finished two days fresh and two days pork. The detachment under the command of Lieut. Collo. Putman may receive this day or tomorrow 2 days fresh provisions and five days pork, which compleats them to the 1st of October inclusively. Collo. Putman to send a return of their number directly to Commissary Wilson and the time that he will receive the provisions.

The Provincials to receive 2 days fresh provisions and 2 days pork tomorrow, begining at 6 o'clock by Rugles and following Whitting, Schuyler, Fitch and Babcock; this compleats them to the 28th inclusively. The tents of the army to be struck at 12 o'clock that the grownd may be thoroughly dryed and aired. A monthly return to be given in tomorrow at orderly time. 1600 working men for the fort tomorrow, the Regulars give 900, Provincials 700, The 12 draughts arraived this day to be drawn for, 4 to the Royall, 3 to the Inniskilling, 3 to Forbess and two to Predeaux; they are to be subsisted by the regiments they are drawn into from the 25th of June and to be immediately provided with blankets, legens, &c., and to have their ammunition compleated to 18 rounds.

Crown Point, 25th September 1759. Parole, Otter River.

For the day tomorrow, Collo. Forster; Field Officers for the picquits this night, Major West, Lieut. Collo. Spencer; tomorrow night, Major John Campbell, Major Douglass; Field Officer for the works tomorrow. Major Gordon; Adjutant of the day tomorrow, Montgomerys. Capt. Smiths companie to receive four days provisions at 12 o'clock this day, which compleats them to the 28 inclusively. 1600 working men for the fort tomorrow, the Regulars give 900, Provincials 700. Lieut. Tolmey (Tolme) of the Royall Highlanders is appointed overseer for the works and to receive his directions from Lieut. Collo. Eyre.

★★★★★★

Kenneth Tolme was commissioned a lieutenant in the 42nd Highlanders, 23rd January, 1756, and promoted to the command of a company 27th July, 1760. His name is dropped after the peace of 1763.

★★★★★★

Crown Point, 26th September 1759. Parole, Jamaica.

For the day tomorrow, Collo. Montgomery; Field Officers for the picquits this night, Major John Campbell, Major Douglass; tomorrow night, Major Reid, Major Whitting; Field Officer for the works, Major

West; Adjutant of the day, Royall.

For the day tomorrow, Collo. Grant; Field Officers for the picquits this night, Major Reid, Major Whitting; tomorrow night, Major Allexander Campbell, Major Baldwin; Field Officer for the works tomorrow. Major Cambbl; Adjutant of the day for tomorrow Forbes. A detachment of 100 Grenadiers and 30 of the Light Infantry of Regiments, non-comissiond officers in proportion, to be commanded by a captain and 2 subalterns of the Light Infantry and 3 subalterns of the Grenadiers, to take 30 *batteaux* this evening and go to Ticonderoga, where the captain will apply to the commissary and load them according to a list that will be given him this day by Lieut. Collo. Robison.

The captain will take a whale boat and crew with arms from his own company; he will keep his boats clos together and as soon as loaded he will return with the whole and see the casks put into the store and the boats returned where received. Officers and non-commissioned officers to carry their arms; the detachment to carry a days provisions with them. Lieut. Collo. Robison will give an order for the *batteaux*. The Regulars to receive 2 days fresh provisions and 2 days salt tomorrow, begining at 6 o'clock by Forbes and following Montgomerys, Royall Highlanders, Inniskilling, Predeaux and Royall, Light Infantry, Grenadiers, Gages and Royall Artillery; this compleats them to the 1st of October inclusively.

All barrells belonging to the brewerie to be sent in tomorrow at 8 o'clock, when the regimints receive spruce beer; each regiment will (send) a serjeant with a partie who will take care that the barrals are always carried and not rolld; the like number of barrells most be collected next day at 12 o'clock and returned to the brewerie in the same manner.

Crown Point, 28th September 1759. Parole, Ligoneer.

For the day tomorrow, Collo. Forster; Field Officers for the picquits this night, Major Allexander Campbell, Major Baldwin; tomorrow night, Major Hamilton, Lieut. Collo. Spencer; Field Officer for the works tomorrow Major Reid; Adjutant of the day tomorrow, Inniskilling. The 62 carpenters of Ruggles first Battalion and Williards Regt. the 27 men of Capt. Smiths companie under the Direction of Major Baldwin, the 31 masons under the comand of Lieut. Pickerin and the remainder of Capt. Smiths companie to receive this afternoon after their work is finished 2 days fresh provisions and 2 days pork.The Provincialls to receive tomorrow morning 2 days fresh provisions and 2 days pork, begining at 6 o'clock by Babcocks and following Fitch, Schuyler,Whitting and Ruggles; this compleats the Provincials to the second of October inclusively.

Crown Point, 29th September 1759. Parole, Kensington.

For the day tomorrow, Collo. Montgomery; Field Officers for the picquits this night, Major Hamilton, Lieut. Collo. Saltenstall; tomorrow night, Major Gordon, Lieut. Collo. Spencer; Field Officer for the works tomorrow, Major Allexander Campbell; Adjutant for the day tomorrow, Royall Highlanders. Major John Whitting of the Rhode Island Regiment has received a comission as Lieut. Collo. to said regiment, and Capt Ebenezer Whitting (Whiting) of said regiment has received a comission as Major, and they are to be obeyed as shuch.

★★★★★★

Ebenezer Whiting, of Conn., was the youngest brother of John. He was born in May, 1735, and married Ann, daughter of Col. Eleazer Fitch. He was a Major in the Army of the Revolution and died at Westfield, Mass., September 6, 1794. His widow died June 27, 1827 (Goodwin).

★★★★★★

Crown Point, 30th September 1759. Parole, King of Prussia.

Collo. of the day tomorrow, Collo. Grant; Field Officers for the picquits this night, Major Gordon, Lieut. Collo. Spencer; tomorrow night, Major West, Lieut. Collo. Whitten; Field Officer for the works tomorrow. Major Hamilton; Adjutant of the day tomorrow, Predeaux.

Crown Point, 1st October 1759. Parole, Burlington.

For the day tomorrow, Collo. Forster; Field Officers for the picquits this night, Major West, Lieut. Collo. Spencer; tomorrow night, Major Campbell, Major Douglass; Field Officer for the day tomorrow. Major Gordon; Adjutant of the day tomorrow, Montgomerys. The Regulars to receive two days fresh and 2 days salt provisions tomorrow, begining at 6 o'clock by the Royall Artillery and following Gages, Grenadiers, Light Infantry, Royall, Predeaux, Inniskilling, Royall Highlanders, Montgomerys, Forbess; this compleats them to the 5th inclusively.

The detachment under the comand of Lieut. Collo. Putman to receive tomorrow 3 days fresh and 2 days salt provisions; this compleats them to the 6th inclusively. A detachment of 100 Grenadiers and 80

Light Infantry of Regiments non-comissiond officers in proportion, to be comanded by a captain and 2 subalterns of Grenadiers and three subalterns of Light Infantry to take eighteen *batteaux* this afternoon at five o'clock from Montgomerys and 12 from Forbess and to proceed to the sawmills without landing at Ticonderoga where the captain will receive orders from Lieut. Collo. Robison as to what provisions the *batteaux* are to be loaded with; the officers and non-commisiond officers to carry their arms; the captain to go in a whale boat and a crew from his own company with arms, and a days bread for the detachment. He is to keep his boats clos together and when loaded to return with the whole and see the casks put into the magazine and the boats returned where received.

The two brigades of Regulars to send each a serjeant or a proper person at 9 o'clock tomorrow morning to the place in the front of Forbes where the boats ly, to see a boats rigged there with two blanketts for sails, and each regiment to rigge 2 *batteaux* in the same manner and when finished to report to Collo. Haviland, who is to examine the whole. Collo. Haviland is to rigg also a sail to a whale boat for a patteron for the Grenadiers, Light Infantry, Gages and Rangers, and each corps to rigg two whale boats after the same pateron.

Crown Point, 2nd October 1759. Parole, Ticonderoga.

For the day tomorrow, Collo. Montgomery; Field Officers for the picquits this night, Major John Campbell, Major Douglass; tomorrow night, Major Reid, Major Baldwin; Field Officer of the works tomorrow. Major West; Adjutant of the day tomorrow, Royall. The 62 carpenters of Ruggles first Batalion and Williards Regiment, the 32 masons under the command of Lieut. Pickerin, and Capt. Smiths companie to receive tomorrow 2 days fresh and 2 days salt provisions after their work is finished. The Provincials to receive tomorrow 2 days fresh and 2 days salt provisions, begining at 6 o'clock by Ruggles and following Schuyler, Whitting, Fitch and Babcock; this compleats the Provincials to the 6 inclusively.

Crown Point, 3rd October, 1759. Parole, Saunders.

For the day tomorrow, Collo. Grant; Field Officers for the picquits this night, Major Reid, Major Baldwin; tomorrow night, Major Allexander Campbell, Major Whitting; Field Officer for the work tomorrow, John Campbell; Adjutant of the day tomorrow, Forbess. A generall courtmartial of the Regulars to set at the Presedents tent tomorrow at 9 o'clock: Collo. Montgomerys, President; Major Hamilton, Major Gordon, one captain of the Royall, 2 of Forbes, one of the Inniskilling, 2 of the Royall Highlanders, one of Predeaux, 3 of Montgomerys, members to try all shuch persons as shall be brought before them; Lieut. George Burton of the Royall, Deputy Judge Advocate, to whom the members names and dates of their comisions, the prisoners names and crimes are to be given in this evening at 6 o'clock.

Crown Point, 4th October, 1759. Parole, Prince Edward.

For the day tomorrow, Collo. Forster; Field Officers for the picquits this night, Major Allexander Campbell; tomorrow night, Major Hamilton, Lieut. Collo. Saltenstall; Field Officer for the works tomorrow. Major Reid; Adjutant of the day tomorrow, Inniskilling. Mr. Napier, Director of the Hospitall, and Mr. Monro to visit the sick of the Provincials tomorrow morning; the surgeons of each regiment to have a list of their sick readie to deliver them at ten o'clock. Mr. Napier is to report to the generall the state the sick is in, and particularly the number of sick in each regiment, who will not be fit for any further service this campaign, whom the generall will order down to the Generall Hospitall at Albany.

The comanding officers of the Provincials Regiments are also to make a report to the generall tomorrow any officers they may have in their regiments, who they think by sickness will not be fit for any further service this campaign, The generall courtmartial of which Collo. Montgomery was President is disolved. The generall approves of the sentences of said courtmartiall; that Joseph Stares of late Predeaux, accused of robbery and found guilty of the crime laid to his charge, is to suffer death; that James Jackson of Forbes Regiment, accused of desertion and found guilty of the crime laid to his charge, is to receive 1000 lashes with the catt and nine tails. The picquits of the regiments to parade in the front of their respective regiments at twelve o'clock tomorrow and to march to the front of late Predeaux Regiment, where a gallows is to be erected for the execution of Joseph Stears.

Crown Point, 5th October, 1759. Parole, Woolff.

For the day tomorrow, Collo. Montgomery; Field Officers of the picquits this night, Major Hamilton, Lieut. Collo. Saltenstall; tomorrow night, Major Gordon, Lieut. Collo. Spencer; Field Officer for the works tomorrow. Major Allexander Cambell; Adjutant of the day tomorrow, Royall Highlanders. Captain Lawlhe (Laulhie) having interceeded with the generall for the pardon of Joseph Stares of late Collo. Predeaux Regiment on account that he will never be guilty of the crime again, the generall hopes that the condemnation of the prisoner, with the order for the execution, will intirley put a stop to that infamous practize of some villians robbing their officers and comerades without making an example of them by death, does therefore at the request of his captain pardon Joseph Stares, and the marching of the picquits this day at 12 o'clock is therefore countermanded.

★★★★★★

John Laulhie was commissioned a Lieutenant in the 55th Regiment 2nd January, 1756; Served at Ticonderoga in 1758, after which he was appointed to a company. His name is not found in the Army List of 1761.

★★★★★★

The Regulars to receive two days fresh and 2 days salt provisions tomorrow, begining at 6 o'clock by Forbes and following Montgomerys, Royall Highlanders, Inniskilling, Predeaux, Royall, Light Infantry, Grenadiers, Gages and Royall Artillery; this compleats them to the 9th inclusive. The Regulars, Grenadiers, Light Infantry and Rangers to send in return this afternoon to the major of brigade at orderly time of what ammunition is wanting to compleat them, the drawghts to only eighteen rounds.

Crown Point, 6th Octoober, 1759. Parole, Portsmouth.

For the day tomorrow, Collo. Grant: Field Officers for the picquits this night, Major Gordon, Lieut. Collo. Spencer; tomorrow night, Major West, Major Whitting; Field Officer for the works tomorrow. Major Hamilton; Adjutant of the day tomorrow, Predeaux. The 62 carpenters of Rugles first Battalion and Williards Regiment, the 31 masons under the comand of Lieut. Pickeren and Capt. Smiths companie to receive 2 days fresh and two days salt provisions this evening after their work is finished. The men of Williards and Worcesters that have joyned Capt. Baldwin, are to receive provisions at the same time to compleat them to the same day as the other artificiers.

The command under the command of Lieut. Collo. Putman to receive tomorrow 2 days fresh and 4 days salt provisions and to send a return of their number this day to Commissary Wilson. The Provincialls to receive 2 days fresh and 2 days salt provisions tomorrow, begining at 6 o'clock by Babcock following Schuyler, Whitting, Fitch and Rugles; this compleats the Provincials to the 11th inclusively, and Lieut. Collo. Putman to the 11th inclusively. The Regular Regiments to give in their cartridges that are damaged this day to the artillery and to receive as much powder, paper, ball and twine as will compleat their ammunition. For the Royall 488 rank and file, Forbess 376, Inniskilling 354, Royall Highlanders 475, late Predeaux 377, Montgomerys 540. They are likewise to receive as many flints as are wanted to compleat the above number; the Grenadiers will receive ammunition and flints by applying to Major Ord to compleat them exclusive of all their artifficiers; the rangers to receive 36 pounds of powder and 126 pound of balls and 222 flints.

A detachment of 180 of the Regulars with non-comisiond officers in proportion, with one captain and 2 subalterns to take 30 *batteaux* this evening at Retreat beating and to proceed to the sawmills without calling at Ticonderoga; the captain will receive a list from Lieut Collo. Robison of what provisions he is to bring; he will take (a whale-boat and crew,) and the officers and non-commissiond officers to carry their arms only; Royall, Royall Highlanders and Montgomerys to furnish 6 *batteaux* each; the other three regiments furnish four *batteaux* each.

The sick of the Provinciall Regiments reported by the Director of the Hospitall unfitt for any further service in the following numbers: Ruggles 48, Schuylers 98, Fitches 95, Whitting 100, Babcock 65, shall be sent to Ticonderoga tomorrow morning, except shuch as are in a condition not to be moved, for which orders will be given at night; their arms, cartridge boxes and ammunition with the tents in proportion to their numbers, unless the officers think the tents will be of use to them between this and Albany, are to be collected this afternoon and given in to Major Ord at 4 o'clock, that the men may be sent to Albany to remain there till the regiments march to their different provinces,

Crown Point, 7th October, 1759. Parole, Gaspee.

For the day tomorrow, Collo. Forster; Field Officers for the picquits this night, Major West, Major Douglass tomorrow night, Major John Campbell, Major Baldwin Field Officer for the works tomorrow, Major Gordon Adjutant of the day tomorrow, Montgomerys. The regiments to prepare their *batteaux* to the following numbers and to have their sails fixed accordingly to the pateron Collo. Haviland approved of: Royall 25, Forbes 16, Inniskilling 15, Royall Highlanders 24, Predeaux 16, Montgomerys 26; one of the *batteaux* of each is to be for the suttler; the comanding officer of each corps to have a whale boat; Gages Light Infantry the 2 boats with the three-pounders; 26

whale boats and a *batteaux* for the suttler; Grenadiers 43 whale boats and a *batteaux* for their suttler; Light Infantry of Regiment 44 whale boats and a *batteaux* for their suttler; the Rangers and Indians are to take all the canoes and as many more whale boats as may be wanted to carry their compleate number and to have one *batteaux* for their suttler. No more hutts to be made, and the comanding officers of corps are orderd not to permit any of their men to go into the woods to cutt any timber for private uses that there may be no stop put to the kings work.

Crown Point, 8th October, 1759. Parole, Scotland.

For the day tomorrow, Collo. Montgomery; Field Officers for the picquitts this night, Major John Campbell, Major Baldwin; tomorrow night, Major Reid, Major Whitting; Field Officer of the works tomorrow. Major West; Adjutant for the day tomorrow, Royall. The Royall, Royall Highlanders and Montgomerys are to take each two *batteaux* more then what were ordered yesterday, late Forbes, Inniskilling and Predeaux one *batteaux* more each; all the artifficiers and overseers imployed at the fortrese are to remaine here at work. Those of the Grenadiers, Light Infantry, and Gages imployed at their respective forts are likewise to remaine. The damaged provisions surveyed this day and condemned is ordered to be thrown into the lake, except the bread which is ordered to be keept for the horses.

Crown Point, 9th October, 1759. Parole, Oswego.

For the day tomorrow, Collo. Grant; Field Officers of the picquits this night, Major Reid, Major Whitting; tomorrow night, Major Alexander Campbell, Lieut. Collo. Saltenstall; Field Officer for the works tomorrow. Major John Campbell; Adjutant of the day tomorrow, Forbes. The Regulars to receive 2 days fresh and 2 days salt provisions tomorrow, begining at 6 o'clock by the Royall Artillery and following Gages, Grenadiers, Light Infantry, Royall, Predeaux, Inniskilling, Royall Highlanders, Montgomerys, and Forbess; this compleats them to the thirteenth inclusively. The undermentioned corps are to send a *batteaux* each at Retreat beating to Ticonderoga to receive tomorrow morning the following number of loves weighting six pound and an half each; they are to pay to the person General Lyman appoints to receive the money, the following sums being one penny sterling for bakeing seven pounds of flower; the quartermasters of each corps or a serjeant doing the duty to go with the party and to give a recipt to Mr. McMullen for the bread he receives for the regiment, which is to be deducted out of the delivery of next provisions at the rate of nine pound of bread for seven pounds of flower. A subaltern officer for this party and six men in each *batteaux* to parade at the left of the Light Infantry and set out at Retreat beating and return as soon as they receive their bread.

Regiments.	Loaves.	Money.
Royall, - - -	480	- - 1: 8:10 Sterling.
Forbes's, - - -	360	- - 1: 1: 8
Innifkilling, - -	340	- - 1: 0: 3
Royall Highlanders,	460	- - 1: 7: 8
Predeaux, - -	360	- - 1: 1: 8
Montgomerys, -	500	- - 1:10: 1
Gages, - - -	360	- - 1: 1: 8
Grenadiers, - -	430	- - 1: 6:10
Light Infantry, -	440	- - 1: 6: 5

Forbes Regiment to take 19 Boats, Inniskilling 18 and Predeaux 19. If any of the regiments think that the number for them ordered are not sufficient, they will report accordingly. The Royall, Royall Highlanders and Montgomerys are to leave each a subaltern officer each, exclusive of officers imployed as overseers at the Kings works, with three serjeants, three corporalls each, with the men that are left behind, and late Forbes, Inniskilling and Predeaux will each two serjeants and two corporalls; when the regiments march, the officers and men of each corps, artificiers included, will encamp on the centre of the encampment of the corps, and what remaines of the two brigades of Regulars will do the duty of the daily guards, and a centry to be keept in the incampment of each corps that nothing may be spoild or taken away during the absence of the regiment.

The regiments are to give the following numbers for the brigge and sloop and will send seamen if they have them: For the brigg the Royall 8 Men, Forbess 16 Men, Inniskilling 15, Royall Highlanders 14, Predeaux 7, Totall 60. For the sloop Montgomerys forty, Predeaux 10, Totall 50. One subaltern to command the detachment on board each. Mr. Ball, surjeons mate, to go on board the sloop as surjeon. Those men are to be readie to go on board when the brigg and sloop arraive, where they will receive their provisions, for which reason they are not included in the number of loaves to be received at Ticonderoga.

The commanding officers will immediately have the same quantity of bread baked here for the serjeants and drumers that will march with the regiment; five days bread is also to be baked here for the Rangers. The Royall, Royall Highlanders and Montgomerys to send

6 *batteaux* each, Forbes, Inniskilling and Predeaux to send 4 each with 6 men in each *batteaux*, to be comanded by a captain and 2 subalterns with non-comisiond officers in proportion, to assemble as soon as possible at the Royall, from whence they are to proceed to the saw-mills and bring up all the stores that the quartermaster has brought for their regiments and to return immediately.

Crown Point, 10th October, 1759. Parole, Ireland.

For the day tomorrow, Collo. Forster; Field Officers for the pic-quits this night, Major Allexander Campbell, Lieut. Collo. Smedley; tomorrow night, Major Hamilton, Lieut. Collo. Saltenstall; Field Officer for the work tomorrow Major Reid; Adjutant of the day tomorrow, Inniskilling. The men that are to embark to dress their 7 days provisions this day, the 52 seamen according to the following list to assemble this night at Retreat beating at the orderly serjeants tents and to be sent on board the brigg and sloop as Captain Loering (Loring) will direct; Ruggles 10, Schuylers eighteen. Fitch 7, Babcock 10; the officers and men under orders as marines to be readie to go on board on the first notice after Retreat beating, Capt. Smiths companie is to encamp at the Grenadiers Fort this evening and to attend the work there under the direction of the officer left for that purpose.

★★★★★★

Commodore Joshua Loring was commissioned a Captain in the Royal Navy 19th Dec. 1757 and had command of the Naval Operations on Lakes George and Champlain in 1759, and on Lake Ontario in 1760, in which year he accompanied Lord Amherst to Montreal. He went to England after the peace and returned to America in 1768; landed at Boston on the 20th of May, his Son, Joshua Loring Jun'r, having been appointed permanent High Sheriff of Massachusetts. Sir John Wentworth Loring and Henry Loyd, Arch Deacon of Calcutta, were his grandsons, He died before 1786 (Beatson's *Pol. Index,* II; Drake's *Hist. of Boston*).

★★★★★★

The 52 men of Babcocks are for the works of the Gages Fort and Brigadier Ruggles 2nd Battalion is to furnish men daily for the works under the direction of the officer left for the Light Infantry Fort, Brigade Ruggles first battalion is to remain where they are encamped. For the works carring on under the direction of Major Skene. The Provincials Regiments who remaine here must furnish all the men they possibly can for the very essential and necessary works that are earring on that they may be finished before Winter comes on and the troops go so much the sooner to winter quarters. Brig. Ruggles is to remaine here with the command of the troops; he will receive further orders from the Generall. Lieut. Collo. Eyre Engineer for the ordering of all the works and Major Skeene to remaine as Major of Brigade.

The collowrs of the regiments are to be lodged with the guard at the fortress after Retreat beating. An officer and 20 men of the picquitt of the Royall will march the collours of the Royall, Predeaux and Inniskilling and the Royall Highlanders. An officer and 20 of the picquit of late Forbess will march the colours of that corps and Montgomerys; the whole to be lodged under the care of the officer of the Fort guard and the detachment of the picquits to return to their corps. The 62 carpenters of Ruggles first Battalion and Williards Regiment, the 31 masons under the comand of Lieut. Pickerin and Capt. Smiths companie to receive two days fresh and two days salt provisions this evening after their work is finished; the men of Williards and Worcesters who have joynd Capt. Baldwin are likewise to receive provisions at the same time to the same day as the other artificiers.

The Provincialls to receive tomorrow morning 2 days fresh and 2 days salt provisions, begining at 6 o'clock by Ruggles and following Schuyler, Fitch and Whitting and Worcester and Babcock; this compleats them to the 14th inclusively. The Provincials most hereafter receive salt provisions untill more live stock arraives, as what are here will be wanted for earring on the works. Capt. Starks to man three whale boats with seven men each and to attend such directions as he shall receive from Capt. Loreing. The surjeons mates to go with their corps, and Mr. Naiper, Director of the Hospital, will take proper care of the sick left behind, to whome a list of them is to be given in this evening.

Crown Point, 10th Oct., 1759.

For Crossing the Lake Shamplaine.

Orders for the troops passing Lake Champlaine: The advanced guard is to consist of Gages Light Infantry with the flat-bottomd English boat on the right, and the 3 boats with the 3 pounders on the left, their whale boats drawen up abreast covering the heads of the collumns, and the comanding officer will keep a partie always near the west shore while the troops advance to make discoverie of boats or any thing left by the enemy in or near the shore. The troops to row in 4 collumns; the right and first collumn to consist of Light Infantry of Regiments, Grenadiers; the second collumn of the brigade of the Royall, and third collumn of all the boats of artillery, stores, tools, comissarys, &c.; the fourth and left collumn is to consist of the 2nd Brigade; the rear guard is composed of all the Rangers and Indians who are to draw up abreast covering the rear of the collumns and the commanding officers will keep a partie always near the east shore for the same purpose as Gages on the west.

The first and 2 collumns will march and embark by the left, the front rank in the boats on the right, and rear in the boats on the left; the comanding officers of corps on the left in a whale boat to lead their corps; the fourth collumn will march and embark by the right, the front rank in the boats on the left, and rear ranks in the boats on the right, the comanding officers of corps in a whale boat on the right of the collumns, the collumns to row always two boats abreast and the boats to follow very clos; the brigg and sloop will cruize and trey to cutt of the enemys vessels from the enemys fort, on the other side of the lake and will not wait for the armie, which the artillery and boats will cover.

The artillery commanded by Major Ord will form the Ligoneer radow in the centre, and the houbitzer on the right and one on the left of the radow; the 12 pounder in the front of the collumn on the right and one in the front of the collumn on the left; and a 12 pounder in the centre in the rear of the whole, following the Rangers. Signals to be made on board the Ligoneer radow at the mainmast, a small Union flag for adjutants to come for orders; a reid flag is for failing or rowing; when struck is for halting and the boats are to dole up to their proper place immediately; a blue flag is for landing; the white pendant is for the three right collumns to close to the left collumn and west shore; a reid pendant is for the three left collumns to close to the right collumn and east shore; a blue pendant is to form to the right if the collumns are to the east shore, and to the left of the collumns are to the west shore.

The collumn of artillery are always to draw up between the first and second brigade, and when the troops land the whale boats and *batteaux* are to be closed in a single range along the shore; the radow and boats with gunns will be posted on the right and left and rear to cover the *batteaux*; when the army is landed the greatest attention most be given to closing in and forming to either shore upon the signal, that no accident may happen on storms arising, but nothing is to be done in a hurrie to create confusion. When the troops land, the comanding officers of corps will immediately advance front platoons or a picquitt; every corps is to fecure his own ground. Fireing in the night is absolutely forbid; the enemy, if any shoud appear, is to be received with fixed bayonetts, and the same orders to be obyed as was given on crossing Lake George. The first collumn is to be comanded by Collo. Haviland, the second by Collo. Forster, and the fourth by Collo. Grant.

The men ordered to remaine here of the Regular Regiments are to take the guards tomorrow; the regiments are to be readie to embark on the shortest notice and to carrie as many tents with them as are neceflarie for their numbers. Lieut. Collo. Eyre will make out a proportion of shuch tools as can be spared from hence, which are to be put on board the boats with the artilliry stores. Each *batteaux* ordered for the regiments, exclusive of the suttlers, to carrie three terces of bread and two barrells and a half of pork each; they will receive orders when to load them. When the generalls guard is taken off a corporall and four men to mount as a guard on the secrateries offices and a corporall and four men on the provosts guard; all the guards of the regiments to report to the officer of the Fort Guard and he to report to Brigadier Rugles and Lieut. Collo. Eyre.

Crown Point, 11th October 1759. Parole, Northfield.

For the day tomorrow, Collo. Montgomery; Field Officers for the picquits this night, Major Hamilton, Lieut. Collo. Saltenstall; tomorrow night, Major Gordon, Lieut. Collo. Spencer; Field Officer for the works tomorrow. Major Baldwin; Adjutant of the day tomorrow, Royall Highlanders. The four artillery boats to sett out immediately and to form according to orders given to Major Ord. The first brigade of Regulars to strick their tents immediately, to load their *batteaux* and embark, begining by the Inniskilling, Predeaux and the Royall, and to draw up in the rear of the 2nd artillery boat on the right; the brigade to strick their tents in an hour and lod their boats and embark by the Royall Highlanders, Montgomerys and Forbess and to draw up in the rear of the artillery boat on the left; the artillery to strick their tents at the same time to embark and form into their line of march.

Gages, Grenadiers, Light Infantry and Rangers to strick their tents likewise in an hour to embark and move into their line of march; great care to be taken that on the lake the men row in turns, and that those that do not, go to sleep, that the army may be able to proceed night

169

and day if it is found necessary.

On Lake Shamplaine, 12 October 1759, Parole, Sunderland.

ORDERS.

Collo, for this day Collo. Montgomery; tomorrow, Collo. Grant; Field Officers for the picquit this night, Major Gordon, tomorrow night, Major West. If the troops land in the day time they are to advance front platoons, in the night time picquits. The troops to form in one column on the west shore in the following manner on the signal of a blew pendant: first, the left brigade is to stand fast, that is the fourth collumn to stand fast, and the artillery boats being the third collumn to row on and get into their front; the first brigade of Regulars being the second collumn to row on at the same time and gitting to the front of the 2nd collumn; Gages and Rangers to keep the same station as yesterday. If the generall orders one sub and 2 serjeant with 50 men on board the Ligoneer radow, they are to be from the Light Infantry and not from the Royall Highlanders, as orderd before. The large boats with the gunns and howbitzcrs always to dress with the radow.

Ligoneer Bay, 13th October 1759. Parole, London
For the day tomorrow, Collo. Forster; Field Officers for the picquits this night, Major West; tomorrow night, Major John Campbell.

★★★★★★

Ligoneer Bay is on the West Shore of Lake Champlain, in the present town of Willsboro, Essex County, N. Y., between the mouth of the River Bouquet and Willsboro Point (Brasier's *Survey of Lake Champlain*).

★★★★★★

Ligonier Bay, the 14th October. Parole, Shaftsbury.
Collo. for the day tomorrow, Collo. Forster; Field Officer for the picquit this night, Major John Campbell; tomorrow night, Major Reid. The regiments to remain encamped as they are now posted and to be readie to embark on the first signall of the Assembly; they are not to be alarmd if they hear some shots fired in the front as, two parties are ordered out that way. An officer and 25 Grenadiers to go on board the Ligoneer radow at sun sett and to return to their corps at day brake. The Royall the Generalls Guard.

Lake Shamplaine, 15th October 1759. Parole, Chester.
For the day tomorrow, Collo. Grant; Field Officer for the picquitts this night, Major Reid; tomorrow night, Major Allexander Campbell.

The commanding officers of corps are to take care that their suttlers do not demand any higher pric for their rum that they sell to the soldiers than what they got at Crown Point. Any suttler that is convicted for taking a higher price after this order will be turned out of camp.

Ligoneer Bay, 16th October, 1759. Parole, Edinburgh.

For the day tomorrow, Collo. Forster; Field Officer for the picquits this night, Major Allexander Campbell; tomorrow night, Major Hamilton. The army to receive four days provisions this day, begining at one o'clock by the Grenadiers who are to receive their provisions from the boats of the 2nd Brigade and following late Forbess, Montgomerys, Royall Highlanders and one half of the Royall Artillery, who are to receive their provisions from that brigade; then the Light Infantry, who are to receive their provisions from the boats of the first brigade; the Inniskilling, late Predeaux, Royall and the remainder of the Royall Artillery, who are to receive their provisions from the boats of the first brigade; this compleats them to the 20th inclusively, and all the pork is to be dressd this day.

Ligoneer Bay, 17th October, 1759. Parole, Trentown.

For the day tomorrow, Collo. Montgomery; Field Officer for the picquits this night, Major Hamilton; tomorrow night, Major Gordon,

Camp at Schuylers Island, 18th October 1759. Parole, Goshen.

For the day tomorrow, Collo. Grant; Field Officer for the picquit this night, Major Gordon; tomorrow night, Major West. The army to be readie on beating the Assembly; if the Assembly begins to beat on the left, the army will march by the left; if the Assembly begins on the right the army will march by the right.

★★★★★★

Schuyler's Island is adjoined to the town of Chesterfield, Essex Co., N. Y. It lies immediately South of Point Trembleau, and between the villages of Port Douglas and Port Kent.

★★★★★★

Camp at Ligoneer Bay, 19th October Parole, Poukepsy.

For the day tomorrow, Collo. Forster; Field Officer for the picquit this night, Major West; tomorrow night, Major John Campbell. The army to be readie to move tomorrow morning on beating the Assembly in the same manner as ordered last night. When the troops arraive at Crownpoint the Rangers, Light Infantry, Grenadiers and Gages will take their boats to the same place where they received them and march directly to camp. The 2 brigades will land their provisions by regiments, the first brigade at the Artillery Wharff, the 2nd brigade to land theirs at the wharff of the magazine; the regiments are then to put up their boats in the same place where they received them, leaving a sufficient number of men to roll the provisions into the magazine, and the officers comanding brigades will take care that the second brigade waits till the first regiment is intierly unloaded their provisions, and the same of the third to the 2nd, and the whole to march then to the grownd where they decamped from.

Lake Shamplaine, 20th October Parole, Scorticock.
For the day tomorrow, Collo. Forster; Field Officer for the picquit this night, Major West; tomorrow night, Major Campbell.

Crown Point, 21st October, 1759. Parole, Gloscester.
For this day, Collo. Montgomery; tomorrow, Collo. Grant; Field Officers for the Picquits this day, Major Reid, Major Douglass; tomorrow night, Major Allexander Campbell, Major Baldwin; Field Officers for the works, Major Hamilton and Major Whitting; Adjutant of the day tomorrow, Inniskilling. The Regulars to receive 2 days fresh and 2 days salt provisions tomorrow, begining at 6 o'clock by Forbes and following Montgomerys, Royall Highlanders, Inniskilling, Predeaux, and Royall Light Infantry, Grenadiers, Gages and the Royall Artillery; this compleats them to the 25th inclusively.

The suttlers have leave to build hutts, but all hutts whatever are to be appropriated for the use of the garrison after the campaign. 1600 working men for the fort tomorrow. Regulars give 900, Provincials 700, The men of Babcocks Regiment who have been employed at Gages Fort are to joyn their regiment.

Crown Point, 22nd October 1759. Parole, Cumberland.
For the day tomorrow, Collo. Forster; Field Officers for the picquits this night, Major Allexander Campbell, Major Baldwin; tomorrow night, Major Hamilton, Major Whitting; Field Officer for the work tomorrow. Major Gordon; Adjutant of the day tomorrow, Royall Highlanders. The 62 carpenters of Ruggles first Battalion and Williards Regiment, the 31 masons under the comand of Lieut. Pickeren, the men of Williards and Worcesters who have joyned Capt. Baldwin, Capt. Smith's companie and the detachment under the comand of Major Williard to receive 2 days fresh and two days salt provisions this evening after their work is finishd. The detachment under the command of Lieut. Collo. Putman to receive 4 days fresh and four days salt provisions; the Provincial Regiments to receive tomorrow 2 days

fresh and 2 days salt provisions, beginning at 6 o'clock by Babcock and following Fitch, Worcester, Whitting, Schuyler and Ruggles; this compleats the Provincials to the 26 inclusively and Lieut. Collo. Putmans partie to the 30 inclusively.

Crown Point, 23rd October 1759. Parole, Philadelphia.

For the day tomorrow, Collo. Montgomery; Field Officers for the picquits this (night), Major Hamilton, Major Waterbury; tomorrow night, Major Gordon, Major Whitting; Field Officer for the works tomorrow. Adjutant of the day, Predeaux. The provost has orders to patrole around the encambment and apprehend any persons he shall find fireing their pieces contrarie to orders; whoever is so apprehended shall be tryed by a court martiall and feverlie punished. The 18 draughts who arraived here the 13 instant to are to joyn the Inniskilling Regiment and are to be acompted with and receive pay from that regiment from the 25th of June last.

The officer and men ordered for the works this day are to parade for the works tomorrow. Collo. Ruggles to acquaint the officers and private men of the Massachusett troops that by a vote of the Assembly that province of the 6th of October which the governour has transmitted to the generall that not withstanding the time for which the troops raised for the present expedition against Canada does expire against the first of November next, if their service should be found necessarie their pay shall be continued to the first of December next. Collo. Schuyler is to acquaint the officers and privats of the Jersey Troops that the governour informs the generall that there is provision made for the troops for the 13th of November, and that if their service is required beyond that time they will be paid till the day of their return.

All the officers and men of the above troops are to be informed of this by their respective commanding officers and to be assured that the generall will not keep them a day longer in the field then what is absolutely necessarie for the security and preservation of his Majestys faithfull subjects in America, and to put it out of the power of the enemy to make any incursions on the inhabitants, which will be effectually done on securing the posts at Crown Point.

Crown Point, 24th October, 1759. Parole, Hanover.

For the day tomorrow, Collo. Grant; Field Officers for the picketts this night, Major Gordon, Major Whitting; tomorrow night, Major West, Lieut. Collo. Smedlie; Field Officers for the works, Major

West, Lieut. Collo. Saltenstall; Adjutant for the day, Montgomerys. A Monthly Return to be given in tomorrow at Orderly Time.

Crown Point, 25th October, 1759. Parole, Plymouth.

For the day tomorrow, Collo. Forster; Field Officers for the picquits this night, Major West; tomorrow Major John Campbell, Lieut. Collo. Saltenstall; Field Officer for the work tomorrow. Major John Campbell; Adjutant of the day tomorrow, Royall. The Regulars to receive two days fresh and 2 days salt provisions tomorrow, begining at 6 o'clock by the Royall Artillery and following Gages, Grenadiers, Light Infantry, Royall, Predeaux, Inniskilling, Royall Highlanders, Montgomerys and Forbess; this compleats them to the 29th inclusively. Some officers of Collo. Babcocks Regiment having been put under arrest for irregularities comitted in the camp, and the collo. having intrested with the generall that they might be released, as they have wrote to him to acknowledge their fauilt and begg pardon for it, the regiment is to be out at 6 o'clock this day and the adjutant is to read their submission which they have made to the men, and the above officers are to be released.

The days now being very short, that the works may be the sooner finished for the men going the sooner into winter quarters, they are only to have an hour for dinner, which is to be from 12 to one. 22 men of the Royall Highlanders are to be sent to the hospital at Fort Edward; 49 men of Gages are to be sent to the hospital at Albany; 49 Men of the Royall and 12 of Predeauxes, 49 of Montgomerys to be sent to the hospitall at Albany. Lists of the above men, signed by the brigade major will be sent to the hospital at Albany and to the comanding officers of regiments this night; an officer is to have the care of the sick on their march, and Lieut. Gardiner, who is ill, is to go at the same time, and the surgeon of the Royall Highlanders is to attend them to Fort Edward, from whence a mate of the hospitall will attend those who go to Albany.

★★★★★★

Valentine Gardiner entered the army as Ensign of the 55th Foot, 4th November, 1755: was promoted to a Lieutenancy 23rd July, 1758, and obtained a company 15th June, 1763. He continued with this regiment until January, 1776, when he became Major of the 16th Foot. That regiment served in the Southern States during the Revolutionary War; a part in the defence of Savannah in 1779, and a part in West Florida, and capitulated at Pensacola in 1781. Major Gardiner is presumed to have died about this time, as his name disappears from the *Army List* 28th April, 1781.

★★★★★★

A subaltern and 18 men of the Royall with 3 *batteaux*, a corporall and 6 men of the Royall Highlanders with one *batoa*, six men of late Predeauxes with one *batteaux*, a serjeant and 18 men of Montgomerys with three *batteaux*, a corporall and 12 men of Gages with 2 *batteaux*, the Royall Highlanders putting 5 men in Predeauxes *batteaux* they are to convey the sick to the sawmills, where the officer will leave the *batteau* with Lieut. Collo. Miller and march the sick to the Landing Place, where he will have orders from Collo. Williard for the same number of *batteaux*, with which number he will transport the sick to Fort George, he will then return to the Landing Place, deliver the *batteaux* to Collo. Williard (Willard) and proceed with the fist *batteaux* to Crownpoint and the officer who has charge of the sick will proceed with them to Fort Edward and Albany.

★★★★★★

Abijah Willard was the Son of Colonel Samuel Willard of Lancaster, Worcester County, Mass., where he was born in the year 1722. He served in the army at the taking of Cape Breton and was a captain in regiment at the Battle of Ticonderoga in 1758, when he was wounded.

In the present expedition he commanded one of the Massachusetts Regiments, which 'tis said he raised in a comparatively short time, and in 1760 entered Montreal by way of the lakes, with the army under the command of Brigadier-General Haviland. In 1774, he was appointed a Mandamus Councillor, in consequence of which he became very unpopular. While at Union, Conn., he was seized and held through the night in confinement, and next day found himself obliged to sign a declaration that he would not act, asking at the same time forgiveness for having taken the Oath of Office.

On the Morning of the 19th of April, 1775, he mounted his horse and was proceeding to Beverly, where he had a farm, to superintend the spring work. While on his way the uprising of the country led him to fear for his personal safety and he turned his horse's head towards Boston, where he proposed remaining only a few days. He was caught by Gage's Proclamation in a trap and was too far compromised to return amongst his old neighbours. He subsequently accompanied the Royal Army to Halifax. Though offered a Commission by General Howe, he refused, saying "he should never fight against his country."

He was afterwards commissary to the British troops at New York, and in 1778 was proscribed and his property confiscated. In July, 1783, he was one of the 55 petitioners in the city of New York to General Carleton, for lands in Nova Scotia. He settled in New Brunswick and called the Town Lancaster, after his native place in Massachusetts. He was a member of the Provincial Council and died at Lancaster, N. B., in May, 1789, aged 67 years. His estate Massachusetts has been redeemed by his family and now belongs to his only surviving daughter and child, Mrs. Anna Goodhue, widow of the Hon. Benjamin Goodhue of Salem (Letter of Joseph Willard, Esq. of Boston; Ward's *Curwen*; Sabine's *Loyalists*).

★★★★★★

The sick and comand are to take 4 days provisions with them and are to parade tomorrow at 11 o'clock in the front of the Royall Highlanders. The following party to receive this afternoon, belonging to the Provincial troops, twelve days bisquitt and 5 days pork, and to parade at the right of the Royall at one o'clock; they are to bring with them all the solling axes belonging to their regiments as they can now spare them, and they are to leave with their regiments what arms and accouterments they have in their possession belonging to the king as they will not have any use for them in the service they are to be imployed in, which arms are to be returned to Major Ord of the Artillery.

After they have performed the service they are sent upon, they will receive from Lieut. Small passports and provisions or money to carry them to their respective abodes, and the generall expects that every man will do his utmost to wards earring on this service, and if any man shoud offer to go home before his passport is given to him, a partie shall be sent to apprehend him; he shall be tryed by a generall courtmartiall and no mercy shall be shown him.

★★★★★★

John Small was born in 1726, in Strathardle, Athole, Scotland, and served originally in the Scotch Brigade, then in the Dutch Service; received a commission as Ensign in the 42nd Highlanders, August 29, 1747, in which year he command a party stationed at Glenelg that was employed hunting the Rebels through the Highlands. The company to which he belonged having been reduced in 1748, he went on half-pay, but was again called into active service in 1756, when he was appointed lieutenant in his old regiment on the eve of its departure for America, to join the expedition under Lord Loudon.

In 1758, the regiment served under Gen. Abercromby against Ticonderoga, and Lieut. Small accompanied the expedition under Amherst the following year to the same part of the country, and in 1760 went down from Oswego to Montreal; he served in the West Indies in 1762, and on the 6th of August of that year was promoted to a company. The second battalion then returned to Scotland, and was reduced in 1763, and Captain Small went on half-pay, where he remained until April, 1765, when he was appointed to a company in the 21st or Royal North British Fusiliers which came soon after to America. He continued with this regiment until 1775, when he received a commission to raise a corps of Highlanders in Nova Scotia in aid of the Crown. No chief of former days ever more firmly secured the attachment of his clan, and no chief, certainly, ever deserved it better.

With an enthusiastic and almost romantic love of his country and countrymen, it seemed as if the principal object of his life had been to serve them and promote their prosperity. Equally brave in leading them in the field, and kind, just, and conciliating in quarters, they would have indeed been ungrateful, if they had regarded him otherwise than as they did. There was not an instance of desertion in this battalion. He was appointed Major, commanding the 2nd Battalion of the 84th Royal Emigrants, with a portion of which he joined the army under Sir Henry Clinton at New York in 1779, and in 1780 was appointed Lieutenant Colonel of his regiment. The Grenadier Company was at the Battle of Eutaw Springs.

In 1782 he was quartered on Long Island and in 1783 the regiment was disbanded. The men who were Americans and had enlisted while the 84th was stationed on Long Island, emigrated to Nova Scotia, where they settled the present town of Douglass. Lieutenant-Colonel Small became a Colonel in the Army on the 18th November, 1790 and was appointed Lieutenant-Governor of Guernsey in 1793; he was promoted to the rank of Major-General 3rd October, 1794, and died at Guernsey on 17th March, 1796, in the 70th year of his age (*Gentleman's Magazine*, LXVI; Browne's *Highland Clans*, IV; Stewart's *Sketches of the Highlanders*, I, II; *Army Lists*; Beatson's *Naval and Military Memoirs*, VI; Haliburton's *Nova Scotia*, II; Onderdonk's *Queen's County*).

★★★★★★

Major Hawkes to comand the partie and will receive further orders from the generall; it is to be composed of Captains Burk and Page, Lieuts Caver (Carver) and Shore with 54 men of Ruggles Regiment, Lieut. Bean of Williards Regt. with 49 men, Lieut. Pearsons and Collins with 39 Men of Whittings Regiment, Capt. Ferris and Lieut. Pringle and Smith with 36 Men of Worcesters, Ens. Hall of Fitches with 36 men, Lieut, Pulling with 36 Men of Babcocks, Lieut. Small with a serjeant and 20 men of Gages, a corporall and 10 men of the Light Infantry, a serjeant and 10 Rangers to parade at the same time with arms, ammunition, kettles and the same quantity of provisions; he will receive his orders from the generall.

★★★★★★

Jonathan Carver, the well known enterprising traveller, was a native, it is believed, of Canterbury, Ct., and was born in 1732. He lost his father (who was a Justice of the Peace) when he was only five years of age. He was intended for the profession of medicine, which he quitted for a military life. He served with reputation in the expedition carried on across the lakes against Canada. After the peace he formed the resolution of exploring the most interior parts of North America, and of even penetrating to the Pacific Ocean, over that broad part of the continent which lies between the forty-third and the forty-sixth degrees of north latitude.

As the English had come in possession of a vast territory by the conquest of Canada, he wished to render this acquisition profitable to his country, while he gratified his taste for adventures. He believed that the French had intentionally kept other nations ignorant of the interior parts of North America. He hoped to facilitate the discovery of a Northwest Passage, or of a communication between the Hudson's Bay and the Pacific Ocean. If he could effect the establishment of a post on the Straits of Annian, he supposed he should thus open a channel for conveying intelligence to China and the English settlements in the East Indies with greater expedition than by a tedious voyage by the Cape of Good Hope or the Straits of Magellan. With these views he set out from Boston in 1766, and in September of that year arrived at Michillimakinac, the most interior English post. He applied to Major Rogers, the governor, to furnish him with a proper assortment of goods, as a present for the Indians living in the track which he intended to pursue. Receiving a supply in part, it was promised that the remainder should be sent to him when he reached the Falls of St. Anthony in the River Mississippi.

In consequence of the failure of the goods, he found it necessary to return to Prairie la Chien in the Spring of 1767. Being thus retarded in his progress westward, he determined to direct his course northward, that by finding a communication between the Mississippi and Lake Superior, he might meet the traders at the grand portage at the northwest side of the lake. Of them he intended to purchase the goods which he needed, and then to pursue his journey by the way of the Lakes La Pluye, du Bois and Ouinipique to the heads of the river of the west.

He reached Lake Superior before the traders had returned to Michillimakinac, but they could not furnish him with goods. Thus, disappointed a second time, he continued some months on the north and east borders of Lake Superior, exploring the bays and rivers which empty themselves into that large body of water, and carefully observing the natural productions of the country, and the customs and manners of the inhabitants. He arrived at Boston in October, 1768, having been absent on this expedition two years and five months, and during that time travelled near seven thousand miles. As soon as he had properly digested his journal and charts, he went to England to publish them.

On his arrival, he presented a petition to his Majesty in council for a reimbursement of the sums which he had expended in the service of government. This was referred to the Lords Commissioners of Trade and Plantations, by whom he was examined in regard to his discoveries. Having obtained permission to publish his papers, he disposed of them to a bookseller. When they were almost ready for press, an order was issued from the Council Board, requiring him to deliver into the Plantation Office all his charts and journals, with every paper relating to the discoveries which he had made. In order to obey this command, he was obliged to purchase them from the bookseller. It was not until ten years after, that he published an account of his travels. Being disappointed in his hopes of preferment, he became Clerk of the Lottery.

As he sold his name to a historical compilation, which was published in 1779, in folio, entitled. *The New Universal Traveler*, containing an account of all the empires, kingdoms and states in the known world, he was abandoned by those whose duty it was to support him, and he died in London in want of the common necessaries of life in 1780, aged 48 years. Captain Carver published a tract on the *Culture of Tobacco*; and *Travels through the Interior Parts of North America in the Years 1766, 1767 and 1768*: London, 8vo, 1778. An edition of this work was published at Philadelphia in 1796, and at Boston in 1797 (Allen).

★★★★★★

The Royall and Montgomerys will send 10 *batteaux* each with 2 men in each at one o'clock to the front of the Royall to carrie Major Hawkes over the lake with his partie. This provisions compleats them to the 31st inclusively and with bread to 7th,

Crown Point, 26th October, 1759. Parole, Dorchester.

For the day, tomorrow, Collo. Montgomery; Field Officers for the picquits this night, Major John Campbell, Lieut. Collo. Spencer; tomorrow night, Major Reid, Lieut. Collo. Saltenstall; Field Officer for the works tomorrow. Major Reid, Major Whitting; Adjutant of the day tomorrow, late Forbes. The detachment under the command of Major Hawkes will compleat the tools they want to 250 and a grindstone, by applying to Serjeant Morrow and giving receipts for them, which will be delivered to Lieut. Small, when they arraive at No. 4 and put up in the store there that they may be sent for.

★★★★★★

In the year 1735, a Committee of the General Court of Massachusetts recommended that a Range of Townships be laid out between the Connecticut and Merrimack Rivers. The townships were afterwards numbered in succession from 1 to 9 inclusively. In this, "No. 4" was the same as that now called Charlestown, N. H. (*Collections N, H. Historical Society*, IV).

★★★★★★

The 62 carpenters of Ruggles first Battalion and Williards Regiment and Worcesters Men who have joynd Captain Baldwin, ye 31 masons under the Command of Lieut. Pickeren and the detachment commanded by Major Williard, to receive 2 days fresh and 2 days salt provisions this evening after their work is finished. The Provincials to receive tomorrow 2 days fresh and 2 days salt provisions, begining at 6 o'clock by Ruggles and following Schuyler, Whitting, Worcester, Fitch and Babcocks; this compleats the Provincials to the 30 inclusively.

★★★★★★

Eleazer Fitch, second son of Joseph Fitch of Norwich, and Ann Whiting of Windham, Conn., was born 27th August, 1726, and married Amy Bowen. He commanded the 4th Connecticut Regiment at the Battle of Ticonderoga in 1758 and down to 1760 (Goodwin's *Genealog.* Notes).

★★★★★★

Crown Point, 27th October, 1759. Parole, Newport.

For the day tomorrow, Collo. Grant; Field Officers for tomorrows Picquits, Major Allexander Campbell, Lieut. Collo. Whitting; this Night, Major Reid, Lieut. Collo. Spencer; Field Officers for the works tomorrow. Major Allexander Campbell, Major Douglass; Adjutant of the day tomorrow, Inniskilling.

Crown Point, 28th October, 1759. Parole, Cork.

For the day tomorrow, Collo. Forster; Field Officers for the picquits this night, Major Allexander Campbell, Lieut. Collo. Whitting; tomorrow night, Major Hamilton, Major Douglass; Field Officers for the works tomorrow. Major Hamilton, Major Baldwin; Adjutant for the day tomorrow, Royall Highlanders,

Crown Point, 29th October, 1759. Parole, Lancaster.

For the day tomorrow, Collo. Montgomerie; Field Officers for the picquitt this night, Major Hamilton, Major Douglass; tomorrow night, Major Gordon, Major Baldwin; Field Officers for the work tomorrow. Major Gordon, Major Waterbury; Adjutant of the day tomorrow, Predeaux. The Regulars to receive 2 days provisions tomorrow, begining by Forbess and following Montgomerys, Royall Highlanders, Inniskilling, Predeaux, Royall, Light Infantry, Grenadiers, Gages, and the Royall Artillery; this compleats them to the 31st inclusively. The Regular Regiments are to prepare their Muster Rolls for one hundred and eighty-three days from the 28 of Aprile to the 24th of this month inclusively. Lieut. Collo. William Eyre is appointed Lieut. Collo. to Major-Generall Abercrombie's Regiment in the room of Lieut. Collo. Farquhar, deceased, and Lieut. Collo. James Robison is appointed Lieut. Collo. to the late Predeaux Regiment in the room of Lieut. Collo. Eyre.

★★★★★★

William Farquhar was commissioned Major of the 15th or General Amherst's Regiment, 12th March, 1754. It served in the expedition against Rochefort in 1757, and at the Siege of Louisbourg in 1758, when Major Farquhar was attached to the Grenadiers, He was next promoted to be Lieutenant-Colonel of the 44th and commanded that regiment at the Siege of Niagara in 1759 (Knox's *Journal*, I., II; *Army Lists*).

★★★★★★

Crown Point, 30th October, 1759. Parole, Newcastle.

For the day tomorrow, Collo. Grant; Field Officers for the picquits this night, Major Gordon, Major Baldwin; tomorrow night, Major West, Major Whitting; Field Officers for the works tomorrow. Major West, Major Whitting; Adjutant for the day tomorrow, Montgomerys. The 62 carpenters of Ruggles first battalion and Williards Regiment, the 31 masons under the comand of Lieut. Pickerin, the men of Williards and Worcesters who have joynd Capt. Baldwin and Capt. Smiths companie to receive 2 days fresh and 2 days salt provisions this evening after their work is finished.

The detachment under the comand of Lieut. Collo. Putman to receive 4 days fresh and 4 days salt provisions tomorrow. The Provincial to receive 2 days fresh and 2 days salt provisions tomorrow at 6 o'clock, begining by Babcocks and following Fitches, Worcesters, Whittings, Schuyler and Ruggles; this compleats the Provincials to the 3rd Inclusively, and Lieut. Collo. Putmans party to the 7th inclusively, Nover. A generall courtmartial to be held at the Presidents tent tomorrow at 9 o'clock, to try all shuch prisoners as shall be brought before them; Collo. Grant, President, Major West, Major John Campbell, one capt. of the Royall, one of late Forbes, one of the Inniskilling, one of the Royall Highlanders, one of Predeaux, 2 of Montgomerys, Grenadiers one. Light Infantry one. Gages one; Lieut. George Burton of the Royall, Deputy Judge Advocate.

Crown Point, 31st October, 1759. Parole, Crown Point.

For the day tomorrow, Collo. Montgomery; Field Officers for the picquits this night, Major Reid, Major Waterbury; tomorrow night, Major Allexander Campbell, Major Whitting; Field Officers for the works tomorrow, Major Allexander Campbell, Lieut. Collo. Smedlie;

Adjutant of the day tomorrow, Royall.

★★★★★★

David Waterbury, sometimes called the 3rd, was a native of Stamford, Conn. He served on the lakes as Lieutenant of Rangers in 1755, in Johnson's Campaign, and through the French War in one of the Connecticut Regiments. In 1775 he was appointed Colonel of a Connecticut Regiment; accompanied the expedition against Canada under Montgomery and was at taking of St Johns and Montreal. In April, 1776, he was recommended to Washington by Gov. Trumbull for promotion as a man who behaved at all times with bravery and honour. In July following he was appointed Brigadier-General by the State of Connecticut and was second in command under Arnold on Lake Champlain, where he was taken prisoner in a naval engagement with the British, 13th October, 1776, and afterwards released on parole the and exchanged (*N.Y. Doc. Hist.* 8vo, IV; 4 *American Arch.*, V; 5 *Am. Arch.*; *Mass. Hist. Coll.* II).

★★★★★★

The Regulars to receive two days fresh provisions tomorrow in the same order as they received the two last days provisions, which compleats them to the 2nd of November inclusively. The men draughted from the Provincial battalions to serve with the Rangers campaign, to joyn their regiments tomorrow, and they are to be paid the difference of the pay to this day inclusively, excepting the men of Limans and Williards Regiment, who are to remaine with the Rangers till their regiments arraive here. All the working men at the fortress and forts are to have at gunn fireing a dram each.

A generall courtmartiall of the line to sett at the Presidents tent at 10 o'clock tomorrow; Collo. Ruggles, President; Major Reid, Major Waterbery, 5 captains of the Regulars and 5 of the Provincials members; Lieut George Burton, Deputy Judge Advocate. The mason and the laberours who attend the mason are not to begin to work till 9 o'clock in the morning and are to continue to work till 4 of the afternoon without intermission. The generall courtmartiall of which Collo. Grant was President is dissolved; the prisoners of the Royall Highland Regiment is acquitted.

Crown Point, 1st November 1759. Parole, Quebeck.

For the day tomorrow, Collo. Grant; Field Officers for the picquit this night, Major Hamilton, Major Whitting; tomorrow night, Major

Gordon, Lieut. Collo. Smeedlie; for the works, Major Gordon, Lieut. Collo. Saltenstall; Adjutant of the day tomorrow, Forbess. The commanding officers of Ruggles, Schuylers, Whittings, Worcesters, Fitches and Babcocks Regiments are each to send a field officer or captain to the camp with Rangers at 12 o'clock this day, to see their men who served as Rangers do receive their additional pay to yesterday inclusively, and to report the same; after which the men are to joyn their regiments. The generall courtmartiall of which Collo. Ruggles was President, to assemble at his tent tomorrow. All the workmen and labrours are not to begin work till 9 in the morning and are to continue working till 4 in the afternoon without ceasing; then they are to be dissmised.

Crown Point, 2nd Nov 1759. Parole, Northumberland.

For the day tomorrow, Collo. Forster; Field Officers for the picquits this night, Major Gordon, Lieut. Collo. Smedlie; tomorrow night, Major West, Lieut. Collo. Saltenstall; For the works tomorrow, Major West, Lieut. Collo. Spencer; Adjutant for the day tomorrow, Inniskilling. The Regulars to receive 2 days fresh and 2 days salt provisions tomorrow, begining at 7 o'clock by the Royall Artillery and following Gages, Grenadiers, Light Infantry, Royall, Predeaux, Inniskilling, Royall Highlanders, Montgomerys and Forbess; this compleats them to the 6th inclusively.

★★★★★★

Archibald Gordon, was commissioned Captain 9th June, 1740, and joined the 27th or Inniskilling Foot, 14th October, 1742; he was wounded in the attack on Ticonderoga, 8th July, 1758, and eight days afterwards was appointed Major of the Regiment. After making this campaign under Amherst he accompanied the division of the army into Montreal, 1760, under Haviland, with whom the regiment afterwards served at Martinico, and Havana in 1762, in which year 'tis supposed Major Gordon died, as his name was then dropped from the *Army Lis.*

★★★★★★

Crown Point, 3rd November 1759. Parole, Bath.

For the day tomorrow, Collo. Montgomery; for the picquits this night, Major West, Lieut. Collo. Saltenstall; tomorrow night, Major John Campbell, Lieut. Collo. Spencer; for the works tomorrow, Major John Campbell, Major Whitting; Adjutant of the day tomorrow, Royall Highlanders. The 62 carpenters of Ruggles first battalion and Williards Regiment, the 31 masons under the comand of Lieut. Pickerin, the men of Williards and Worcesters who have joyned Capt. Baldwin and Capt. Smiths companie, to receive 2 days fresh and 2 days salt provisions this evening after their work is finished; the Provincials to receive 2 days fresh and 2 days salt provisions tomorrow, begining at seven o'clock by Ruggles and following Schuyler, Fitch, Whitting, Worcesters and Babcocks; this compleats the Provincials to the 7th inclusively.

Fort Duquesne and Fort Pitt
By Pittsburgh Chapter Daughters of the American Revolution

This little sketch of Fort Duquesne and Fort Pitt is compiled from extracts taken mainly from. Parkman's histories; *The Olden Time*, by Neville B. Craig; *Fort Pitt*, by Mrs. Wm. Darlington; *Pioneer History*, by S. P. Hildreth, etc.

CHRONOLOGY

1753.—The French begin to build a chain of forts to enforce their boundaries.

Dec. 11, 1753.—Washington visits Fort Le Boeuf.

Jan., 1754.—Washington lands on Wainwright's Island in the Allegheny River.—Recommends that a fort be built at the "Forks of the Ohio."

Feb. 17, 1754.—A fort begun at the "Forks of the Ohio" by Capt. Wm. Trent.

April 16, 1754.—Ensign Ward, with thirty-three men, surprised here by the French, and surrenders June, 1754.—Fort Duquesne completed.

May 28, 1754.—Washington attacks Coulon de Jumonville at Great Meadows.

July 9, 1755.—Braddock's defeat.

April, 1758.—Brig. Gen. John Forbes takes command.

August, 1758.—Fort Bedford built.

October, 1758.—Fort Ligonier built.

Nov. 24, 1758.—Fort Duquesne destroyed by the retreating French.

Nov. 25, 1758.—Gen. Forbes takes possession.

BLOCK HOUSE OF FORT PITT. BUILT 1764.

August, 1759.—Fort Pitt begun by Gen. John Stanwix.

May, 1763.—Conspiracy of Pontiac.

July, 1763.—Fort Pitt besieged by Indians.

1764.—Col. Henry Bouquet builds the Redoubt.

Oct. 10, 1772.—Fort Pitt abandoned by the British.

Jan., 1774.—Dr. James Connelly occupies Fort Pitt with Virginia militia, and changes name to Fort Dunmore.

July, 1776.—Indian conference at Fort Pitt—Pontiac and Guyasuta.

June 1, 1777.—Brig. Gen. Hand takes command of the fort.

1778.—Gen. Mcintosh succeeds Hand.

Nov., 1781.—Gen. William Irvine takes command.

May 19, 1791.—Maj. Isaac Craig reports Fort Pitt in a ruinous condition.—Builds Fort Lafayette.

Sept. 4, 1805.—The historic site purchased by Gen. James O'Hara.

April 1, 1894.—Mrs. Mary E. Schenley, granddaughter of Gen. James O'Hara, presents Col. Bouquet's Redoubt to the Daughters of the American Revolution of Allegheny County.

FORT PITT

CONFLICTING CLAIMS OF FRANCE AND ENGLAND IN NORTH AMERICA.

On maps of British America in the earlier part of the eighteenth century, one sees the eastern coast, from Maine to Georgia, gashed with ten or twelve coloured patches, very different in size and shape, and defined more or less distinctly by dividing lines, which in some cases are prolonged westward until they reach the Mississippi, or even cross it and stretch indefinitely towards the Pacific.

These patches are the British Provinces, and the western prolongation of their boundary represents their several claims to vast interior tracts founded on ancient grants, but not made good by occupation or vindicated by any exertion of power. . . . .

Each province remained in jealous isolation, busied with its own work, growing in strength, in the capacity of self-rule, in the spirit of independence, and stubbornly resisting all exercise of authority from without. If the English-speaking population flowed westward, it was in obedience to natural laws, for the king did not aid the movement, and the royal governor had no authority to do so. The power of the colonies was that of a rising flood, slowly invading and conquering by the unconscious force of its own growing volume, unless means be found to hold it back by dams and embankments within appointed limits.

In the French colonies it was different. Here the representatives of the Crown were men bred in the atmosphere of broad ambition and masterful, far-reaching enterprise. They studied the strong and weak points of their rivals, and with a cautious forecast and a daring energy set themselves to the task of defeating them. If the English colonies were comparatively strong in numbers these numbers could not be brought into action, while if French forces were small they were vigorously commanded and always ready at a word.

It was union confronting division, energy confronting apathy, and military centralization opposed to industrial democracy, and for a time the advantage was all on one side. Yet in view of what France had achieved, of the patient gallantry of her explorers, the zeal of her missionaries, the adventurous hardihood of her bush-rangers, revealing to mankind the existence of this wilderness world, while her rivals plodded at their workshops, their farms, their fisheries; in view of all this, her pretensions were moderate and reasonable compared to those of England.

FORKS OF THE OHIO.—WASHINGTON'S FIRST VISIT.

The Treaty of Utrecht had decided that the Iroquois or Five Nations were British subjects; therefore, it was insisted that all countries conquered by them belonged to the British crown. The range of the Iroquois war parties was prodigious, and the English laid claim to every mountain, forest and prairie where an Iroquois had taken a scalp. This would give them not only all between the Alleghanies and the Mississippi, but all between Ottawa and Huron, leaving nothing to France but the part now occupied by the Province of Quebec.

The Treaty of Utrecht in 1713, and that of Aix la Chapelle in 1745, were supposed to settle the disputed boundaries of the French and English possessions in America; France, however, repented of her enforced concessions, and claimed the whole American continent as hers, except a narrow strip of sea coast. To establish this boundary, it was resolved to build a line of forts from Canada to the Mississippi, following the Ohio, for they perceived that the forks of the Ohio, so strangely neglected by the English, formed together with Niagara the key of the great West.

This chain of forts began at Niagara; then another was built of squared logs at Presque Isle (now Erie), and a third called Fort Le Boeuf on what is now called French Creek. Here the work stopped for a time, and Legardeur de St. Pierre went into winter quarters with a small garrison at Fort Le Boeuf.

On the 11th of December, 1753, Major George Washington, with Christopher Gist as guide, Abraham Van Braam as interpreter, and four or five woodsmen, presented himself as bearer of a letter from Governor Dinwiddie of Virginia to the commander of Fort Le Boeuf. He was kindly received. In fact, no form of courtesy was omitted during the three days occupied by St. Pierre in framing his reply to Governor Dinwiddie's letter. This letter expressed astonishment that his (St. Pierre's) troops should build forts upon lands so notoriously known to be the property of Great Britain and demanded their immediate and peaceable departure. In his answer, St. Pierre said he had acted in accordance with the commands of his general, that he would forward Governor Dinwiddie's letter to the Marquis Duquesne and await his orders.

It was on his return journey that Washington twice escaped death. First from the gun of a French Indian; then in attempting to cross the Allegheny, which was filled with ice, on a raft, which he and his companions had hastily constructed with the help of one hatchet between them. He was thrown into the river and narrowly escaped drowning; but Gist succeeded in dragging him out of the water, and the party landed on Wainwright's Island, about opposite the foot of Thirty-Third Street. On making his report Washington recommended that a fort be built at the "Forks of the Ohio."

Men and money were necessary to make good Governor Dinwiddie's demand that the French evacuate the territory they had appropriated; these he found it difficult to get. He dispatched letters, orders, couriers from New Jersey to South Carolina, asking aid. Massachusetts and New York were urged to make a feint against Canada, but as the land belonged either to Pennsylvania or Virginia, the other colonies did not care to vote money to defend them.

In Pennsylvania the placid obstinacy of the Quakers was matched by the stolid obstinacy of the German farmers, and Pennsylvania refused to move. All Dinwiddie could muster was the promise of three or four hundred men from North Carolina, two companies from New York and one from South Carolina, with what recruits he could gather in Virginia. In accordance with Washington's recommendation,

Capt. William Trent, an Indian trader of the better class, had been sent with a company of backwoodsmen to build a fort at the forks of the Ohio, and it was hoped he would fortify himself sufficiently to hold the position. Trent began the fort but left it with forty men under Ensign Ward and went back to join Washington. The recruits gathered in Virginia were to be commanded by Joshua Fry, with Washington as second in command.

FORT DUQUESNE.—WASHINGTON AT FORT NECESSITY

On the 17th of April, 1754, Ward was surprised by the appearance of a swarm of canoes and *bateaux* descending the Allegheny, carrying, according to Ward, about one thousand Frenchmen, who landed, planted their cannon, and summoned the ensign to surrender. He promptly complied and was allowed to depart with all his men. The French soon demolished the unfinished fort and built in its place a much larger and better one, calling it Fort Duquesne, in honour of the Marquis Duquesne, then Governor of Canada,

Washington, with his detachment of ragged recruits, without tents and scarcely armed, was at Will's Creek, about one hundred and forty miles from the "Forks of the Ohio," and he was deeply chagrined when Ward joined him and reported the loss of the fort. Dinwiddie then ordered Washington to advance. In order to do so a road must be cut for wagons and cannon, through a dense forest; two mountain ranges must be crossed, and innumerable hills and streams. Towards the end of May he reached Great Meadows with one hundred and fifty men. While encamped here, Washington learned that a detachment of French had marched from the fort in order to attack him. They met in a rocky hollow, and a short fight ensued. Coulon de Jumonville, the commander, was killed; all the French were taken prisoners or killed except one Canadian.

This skirmish was the beginning of the war. Washington then advanced as far as Christopher Gist's settlement, twelve or fourteen miles on the other side of the Laurel Ridge. He soon heard that strong reinforcements had been sent to Fort Duquesne, and that another detachment was even then on the march under Coulon de Villiers, so on June 28th he began to retreat. Not having enough horses, the men had to carry the baggage on their backs and drag nine swivels over miserable roads. Two days brought them to Great Meadows, and they had but one full day to strengthen the slight fortification they had made there, and which Washington named Fort Necessity.

The fighting began at about 11, and lasted for nine hours; the English, notwithstanding their half-starved condition, and their want of ammunition, keeping their ground against double their number. When darkness came a parley was sounded, to which Washington at first paid no attention, but when the French repeated the proposal, and requested that an officer might be sent, he could refuse no longer. There were but two in Washington's command who could understand French, and one of them was wounded. Capt. Van Braam, a Dutchman, acted as interpreter. The articles were signed about midnight. The English troops were to march out with drums beating, carrying with them all their property. The prisoners taken in the Jumonville affair were to be released, Capt. Van Braam and Major Stobo to be detained as hostages for their safe return to Fort Duquesne.

This defeat was disastrous to the English. There was now not an English flag waving west of the Alleghanies Villiers went back exultant to Fort Duquesne, and Washington began his wretched march to Will's Creek. No horses, no cattle, most of the baggage must be left behind, while the sick and wounded must be carried over the Alleghanies on the backs of their weary, half-starved comrades. And this was the Fourth of July, 1754.

The conditions of the surrender were never carried out. The prisoners taken in the skirmish with Jumonville were not returned. Van Braam and Stobo were detained for some time at Fort Duquesne. Van Braam was at last released, but Major Stobo was sent to Quebec, where he was kept a prisoner for several years. While a prisoner on parole he made good use of his opportunities by acquainting himself with the neighbourhood; afterwards he was kept in close confinement and endured great hardships; but in the spring of 1759 he succeeded in making his escape in the most miraculous manner. While Wolfe was besieging Quebec, he returned from Halifax, and, it is said, it was he who guided the troops up the narrow, wooded path to the Heights of Abraham. Strange, that one taken prisoner in a far distant province, in a skirmish which began the war, should guide the gallant Wolfe to the victory at Quebec, which virtually closed the war in America.

BRADDOCK.

Nothing of importance was done in Virginia and Pennsylvania until the arrival of Braddock in February, 1755, bringing with him two regiments. Governor Dinwiddie hailed his arrival with joy, hoping that his troubles would now come to an end. Of Braddock, Governor

Dinwiddie's Secretary Shirley wrote to Governor Morris:

We have a general most judiciously chosen for being disqualified for the service he is in, in almost every respect.

Braddock issued a call to the provincial governors to meet him in council, which was answered by Dinwiddie of Virginia, Dobbs of North Carolina, Sharpe of Maryland, Morris of Pennsylvania, Delancy of New York, and Shirley of Massachusetts. The result was a plan to attack the French at four points at once. Braddock was to advance on Fort Duquesne, Fort Niagara was to be reduced. Crown Point seized, and a body of men from New England to capture Beausejour and Arcadia.

We will follow Braddock. In his case prompt action was of the utmost importance, but this was impossible, as the people refused to furnish the necessary supplies. Franklin, who was Postmaster General in Pennsylvania, was visiting Braddock's camp with his son when the report of the agents sent to collect wagons was brought in. The number was so wholly inadequate that Braddock stormed, saying the expedition was at an end. Franklin said it was a pity he had not landed in Pennsylvania, where he might have found horses and wagons more plentiful.

Braddock begged him to use his influence to obtain the necessary supply, and Franklin on his return to Pennsylvania issued an address to the farmers. In about two weeks a sufficient number was furnished, and at last the march began. He reached Will's Creek on May 10, 1755, where fortifications had been erected by the colonial troops, and called Fort Cumberland. Here Braddock assembled a force numbering about twenty-two hundred. Although Braddock despised the provincial troops and the Indians, he honoured Col. George Washington, who commanded the troops from Virginia, by placing him on his staff.

A month elapsed before this army was ready to leave Fort Cumberland. Three hundred axemen led the way, the long, long train of pack horses, wagons, and cannon following, as best they could, along the narrow track, over stumps and rocks and roots. The road cut was but twelve feet wide, so that the line of march was sometimes four miles long, and the difficulties in the way were so great that it was impossible to move more than three miles a day.

On the 18th of June they had reached Little Meadows, not thirty miles from Fort Cumberland, where a report reached them that five hundred regulars were on their way to reinforce Fort Duquesne. Washington advised Braddock to leave the heavy baggage and press forward, and following this advice, the next day, June 19th, the advance corps of about twelve hundred soldiers, with what artillery was thought indispensable, thirty wagons, and a number of pack-horses, began its march; but the delays were such that it did not reach the mouth of Turtle Creek until July 7th. The distance to Fort Duquesne by a direct route was about eight miles, but the way was difficult and perilous, so Braddock crossed the Monongahela and re-crossed farther down, at one o'clock,

Washington describes the scene at the ford with admiration. The music, the banners, the mounted officers, the troops of light cavalry, the naval detachment, the red-coated regulars, the blue-coated Virginians, the wagons and tumbrils, the cannon, howitzers and coehorns, the train of pack-horses and the droves of cattle passed in long procession through the rippling shallows and slowly entered the forest.

Fort Duquesne was a strong little fort, compactly built of logs, close to the point where the waters of the Allegheny and Monongahela unite. Two sides were protected by these waters, and the other two by ravelins, a ditch and glacis and a covered way, enclosed by a massive stockade. The garrison consisted of a few companies of regulars and Canadians and eight hundred Indian warriors, under the command of Contrecoeur. The captains under him were Beaujeu, Dumas and Ligneris.

When the scouts brought the intelligence that the English were within six leagues of the fort, the French, in great excitement and alarm, decided to march at once and ambuscade them at the ford. The Indians at first refused to move, but Beaujeu, dressed as one of them, finally persuaded them to march, and they filed off along the forest trail that led to the ford of the Monongahela—six hundred Indians and about three hundred regulars and Canadians. They did not reach the ford in time to make the attack there.

BRADDOCK'S DEFEAT.

Braddock advanced carefully through the dense and silent forest, when suddenly this silence was broken by the war-whoop of the savages, of whom not one was visible. Gage's column wheeled deliberately into line and fired; and at first the English seemed to carry everything before them, for the Canadians were seized by a panic and fled; but the scarlet coats of the English furnished good targets for their invisible enemies. The Indians, yelling their war cries, swarmed in the forest, but were so completely hidden in gullies and ravines, behind trees and bushes and fallen trunks, that only the trees were struck by the volley after volley fired by the English, who at last broke ranks and huddled together in a bewildered mass.

Both men and officers were ignorant of this mode of warfare. The Virginians alone were equal to the emergency, and might have held the enemy in check, but when Braddock found them hiding behind trees and bushes, as the Indians, he became so furious at this seeming want of courage and discipline, that he ordered them with oaths to join the line, even beating them with his sword, they replying to his threats and commands that they would fight if they could see any one to fight with. The ground was strewn with the dead and dying, maddened horses were plunging about, the roar of musketry and cannon, and above all the yells that came from the throats of six hundred invisible savages, formed a chaos of anguish and terror indescribable.

Braddock saw that all was lost and ordered a retreat but had scarcely done so when a bullet pierced his lungs. It is alleged that the shot was fired by one of his own men, but this statement is without proof. The retreat soon turned into a rout, and all who remained dashed pell-mell through the river to the opposite shore, abandoning the wounded, the cannon, and all the baggage and papers to the mercy of the Indians. Beaujeu had fallen early in the conflict. Dumas and Ligneris did not pursue the flying enemy, but retired to the fort, abandoning the field to the savages, which soon became a pandemonium of pillage and murder. Of the eighty-six English officers all but twenty-three were killed or disabled, and but a remnant of the soldiers escaped.

When the Indians returned to the fort, they brought with them twelve or fourteen prisoners, their bodies blackened and their hands tied behind their backs. These were all burned to death on the bank of the Allegheny, opposite the fort. The loss of the French was slight; of the regulars there were but four killed or wounded, and all the Canadians returned to the Fort unhurt except five.

The miserable remnant of Braddock's army continued their wild flight all that night and all the next day, when before nightfall those who had not fainted by the way reached Christopher Gist's farm, but six miles from Dunbar's Camp. The wounded general had shown an incredible amount of courage and endurance. After trying in vain to stop the flight, he was lifted on a horse, when fainting from the effects of his mortal wound, some of the men were induced by large bribes to carry him in a litter. Braddock ordered a detachment from the camp to go to the relief of the stragglers, but as the fugitives kept coming in with their tales of horror, the panic seized the camp, and soldiers and teamsters fled.

The next day, whether from orders given by Braddock or Dunbar is not known, more than one hundred wagons were burned, cannon, coehorns and shells were destroyed, barrels of gunpowder were staved and the contents thrown into a brook, and provisions scattered about through the woods and swamps, while the enemy, with no thought of pursuit, had returned to Fort Duquesne. Braddock died on the 13th of July, 1755, and was buried on the road; men, horses and wagons passing over the grave of their dead commander as they retreated to Fort Cumberland, thus effacing every trace of it, lest it should be discovered by the Indians and the body mutilated. Thus, ended the attempt to capture Fort Duquesne, and for about three years, while the storm of blood and havoc raged elsewhere, that point was undisturbed.

BRIGADIER GENERAL FORBES.

In the meantime, Dinwiddie had gone, a new governor was in his place, while in the plans of Pitt the capture of Fort Duquesne held an important place. Brigadier General John Forbes was charged with it. He was Scotch by birth, a well-bred man of the world, and unlike Braddock, by his conduct toward the provincial troops, commanded both the respect and affection of the colonists. He only resembled Braddock in his determined resolution, but he did not hesitate to embrace modes of warfare that Braddock would have scorned. He wrote to Bouquet:

> I have been long of your opinion of equipping numbers of our men like the savages, and I fancy Col. Burd of Virginia has most of his men equipped in that manner. In this country we must learn our art of war from the Indians, or anyone else who has carried it on here.

He arrived in Philadelphia in April, 1758, but it was the end of June before his troops were ready to march. His force consisted of Montgomery's Highlanders, twelve hundred strong; Provincials from Pennsylvania, Virginia, Maryland, North Carolina, and a detachment of Royal Americans, amounting to about six or seven thousand men. The Royal Americans were Germans from Pennsylvania, commanded by European officers, the lieutenant-colonel being Henry Bouquet, a Swiss.

197

General Forbes was detained in Philadelphia by a painful and dangerous malady. Bouquet advanced, and encamped at Raystown, now Bedford. Then arose the question of opening a new road through Pennsylvania to Fort Duquesne, or following the old road made by Braddock. Washington, who commanded the Virginians, foretold the ruin of the expedition unless Braddock's road was chosen, but Forbes and Bouquet were firm, and it was decided to adopt the new route through Pennsylvania. Forbes was able to reach Carlisle early in July, but his disorder was so increased by the journey that he was not able to leave that place until the 11th of August, and then in a kind of litter swung between two horses.

In this way he reached Shippensburg, where he lay helpless until far into September. His plan was to advance slowly, establishing fortified magazines as he went, and at last when within easy distance of the fort, to advance upon it with all force, as little impeded as possible with wagons and packhorses. Having secured his magazines at Raystown and built a fort which he called Fort Bedford in honour of his friend and patron, the Duke of Bedford, Bouquet was sent with his command to forward the heavy work of road making over the main range of the Alleghanies and the Laurel Hills; "hewing, digging, blasting, laying fascines, and gabions, to support the track along the sides of the steep declivities, or worming their way like moles through the jungle of swamp and forest."

★★★★★★

In recognition of this honour, the Duke of Bedford presented to the fort a large flag of crimson brocade silk. In 1895 this flag was in the possession of Mrs. Moore, of Bedford, who kindly lent it to the Pittsburgh Chapter, Daughters of the American Revolution, for exhibition at a reception given by them at Mrs. Park Painter's, February 15th, 1895.

★★★★★★

As far as the eye or mind could reach a prodigious forest vegetation spread its impervious canopy over hill, valley and plain. His next post was on the Loyalhanna Creek, scarcely fifty miles distant from Fort Duquesne, and here he built a fortification, naming it Fort Ligonier, in honour of Lord Ligonier, commander-in-chief of His Majesty's armies. Forbes had served under Ligonier, and his influence, together with that of the Duke of Bedford, secured to Forbes his appointment.

Now came the difficult and important task of securing Indian allies. Sir William Johnson for the English, and Joncaire for the French,

Henry Bouquet

LORD VISCOUNT LIGONIER.

were trying in every way to frighten or cajole them into choosing sides; but that which neither of them could accomplish was done by a devoted Moravian missionary, Christian Frederic Post. Post spoke the Delaware language, had married a converted squaw, and by his simplicity, directness and perfect honesty, had gained their full confidence. He was a plain German, upheld by a sense of duty and singlehearted trust in God. The Moravians were apostles of peace, and they succeeded in a surprising way in weaning their converts from their ferocious instincts and savage practices, while the mission Indians of Canada retained all their native ferocity, and their wigwams were strung with scalps, male and female, adult and infant. These so-called missions were but nests of baptized savages, who wore the crucifix instead of the medicine-bag.

Post accepted the dangerous mission as envoy to the camp of the hostile Indians and making his way to a Delaware town on Beaver Creek, he was kindly received by the three kings; but when they conducted him to another town he was surrounded by a crowd of warriors, who threatened to kill him. He managed to pacify them, but they insisted that he should go with them to Fort Duquesne. In his Journal he gives thrilling accounts of his escape from dangers threatened by both French and Indians. But he at last succeeded in securing a promise from both Delaware and Shawnees, and other hostile tribes, to meet with the Five Nations, the Governor of Pennsylvania and commissioners from other provinces, in the town of Easton, before the middle of September.

The result of this council was that the Indians accepted the white *wampum* belt of peace and agreed on a joint message of peace to the tribes of Ohio. A few weeks before this. Col. Bouquet, from his post at Fort Ligonier, forgot his usual prudence, and at his urgent request allowed Major Grant, commander of the Highlanders, to advance. On the 14th of September, at about 2 a. m., he reached an eminence about half a mile from the Fort. He divided his forces, placing detachments in different positions, being convinced that the enemy was too weak to attack him. Infatuated with this idea, when the fog had cleared away, he ordered the reveille to be sounded.

It was as if he had put his foot into a hornet's nest. The roll of the drums was answered by a burst of war-whoops, while the French came swarming out, many of them in their night shirts, just as they had jumped from their beds. There was a hot fight for about three-quarters of an hour, when the Highlanders broke away in a wild flight.

Captain Bullit and his Virginians tried to cover the retreat and fought until two-thirds of them were killed and Grant taken prisoner. The name of "Grant's Hill" still clings to the much-abused "hump" where the Court House now stands.

The French pushed their advantages with spirit, and there were many skirmishes in the forest between Fort Ligonier and Fort Duquesne, but their case was desperate. Their Indian allies had deserted them, and their supplies had been cut off; so Ligneris, who succeeded Contrecoeur, was forced to dismiss the greater part of his force. The English too were enduring great hardships. Rain had continued almost without cessation all through September; the newly made road was liquid mud, into which the wagons sunk up to the hubs. In October the rain changed to snow, while all this time Forbes was chained to a sick-bed at Raystown, now Fort Bedford. In the beginning of November, he was carried from Fort Bedford to Fort Ligonier in a litter, and a council of officers, then held, decided to attempt nothing more that season; but a few days later a report of the condition of the French was brought in, which led Forbes to give orders for an immediate advance. On November 18, 1758, two thousand five hundred picked men, without tents or baggage, without wagons or artillery except a few light pieces, began their march.

FRENCH ABANDON FORT DUQUESNE—FORT PITT IS BUILT.

On the evening of the 24th they encamped on the hills around Turtle Creek, and at midnight the sentinels heard a heavy boom as if a magazine had exploded. In the morning the march was resumed. After the advance guard came Forbes, carried in a litter, the troops following in three columns, the Highlanders in the centre headed by Montgomery, the Royal Americans and Provincials on the right and left under Bouquet and Washington. Slowly they made their way beneath an endless entanglement of bare branches. The Highlanders were goaded to madness by seeing as they approached the Fort the heads of their countrymen, who had fallen when Grant made his rash attack, stuck on poles, around which their plaids had been wrapped in imitation of petticoats.

Foaming with rage they rushed forward, abandoning their muskets and drawing their broadswords; but their fury was in vain, for when they reached a point where the Fort should have been in sight, there was nothing between them and the hills on the opposite banks of the Monongahela and Allegheny but a mass of blackened and smouldering ruins. The enemy, after burning the barracks and store-houses, had blown up the fortifications and retreated, some down the Ohio, others overland to Presqu' Isle, and others up the Allegheny to Venango.

There were two forts, and some idea may be formed of their size, with the barracks and store-houses, from the fact that John Haslet writes to the Rev. Dr. Allison, two days after the English took possession, that there were thirty chimney stacks standing.

Col. Bouquet, in a letter written to Chief Justice Allen of Pennsylvania on November 26th, enumerated the needs of the garrison, which he hopes the Provinces of Pennsylvania and Virginia will immediately supply. He adds:

> After God, the success of this expedition is entirely due to the general. He has shown the greatest prudence, firmness and ability. No one is better informed than I am, who had an opportunity to see every step that has been taken from the beginning and every obstacle that was thrown in his way.

Forbes' first care was to provide defence and shelter for his troops, and a strong stockade was built around the traders' cabins and soldiers' huts, which he named Pittsburgh, in honour of England's great minister, William Pitt. Two hundred Virginians under Col. Mercer were left to defend the new fortification, a force wholly inadequate to hold the place if the French chose to return and attempt to take it again. Those who remained must for a time depend largely on stream and forest to supply their needs, while the army, which was to return, began their homeward march early in December, with starvation staring them in the face.

No sooner was his work done than Forbes utterly succumbed. He left with the soldiers and was carried all the way to Philadelphia in a litter, arriving there January 18, 1759. He lingered through the winter, died in March, and was buried in Christ Church, March 14, 1759. Parkman says:

> If his achievement was not brilliant, its solid value was above price; it opened the Great West to English enterprise, took from France half her savage allies, and relieved the western borders from the scourge of Indian war. From southern New York to North Carolina the frontier population had cause to bless the memory of this steadfast and all-enduring soldier.

Just sixty days after the taking of Fort Duquesne, William Pitt wrote a letter, dated Whitehall, January 23, 1759, of which the following extract will show how important this place was considered in Great Britain.

Sir:—I am now to acquaint you that the king has been pleased immediately upon receiving the news of the success of his arms on the River Ohio, to direct the commander-in-chief of His Majesty's forces in North America, and General Forbes, to lose no time in concerting the properest and speediest means for completely restoring, if possible, the ruined Fort Duquesne to a defensible and respectable state, or for erecting another in the room of it of sufficient strength, and every way adequate to the great importance of the several objects of maintaining His Majesty's subjects in the undisputed possession of the Ohio, etc., etc.

There was no attempt made to restore the old fortifications, but about a year afterward work was begun on a new fort. Gen. John Stanwix, who succeeded Gen. Forbes, is said to have been a man of high military standing, with a liberal and generous spirit. In 1760, he appeared on the Ohio at the head of an army, and with full power to build a large fort where Fort Duquesne had stood. The exact date of his arrival and the day when work was commenced is not known, but the work must have been begun the last of August or the first of September, 1759. A letter dated September 24, 1759, gives the following account:

It is now near a month since the army has been employed in erecting a most formidable fortification, such a one as will to latest posterity secure the British empire on the Ohio. There is no need to enumerate the abilities of the chief engineer (Retzer), nor the spirit shown by the troops in executing the important task; the fort will soon be a lasting monument of both.

The fort was built near the point where the Allegheny and Monongahela unite their waters, but a little farther inland than the site of Fort Duquesne. It stood on the present site of the Duquesne Freight Station, while all the ground from the Point to Third Street and from Liberty Street to the Allegheny River was enclosed in a stockade and surrounded by a moat. It was a solid and substantial building, constructed of Flemish brick, at a cost to the English Government of sixty

WILLIAM PITT.

MAJ. GEN. ARTHUR ST. CLAIR.

thousand pounds or three hundred thousand dollars It was five-sided, the two sides facing the land of brick, the others stockade. The earth around was thrown up so all was enclosed by a rampart of earth, supported on the land side by a perpendicular wall of brick; on the other sides a line of pickets was fixed on the outside of the slope, and a moat encompassed the entire work.

Casemates, barracks and store-houses were completed for a garrison of one thousand men and officers, and eighteen pieces of artillery mounted on the bastions. This strong fortification was thought to establish the British dominion on the Ohio. The exact date of its completion is not known, but on March 21, 1760, Maj. Gen Stanwix, having finished his work, set out on his return journey to Philadelphia.

CONSPIRACY OF PONTIAC AND COL. BOUQUET.

The effect of this stronghold was soon apparent in the return of about four thousand settlers to their lands on the frontiers of Pennsylvania, Virginia and Maryland, from which they had been driven by their savage enemies, and the brisk trade which at once began to be carried on with the now, to all appearance, friendly Indians. However, this security was not of long duration. The definite treaty of peace between England, Spain and France was signed February 10, 1763, but before that time, Pontiac, the great chief of the Ottawas, was planning his conspiracy, which carried death and desolation throughout the frontier.

The French had always tried to ingratiate themselves with the Indians. When their warriors came to French forts they were hospitably welcomed, and liberally supplied with guns, ammunition and clothing, until the weapons and garments of their forefathers were forgotten. The English, on the contrary, either gave reluctantly or did not give at all. Many of the English traders were of the coarsest stamp, who vied with each other in rapacity and violence. When an Indian warrior came to an English fort, instead of the kindly welcome he had been accustomed to receive from the French, he got nothing but oaths, and menaces, and blows, sometimes being assisted to leave the premises by the butt of a sentinel's musket. But above and beyond all, they watched with wrath and fear the progress of the white man into their best hunting grounds, for as the English colonist advanced their beloved forests disappeared under the strokes of the axe. The French did all in their power to augment this discontent.

In this spirit of revenge and hatred a powerful confederacy was formed, including all the western tribes, under the command of Pontiac, alike renowned for his warlike spirit, his wisdom and his bravery, and whose name was a terror to the entire region of the lakes. The blow was to be struck in the month of May, 1763. The tribes were to rise simultaneously and attack the English garrisons. Thus, a sudden attack was made on all the western posts. Detroit was saved after a long and close siege. Forts Pitt and Niagara narrowly escaped, while Le Boeuf, Venango, Presqu' Isle, Miamis, St. Joseph, Ouachtanon, Sandusky, and Michillimackinac all fell into the hands of the Indians. Their garrisons were either butchered on the spot or carried off to be tortured for the amusement of their cruel captors.

The savages swept over the surrounding country, carrying death and destruction wherever they went. Hundreds of traders were slaughtered without mercy, while their wives and children, if not murdered, were carried off captives. The property destroyed or stolen amounted, it is said, to five hundred thousand pounds. Attacks were made on Forts Bedford and Ligonier, but without success. Fort Ligonier was under siege for two months. The preservation of this post was of the utmost importance, and Lieut. Blaine, by his courage and good conduct, managed to hold it until August 2, 1763, when Col. Bouquet arrived with his little army.

In the meantime, every preparation was made at Fort Pitt for an attack. The garrison at that post numbered three hundred and thirty, commanded by Capt. Simeon Ecuyer, a brave Swiss. The fortifications having been badly damaged by floods, were with great labour repaired. The barracks were made shot-proof to protect the women and children, and as the buildings inside were all of wood, a rude fire-engine was constructed to extinguish any flames kindled by the fire-arrows of the Indians. All the houses and cabins outside the walls were levelled to the ground. The fort was so crowded by the families of the settlers who had taken refuge there, that Ecuyer wrote to Col. Bouquet:

> We are so crowded in the fort that I fear disease, for in spite of every care I cannot keep the place as clean as I should like. Besides, the smallpox is among us, and I have therefore caused a hospital to be built under the drawbridge.

Several weeks, however, elapsed before there was any determined attack from the enemy. On July 26th some chiefs asked for a *parley* with Capt. Ecuyer, which was granted. They demanded that he and all in the fort should leave it immediately or it and they would all be destroyed. He replied, that they would not go, closing his speech with these words:

> Therefore, my brother, I will advise you to go home. . . . . More-over, I tell you if any of you appear again about this fort, I will throw bomb-shells which will burst and blow you to atoms, and fire cannon upon you loaded with a whole bagful of bul-lets. Take care, therefore, for I don't want to hurt you.

On the night succeeding this parley the Indians approached in great numbers, crawling under the banks of the two rivers, digging holes with their knives, in which they were completely sheltered from the fire of the fort. On one side the entire bank was lined with these burrows, from which they shot volleys of bullets, arrows and fire-arrows into the fort. The yelling was terrific, and the women and children in the crowded barracks clung to each other in abject terror. This attack lasted for five days. On August 1st the Indians heard the rumour of Col. Bouquet's approach, which caused them to move on, and so the tired garrison was relieved.

When the news of this Indian uprising reached Gen. Amherst, he ordered Col. Bouquet to march with a detachment of five hundred men to the relief of the besieged forts. This force was composed of companies from the Forty-Second Highlanders and Seventy-Seventh Regulars, to which were added six companies of Rangers. Bouquet established his camp in Carlisle at the end of June. Here he found every building, every house, every barn, every hovel, crowded with refugees. He writes to Gen, Amherst on July 13th, as follows:

> The list of people known to be killed increases every day. The desolation of so many families, reduced to the last extremity of want and misery; the despair of those who have lost their par-ents, relations and friends, with the cries of distracted women and children who fill the streets, form a scene painful to hu-manity and impossible to describe.

Strange as it may seem, the Province of Pennsylvania would do nothing to aid the troops who gathered for its defence. The Quak-ers, who held a majority in the Assembly, were non-combatants from principle and practice; and the Swiss and German Mennonists, who were numerous in Lancaster County, professed, like the Quakers, the principle of non-resistance, and refused to bear arms. Wagons and horses had been promised, but promises were broken. Bouquet writes again to Amherst:

> I hope we shall be able to save that infatuated people from destruction, notwithstanding all their endeavours to defeat your vigorous measures.

While Bouquet, harassed and exasperated, laboured on at his difficult task, the terror of the country people increased, until at last, finding that they could hope for but little aid from the Government, they bestirred themselves with admirable spirit in their own defence. They raised small bodies of riflemen, who scoured the woods in front of the settlements, and succeeded in driving the enemy back. In some instances, these men dressed themselves as Indian warriors, painted their faces red and black, and adopted the savage mode of warfare.

On the 3rd of July a courier from Fort Bedford rode into Carlisle, and as he stopped to water his horse he was immediately surrounded by an anxious crowd, to whom he told his tale of woe, adding, as he mounted his horse to ride on to Bouquet's tent, "The Indians will soon be here." Terror and excitement spread everywhere, messengers were dispatched in every direction to give the alarm, and the reports, harrowing as they had been, were fully confirmed by the fugitives who were met on every road and by-path hurrying to Carlisle for refuge. A party armed themselves and went out to warn the living and bury the dead. They found death and desolation everywhere and sickened with horror at seeing groups of hogs tearing and devouring the bodies of the dead.

After a delay of eighteen days, having secured enough wagons, horses and oxen. Bouquet began his perilous march, with a force much smaller than Braddock's, to encounter a foe far more formidable. But Bouquet, the man of iron will and iron hand, had served seven years in America, and understood his work.

On July 25th he reached Fort Bedford, when he was fortunate in securing thirty backwoodsmen to go with him. This little army toiled on through the blazing heat of July over the Alleghanies, and reached Fort Ligonier August 2nd, the Indians, who had besieged the fort for two months, disappearing at the approach of the troops. Here Bouquet left his oxen and wagons and resumed his march on the 4th. On the 5th, about noon, he encountered the enemy at Bushy Run. The battle raged for two days and ended in a total rout of the savages.

The loss of the British was one hundred and fifteen and eight officers. The distance to Fort Pitt was twenty-five miles, which place was reached on the 10th. The enemy had abandoned the siege and marched to unite their forces with those which attacked Col. Bouquet at Bushy Run. The savages continued their hasty retreat, but Col. Bouquet's force was not sufficient to enable him to pursue the enemy beyond the Ohio, and he was obliged to content himself with supplying Fort Pitt and other forts with provisions, ammunition and stores.

It was at this time that Col. Bouquet built the little Redoubt which is now not only all that remains of Fort Pitt, but the only existing monument of British occupancy in this region.

The Indians abandoned all their former settlements and retreated to the Muskingum; here they formed new settlements, and in the spring of 1764 again began to ravage the frontier. To put an end to these depredations, Gen. Gage planned a campaign into this western wilderness from two points—Gen. Bradstreet was to advance by way of the lakes, and Col. Bouquet from Fort Pitt. After the usual delays and disappointments in securing troops from Pennsylvania and Virginia to aid in this expedition, the march from Carlisle was begun, and Col. Bouquet arrived at Fort Pitt September 17th, and was detained there until October 3rd.

He followed the north bank of the Ohio until he reached the Beaver, when he turned towards Central Ohio. Holding on his course, he refused to listen to either threats or promises from the Indians, declining to treat with them at all until they should deliver up the prisoners. Although not a blow was struck, the Indians were vanquished. Bouquet continued his march down the valley of the Muskingum until he reached a spot where some broad meadows offered a suitable place for encampment. Here he received a deputation of chiefs, listened to their offers of peace, and demanded the delivery of the prisoners. Soon band after band of captives arrived, until the number exceeded three hundred.

The scenes which followed the restoring of the prisoners to their friends beggar all description; wives recovering their husbands, parents seeking for children whom they could scarcely recognise, brothers and sisters meeting after a long separation, and sometimes scarcely able to speak the same language. The story is told of a woman whose daughter had been carried off nine years before. The mother recognised her child, but the girl, who had almost forgotten her mother tongue, showed no sign of recognition. The mother complained to Col. Bouquet that the daughter she had so often sung to sleep on her knee had forgotten her.

"Sing the song to her that you used to sing when she was a child," said Col. Bouquet. She did so, and with a passionate flood of tears the long-lost daughter flung herself into her mother's arms.

Everything being settled the army broke camp November 18th and arrived at Fort Pitt on the 28th. Early in January Col. Bouquet returned to Philadelphia, receiving wherever he went every possible mark of gratitude and esteem from the people. The Assembly of Pennsylvania and the House of Burgesses of Virginia each unanimously voted him addresses of thanks, and on the arrival of the first account of this expedition the king promoted him to the rank of Brigadier General, to command the Southern District of North America.

CONFLICT BETWEEN PENNSYLVANIA AND VIRGINIA.

We have seen two of the most powerful nations of Europe contending for the possession of the "Forks of the Ohio." We have seen the efforts of the Indians to destroy the Fort and regain possession of their hunting grounds.

In October, 1770, Washington again visited the "Forks of the Ohio," this time on a peaceful errand. He reached Fort Pitt October 17, 1770, and he says in his *Journal*:

> Lodged in what is called the town; distant about three hundred yards from the fort, at one Semple's, who keeps a very good house of entertainment.

He describes both the town and the fort, where the garrison at this time consisted of two companies of Royal Irish, commanded by Capt. Edmondson. In this *Journal* we find the following entry on October 18th:

> Dined in the fort with Col. Croghan and the officers of the garrison; supped there also, meeting with great civility from the gentlemen, and engaged to dine with Col. Croghan the next day, at his seat about four miles up the Allegheny.

Washington and his party, numbering nine or ten persons, with three Indians, continued their journey down the Ohio in a large canoe. On November 2nd, we find that the party:

> Encamped and went a-hunting, killed five buffaloes and wounded some others, three deer, &c. This country abounds in buffaloes and wild game of all kinds, as also in all kinds of

wild fowl, there being in the bottoms a great many small, grassy ponds or lakes, which are full of swan, geese and ducks of different kinds.

The party returned to Pittsburgh November 21st, were again hospitably entertained, and on the 23rd mounted their horses for their return journey to Virginia. This was Washington's last visit to Fort Pitt.

Now, after the season of rest and quiet, there comes another contest, this time between the Provinces of Pennsylvania and Virginia. The British Government, as the trouble with the colonies increased, deemed it advisable to abandon Fort Pitt and withdraw the troops. Maj. Edmondstone, then in command, sold the buildings and material October 10, 1772, to Alexander Ross and William Thompson, for fifty pounds New York currency. The fort was evacuated by the British forces in October, 1772, and in January, 1774, troops from Virginia sent by the Governor, Lord Dunmore, under command of Dr. James Connelly, took possession and changed the name to Fort Dunmore.

Dr. Connelly was arrested by Arthur St. Clair, then a magistrate of Westmoreland County, of which Allegheny County was at that time a part, and put in jail, but was soon released on bail. He went back to Virginia, but shortly returned with civil and military authority to enforce the laws of Virginia. This contest continued for several years, until a prominent citizen wrote to Governor Penn:

> The deplorable state of affairs in this part of your government is truly distressing. We are robbed, insulted and dragooned by Connelly and his militia in this place and its environs.

Maryland, too, had contended sometimes with the shedding of blood for the possession of this important point. It was not until 1785 that commissioners were appointed, the boundary of the western part of the State finally run, and Pennsylvania established in the possession of her territory.

Revolutionary Period.

During the struggle for independence the settlements west of the Alleghanies had little to fear from the invading armies of Great Britain; but influenced by the English, the Indians again began their ravages.

Fort Pitt was at this time under the command of Capt. John Neville, and was the centre of government authority. Just two days after the Declaration of Independence, but long before the news of it could have crossed the mountains, we read of a conference at Fort Pitt between Maj. Trent, Maj. Ward, Capt. Neville and other officers of the garrison, with the famous Pontiac, Guyasuta, Capt. Pipe and other representatives of the Six Nations. Guyasuta was the chief speaker. He produced a belt of *wampum*, which was to be sent from the Six Nations to other Western tribes, informing them that the Six Nations would take no part in the war between England and America and asking them to do the same. In his address Guyasuta said:

> Brothers: We will not suffer either the English or Americans to pass through our country. Should either attempt it, we shall forewarn them three times, and should they persist they must take the consequences. I am appointed by the Six Nations to take care of this country; that is, of the Indians on the other side of the Ohio (which included the Allegheny) and I desire you will not think of an expedition against Detroit, for, I repeat, we will not suffer an army to pass through our country.

The Six Nations was the most powerful confederacy of Indians in America, and whichever side secured their allegiance might count on the other tribes following them.

Instigated by the agents of Great Britain, it was not long before a deadly struggle began. Scalping parties of Indians ravaged the frontier, sparing neither age nor sex, and burning and destroying all that came in their path. Companies were formed to protect the settlements, whose headquarters were at Fort Pitt, and expeditions were made into the enemy's country, but with no very great success.

On June 1, 1777, Brig. Gen. Edward Hand took command of the post and issued a call for two thousand men. He did not receive a very satisfactory response to this call. After considerable delay, he made several expeditions against the Indians, but was singularly unfortunate in his attempts. These fruitless efforts only emboldened the savages to continue their ravages.

In 1778, Gen. Hand, at his own request, was recalled, and Brig. Gen. Mcintosh succeeded him. Gen. Mcintosh planned a formidable expedition into the enemy's country. He marched to the mouth of the Beaver, where he built a fort and called it Fort Mcintosh; then he advanced seventy-five miles farther, built another fort, and called it Fort Laurens; but on hearing alarming reports of the Indians and for want of supplies, he left Col. John Gibson with one hundred and fifty men there and returned to Fort Pitt. The depredations of the Indians continued, and Gen. Mcintosh, utterly disheartened from the want of men and supplies, asked to be relieved of his command. He was succeeded by Col. Daniel Brodhead, who like his predecessors planned great things, but never had the means of carrying out his plans.

By this time Fort Pitt was badly in need of repairs, and the garrison, half-fed and badly equipped, was almost mutinous. In November, 1781, Gen. William Irvine took command of the post. He describes the condition of the fort and of the soldiers as deplorable. He writes:

> The few troops that are here are the most licentious men and worst-behaved I ever saw, owing, I presume, in a great measure to their not being hitherto kept under any subordination or tolerable degree of discipline.

The firmness of the commander soon restored order, but not without the free application of the lash and the execution of two soldiers.

The winter of 1782 and 1783 was comparatively quiet, and on Oct. 1st, 1783, Gen. Irvine took his final leave of the western department. The State of Pennsylvania acknowledged her gratitude for his services by donating him a valuable tract of land.

In 1790 there was another Indian outbreak. Maj. Isaac Craig was then acting as Quartermaster in Pittsburgh. On May 19th, 1791, he wrote to Gen. Knox, representing the terror occasioned by the near approach of the Indians, and asking permission to erect another fortification, as Fort Pitt was in a ruinous condition. This request was granted, and Maj. Craig erected a fortification occupying the ground from Garrison Alley to Hand (now Ninth) Street, and from Liberty to the Allegheny River. This he named Fort Lafayette.

The expeditions of Gen. Harmar and of Gen. St. Clair against the Indians had been ineffectual and disastrous. In 1794, Gen. Anthony Wayne was more successful, and defeated and scattered the Indians so effectually that they never again gave trouble in this region.

THE OLD BLOCK HOUSE,

MRS. MARY E. SCHENLEY'S GIFT TO THE DAUGHTERS OF THE AMERICAN REVOLUTION OF ALLEGHENY COUNTY.

The close of the century found Fort Pitt in ruins, and this spot over which waved the flags of three nations, and the banners of two States, was left to the peaceable possession of the mechanic and artisan, the trader and farmer. The little redoubt built by Col. Bouquet in 1764, and the names of the streets in Pittsburgh, are all that is left as reminders of the struggle for the "Forks of the Ohio,"—the only relics

THE BLOCK HOUSE USED AS A DWELLING.

of the contest of the courtly Frenchman with the intrepid British, of the daring of the indomitable colonist and the craft and cruelty of the Indian. This redoubt was not built by Gen. Stanwix when the fort was erected in 1761, but by Col. Bouquet in 1764.

At the time of Pontiac's War, when Col. Bouquet came to Pittsburgh, he found that the moat which surrounded the fortifications was perfectly dry when the river was low, so that the Indians could crawl up the ditch and shoot any guard or soldier who might show his head above the parapet. To prevent this, Col. Bouquet ordered the erection of the Redoubt or Block House, which completely commanded the moat on the Allegheny side of the fort. The little building is of brick, five-sided, with two floors, having a squared oak log with loop holes on each floor. There were two underground passages, one connecting it with the fort, and the other leading to the Monongahela river.

The ground from Fort Pitt to the Allegheny River was sold in 1784 to Isaac Craig and Stephen Bayard, and after passing through various hands was purchased by Gen. James O'Hara, Sept. 4, 1805. When Gen. O'Hara died in 1S19, the property passed to his daughter Mary, who in 182 1 married William Croghan. Mrs. Croghan died in 1827, and her daughter, Mary Elizabeth, an infant barely a year old, became her sole heir. She married Capt. E. W. H. Schenley, of the English Army, and to Mrs. Mary E. Schenley, who might be called Pittsburgh's "Fairy Godmother," the Daughters of the American Revolution of Allegheny County are indebted for the gift of the old Block House and surrounding property.

While the property was in possession of Craig and Bayard, a large dwelling house was built and connected with the Block House. This was occupied one year by Mr. Turnbull, and for two years subsequently by Maj. Craig. From that time, 1785, until it came into the possession of the Daughters of the American Revolution, April 1, 1894, it continued to be used as a dwelling house. Time and decay had done their work in one hundred and thirty years, and the "Daughters" found the old Block House fast crumbling away. If it had been left much longer without repairs, it would soon have been nothing but a heap of broken brick. Mrs. Schenley's gift to the Daughters of the American Revolution was the Block House, with a plot of ground measuring one hundred by ninety feet, and a passage way leading to Penn avenue of ninety feet by twenty.

As soon as the Daughters of the American Revolution received the deed for the property, the work of clearing away the tumble-down tenements which covered the ground was commenced. It was not without great difficulty, and no little expense, that the occupants of these houses were induced to give them up. An ordinance to close Fort Street passed the City Councils some years ago, but it has never been enforced. As soon as that ordinance is carried into effect, the line of the Block House property will be extended to the middle of the street, when the passage way to Penn Avenue will be opened, and a substantial fence take the place of the temporary one at present on the ground. While the Block House was used as a dwelling the stone tablet placed over the door with the inscription,

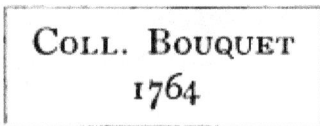

> COLL. BOUQUET
> 1764

was removed and inserted in the wall of the staircase of City Hall. The Daughters of the American Revolution petitioned Councils for permission to restore it to its original position. The petition was granted, and the tablet now fills the space which it occupied one hundred and thirty-four years ago, (as at 1899).

I do love these ancient ruins.
We never tread upon them but we set
Our foot upon some rev'rend history.

NAMES OF PITTSBURGH STREETS.

Their Historical Significance.
By Julia Morgan Harding.
(From the *Pittsburgh Bulletin,* February 15, 1893.)

We are told in his *Autobiography* that Benjamin Franklin "ever took pleasure in obtaining any little anecdotes of his ancestors," and in these days of reawakened interest in things of the past, many people may be found who, like the great prototype of American character, Pennsylvania's apostle of common sense, take pleasure in looking into the old records of their family history. A still richer inheritance is the story of the lives of the men who conquered the wilderness and subdued the Indians, French, and British; and this inheritance is held in common by all good citizens of Pittsburgh, whether or not their ancestors fought with Braddock or Bouquet or marched with Forbes.

In the stir and bustle of the busy city, above the noise of the trolley and the iron wagon, one faintly hears the names of streets whose unfamiliar sounds recall to our minds these illustrious dead. With but little effort the inward eye quickly sees an impenetrable forest clothing hills and river banks—dark, mysterious, forbidding, crossed by occasional narrow and obstructed paths; war parties of painted savages; a few scattered settlers' and traders' cabins; here and there a canoe on the swift and silent rivers; a silence too often broken by the war-whoop of the Indian and the scream of his tortured victim.

From the eastern slope of the Endless Hills to the unknown and unbounded "Indian Country" that lay beyond the Forks of the Ohio, such was the region into which Washington, Braddock, Forbes and Bouquet led their "forlorn hopes." In days when a less utilitarian spirit prevailed, and association was still powerful, the City of Pittsburgh acknowledged its debt of gratitude to the soldiers, statesmen and early settlers who made its unexampled prosperity possible, by naming for them many of its streets and suburbs.

Its early history can be traced thereby, much as the historian and archaeologist discovers the successive Roman, Saxon, Danish and Norman occupations of London and other English towns. Alliquippa, Mingo, Shannopin, Shinghiss, Guyasuta and Killbuck recall the Indian tribes and chiefs who once possessed the country; Gist, Montour, Girty, McKee, Chartiers and Van Braam the guides and traders who first penetrated the wilderness. Dinwiddie brings to mind the crusty but far-seeing Scotch governor of Virginia, who first comprehended the value of the disputed land. Forbes, Bouquet, Ligonier, Halket, Grant, Stanwix, Neville, Crawford, Hay, Marbury, Ormsby, Tannehill, O'Hara, Butler, Wayne, Bayard, Stobo, Steuben, St. Clair, Craig, Smallman and Irwin recall, or did recall, the soldiers and commandants who won the West. Duquesne, St. Pierre and Jumonville speak of the French governor of Canada, the officer who received Washington at Fort Le Boeuf, and the captain who fell at Great Meadows. Smithfield owes its name to Devereaux Smith, prominent in colonial and revolutionary days; and Wood Street was called for George Woods, surveyor.

In Penn Avenue, or street, as it used and still ought to be called, the name of the founder of the Commonwealth, the Quaker feudal proprietor, is preserved; and the great city itself, as well as two shabby, sooty little streets, forever immortalizes William Pitt, the friend of America, and makes for him a splendid and enduring monument.

But let us dig into the lowest historical *stratum* and discover the local relationships of names and places with the first occupants of the land. Alliquippa tells us of the great queen of the Delawares, who lived at the mouth of the Youghiogheny, where McKeesport now is, and whom it must be remembered Washington visited on his first memorable journey to the Ohio. From what he relates to us she could not have been a very temperate sovereign lady, but she was a celebrity and a power in her day, with a prestige that long survived her; and when in full savage regalia, surrounded by her warriors, she granted an audience to the young Virginian she was doubtless most impressive and condescending.

Shinghiss, who bore a name which suggests a subject of Queen Wilhelmina rather than a North American Indian, was a mighty warrior in his day, and a king of the Delawares. Some of the chroniclers give him a very bad name and tell us that his exploits in war would "form an interesting though shocking document;" others, among them Christian Post, give him a much better character. Nevertheless, it is true that the colony of Pennsylvania offered a thousand dollars for his scalp. Washington met him on his first visit to the Ohio and speaks of him in his Journal. This brave and much feared chief was small in stature for an Indian and lived near the Ohio on Chartiers Creek.

A chieftain as renowned as Shinghiss, and more frequently mentioned in the histories of the olden time, was Guyasuta, or Kiashuta, a Seneca, who first appears on the scene as one of the three Indians who accompanied Washington to Fort Le Boeuf. He was a conspicuous figure in all the Indian wars and treaties which followed that event and was present at the treaty Colonel Bouquet held with the Shawnees, Delawares and Senecas on the Muskingum. We hear of him again in Lord Dunmore's war. He was frequently at or in the neighborhood of Fort Pitt, and had unbounded influence with his people, an influence he generally exerted for good and in the interest of the colonies, though finally won over to the British during the Revolution. His speeches at the various councils he attended were eloquent, and his language that of an autocrat who had unquestioning confidence in the power of his people and in his own might.

He was deeply concerned in the conspiracy of Pontiac and is believed to have inspired the attack on Hannahstown. Guyasuta found his last resting place near the banks of the Allegheny on General O'Hara's farm, which is still called by his name.

The stray visitor who from time to time threads his devious way through the alleys and courts which surround the Block House may find himself perhaps in Fort street, on historic ground once trodden by Washington, Forbes, Bouquet, and the Indian kings of whom we have just been speaking. The echoes of the English drums, Scottish bagpipes and clash of arms have long since died away from the scarred sides of Mt. Washington and Duquesne Heights, and in their stead we hear the steam whistle and hollow reverberations from neighbouring boiler shops. Hibernians and Italians inhabit the fields and river banks where Killbuck, White Eyes, Shinghiss and Cornstalk once lit their campfires and held eloquent council with Jumonville, De Ligneris and Bouquet.

Squalid tenements crowd the narrow promontory where Robert de la Salle stood at the headwater of the Ohio, in all probability the discoverer of the three rivers. The fort that Pontiac besieged has disappeared. The painted post to which the Indian tied his victim, the wigwam, the *wampum* belts, have vanished; the tomahawk is buried forever, though the readiness once observed among the residents at the "Point" to draw knives upon each other on occasions of super-hilarity may be but the survival of the good old customs which prevailed in that neighborhood more than one hundred years ago, (as at 1899).

Inspired by suggestions of heredity, the imaginative mind turns to the past for other instances. On any pleasant Monday morning during the spring or summer months the thrifty housekeepers in Fort Street or Point Alley, and in the shadow of the Block House itself, may be seen doing their week's washing in front of their houses. But little are they thinking of those Monday mornings in the middle of the last century when the women of the fort were escorted by bands of soldiers to the banks of the Allegheny, where laundry work was carried on under rather embarrassing circumstances. For Indians were dodging about behind trees and bushes, and dancing in full view on the opposite shore, with threatening cries, and only kept at a distance by the presence of a guard. The custom seems still to prevail on this classic ground, but do the conveniences of soap and hydrant water make up for the spice and variety that characterized the lives of colonial laundresses?

Pittsburgh has always been pre-eminently a hospitable city, and it is possible that in no other town of its size is there as much entertaining. At weddings, too, the display of presents is an object of surprise to the out-of-town guest, unused to such lavishness. Tracing our provincial characteristics back to their remote origins, we discover that Pittsburgh at the end of the nineteenth century, in the grip of heredity, imitates the traders and early settlers in this region, who were in the

219

habit of entertaining whole tribes of Indians, and of making them frequent gifts. Gay blankets, red paint, strings of *wampum* and barrels of whiskey are not now exchanged at Christmas and on New Year's Day, or shown at wedding feasts, as we have improved somewhat upon the primitive customs of our forefathers, but the instinct is unchanged.

Noted for the beauty and brilliancy of our balls, and the excellence of our dinners, it may be interesting to know something of our first attempts in the art of social entertaining. In a letter from Captain Ecuyer, commandant at Fort Pitt, dated January 8th, 1763, written to Colonel Bouquet, he informs the latter that they have a ball every Saturday evening, graced by the presence of the most beautiful ladies of the garrison. No mention is made of any solid refreshment, but we are informed that "the punch was abundant," and it is also intimated that if the fair sex did not find it strong enough for their taste, they knew where the whiskey was kept and how to remedy the fault. Gay indeed must have been the dancing and the merriment inspired by frontier punch and the shrieks of the Indians outside the stockade, for at that very time hostile savages surrounded and threatened the lonely fort. No wonder the revellers needed strong drinks to keep up their spirits! It is indeed doubtful if the very strongest ever brewed would give nerve enough to Pittsburgh *belles* of today (1899) to enable them to dance a cotillon to the tune of Indian whoops and yells.

As to more intellectual pursuits, it would at first seem impossible to discover what our frontier ancestors did in the way of reading. News from the outside world was not to be depended upon, and books a rare article, one would presume; but information often comes from unexpected sources, and in an edition of Robertson's *Charles Fifth*, "printed for the subscribers in America in 1770," is:

A list of subscribers whose names posterity may respect, because by their seasonable encouragement the American edition hath been accomplished at a price so moderate that the man of the woods, as well as the man of the court, may solace himself with sentimental delight.

In this list we find the name of "Ensign Francis Howard of the Royal Irish at Fort Pitt," the only subscriber west of the mountains.

We can imagine the young soldier, far from home and friends, reading of those far off times of war and peril, the winter wind howling up and down the river and beating against the Block House, carrying with it the echo, perhaps, of an Indian death halloo! Doubtless he wondered what the stern Spanish campaigner would have done if brought to the western wilderness to fight the red man, and, if he lived to return to his English home with his scalp intact, it is more than probable that Ensign Francis Howard's tales of American warfare and adventure were the delight of many a hunting dinner or evening fireside.

Few indeed are the tangible relics of the most romantic period of our local history. The writer owns a copy of the edition of *Charles Fifth*, and in all probability, it is the one that the English ensign read at Fort Pitt. A few old letters, maps and account books, some cannon balls, rusty swords and bayonets, the handsome carved stone sun-dial which the Chapter has placed for safe-keeping in Carnegie Museum until its own home is built, are about all we can show of the works and possessions of the men who made our early history.

Here was the scene of a mighty struggle for empire, a struggle of which the only vestiges left are the Block House, and the names of our streets, too many of which have been changed in recent years to suit the vulgar needs of convenience, and at the cost of our historical identity.

A Journal kept during the Siege of Fort William Henry, August, 1757

By I. Minis Hays

(Read April 15, 1898)

One hundred and fifty years ago the French claimed all of North America from the Atlantic coast range to the Rocky Mountains and from Mexico and the Gulf to the northernmost limit, and they had planted flourishing colonies at the mouth of the St. Lawrence and of the Mississippi to control these great waterways, with their tributaries, to the North and West. These vast possessions, which they called New France, had a white population of about 80,000 souls.

The thirteen British colonies were scattered along the Atlantic seaboard from Maine to Georgia, with a white population of about 1,160,000, who were continually extending further and further inland and encroaching upon the undefined area beyond the mountains claimed by both French and English.

To maintain their territorial claims by force of arms, with the aid of their numerous Indian allies, and to keep in check the British colonists with their vastly larger population, and to drive back those who were already intruding into the broad valley of the Ohio, the French established a chain of forts and trading posts from Canada to Louisiana. They recognised that the fork of the Ohio and Niagara were the gateways to the great West and they therefore strongly entrenched themselves at these points. Lake Champlain and Lake George on the direct line between Montreal and New York, controlling the gateway to the Hudson, were also important strategic points for the mastery of which both French and English stubbornly contended.

In September, 1755, Gen. Johnson defeated the French under Dieskau at the Battle of Lake George, and in the following spring

Montcalm was sent out to command the French forces and to retrieve their fortunes. Ticonderoga at the head of Lake Champlain was their most advanced post, while the British troops were entrenched at Fort William Henry at the head of Lake George.

Montcalm in planning his campaign for the summer of 1757 determined, with the aid of his Indian allies, to drive the English back from Lake George, perhaps to capture Fort Edward, fourteen miles to the south, and even to make a demonstration against Albany.

In the latter part of July, he concentrated his forces at Ticonderoga, and on the 1st of August, with about 7600 men, of whom more than 1600 were Indians, he started his expedition against Fort William Henry, which was commanded by Lieut.-Col. Monro, a brave Scotch veteran, and garrisoned by a force of little more than 2000 men. Gen. Webb was in command at Fort Edward with a force of about 1600 men, with half as many more distributed at Albany and the intervening forts.

He promised his assistance, and Col. Monro had every reason to expect it, when Fort William Henry was attacked, but he failed at the last moment to give that support which it was his duty to have rendered. The rest of the sad story is told in the accompanying Journal which was recently found among the papers of Col. James Burd in the possession of this Society.

Col. James Burd was the third son of Edward Burd, a Scottish gentleman, who lived on his estate of Ormiston, near Edinburgh, by his wife, Jane Halliburton, a daughter of the Lord Provost of Edinburgh. He married Sarah Shippen, daughter of Edward Shippen, of Lancaster, Pennsylvania. He held a prominent position in the military forces of this colony, and at the time of the French attack on Fort William Henry he commanded Fort Augusta at the fork of the Susquehanna on the site of the present town of Sunbury, which was one of the long chain of forts that had recently been built by the Province of Pennsylvania to protect its territory in the war with the French and Indians.

Although the individual colonies maintained their independence they were forced to cooperate against the common foe, and the commanders of the frontier posts were kept advised of the movements of the enemy at all points along the line. The following interesting letter from Capt. Thomas Lloyd, also found among the Burd papers, conveyed to Col. Burd information in reference to the French attack on Fort William Henry:

To Major James Burd, Esquire.

Philadelphia, August 9, 1757.

Sir:—We have just now recd, an Express from York informing that Governor De Lancy has marched with an escort to be shortly followed by the whole militia of that government and a demand made of a thousand from the Jerseys to the relief of Fort William Henry which is now invested by two thousand five hundred French regulars four thousand five hundred Canadians and two thousand Indians with a train of 36 cannon and five mortars against all which damned execrable combination 'tis impossible for that fortress to hold out and the next news that arrives we expect will confirm their mastery of it. I need tell you no more than that I am Sir

    Yours etc.

T. Lloyd.

Endorsed as "Rec'd 10th Sept. 1757."

It can be readily understood that this accompanying *Journal* of the capture of Fort William Henry and the subsequent massacre its garrison had a deep personal interest to Col. Burd, which suffices to account for its having been copied and sent to him. Fortunately, he was a man of methodical habits and appears to have made a custom of filing and keeping all papers coming into his possession. Hence this copy has been preserved, while the original is unpublished and unknown, and has probably been lost or destroyed.

The French records give full data concerning the capture of Fort William Henry, but accounts written by observers on the English side are very few and, with the exception of Col. Frye's *Journal*, (*The Port Folio,* May, 1819, p. 356) most meagre. The accompanying *Journal* by an unknown writer who was evidently an officer within the fort has considerable historical value in not only confirming Col. Frye's account, but also in furnishing some additional details to complete the picture of the bravery of Col. Monro, of the incapacity of the British commander at Fort Edward, and of the treacherous apathy of the French in the face of the savage cruelties committed by their Indian allies on their capitulated foe.

COPY OF A JOURNAL KEPT DURING THE SIEGE

Tuesday

August 2nd 1757

In the evening Col. Young of the 3rd Battalion of the Royal Americans and Col. Fry of the N. England Forces came to the camp at Lake George with a reinforcement of 1100 men Regulars and Provincials making with what we had before upwards of 2400 men the whole under command of Col. Monro of the 35th Regiment.

Lieut. Forty of the 35th Regt. and captain of one of ye gallies detached 14 of his sailors to reconitre the lake this evening who returned about midnight and reported that they saw a large number of the enemys boats which gave them chace and had like to have been taken. During this night the camp was frequently alarmed by the enemys firing on ur centurys.

Wednesday 3rd Early this morning our century discovered a large number of boats on the lake close under a point of land on the west shore distance about 5 miles upon which we fired our warning guns (32 pounders) a signal agreed on upon the approach of the enemy. The French fired at the fort from their boats lying at the point but their shot did not reach half way: At this point the enemy landed their forces and artillery. This morning we brought in our live stock put them into the picquet store yard but being neglected afterwards strayed and fell into the enemy's hands.

Capt. William Arbuthnot was ordered out with a party of his N. England Forces to burn and destroy some huts and hedges on the west of the fort, which he did with difficulty. Nine o'clock discovered a number of French Regulars marching S. W. near the foot of a hill distant about 1000 yds which we apprehended were intended to cut off our communication with Fort Edward. Lieut. Collins of the Royal Regiment of Artillery gave orders to cannonade them as they marched which was done. Our rangers and a party of Provincials were smartly engaged with enemy S. W. of the camp on the ground where Sir William Johnson engaged and beat the enemy in the year 1755 and beat them off several times.

Twelve o'clock we could plainly see from the fort that the enemy were throwing up an entrenchment and erecting a battery at the distance of about 7 or 800 yards on a clear ground bearing N, B, W, saw several large boats coming to the point where the enemy landed.

Two o'clock Mons. Mont Calmn sent an officer with a flag to demand the fort but the brave Col. Monro rejected the summons with scorn. The remainder of this day was spent in bombarding the enemys works, Capt. McCloud commanding and cannonading. The artillery fired several shot from the camp which did great service in beating back the Indians. One of our balls fell on an Indian hutt and killed many.

Tuesday (sic) 4th Early this morning the enemy's works were in great forwardness with a ten gun battery almost finished. Their entrenchment approached towards the fort thus ~~~~~~~~~~ Saw several large boats coming to the point where the enemy landed from Ticonderoga: this day we had several skirmishes from all quarters in which our people behaved with great bravery, a mortar being pointed towards another Indian hutt fell on it and killed several. During this day we cannonaded the French battery and threw a large number of shells into their entrenchments. The Artillery at the camp kept a constant fire on the enemy as they came to attack our out guards and Rangers who drove them off into the woods. The Rangers brought in an enemy wounded Indian but he soon died.

Friday 5th This morning the enemy began to cannonade our forts with nine pieces of cannon 18 & 12 pounders. It was some time before they could find their mark. At eleven they tried their shells, mostly 13 inches diameter, which fell short but towards the afternoon they got their distance very well, several of their small shells falling into the parade. One of their shott carried away the pully of our flag staff and the falling of our flag much rejoyced the enemy; but it was soon hoisted though one of the men that was doing this had his head shot off with a ball, and another wounded.

A part of the enemy and their Indian (allies) advanced near our camp on which the brave Capt. Waldo of the N. England forces went out to take possession of a piece of rising ground near the wood on which a brisk fire unsued on both sides. Col. Monro sent out a second party to surround the enemy, but they were forced back and the enemy advanced up to our quarter guard. Capt. M. Cloud brought his cannon to bear upon them soon dispersed them. Here an unlucky accident happened, as some of our men were returning to camp were taken for the enemy and fired upon by which several were killed and wounded. During this attack poor Capt. Waldo was shot and soon expired. Capt. Cunningham of the 35th Regt. was wounded in the right arm.

Saturday (6th) Last night the enemy carried on their entrenchments and erected a battery of 10 guns mostly 18 pounders about 6 or 700 yards from us bearing N. W. both of cannon & mortars. This was the hotest days action from all quarters; though as yet our garrison remained in high spirits expecting Sir W. Johnson with the militia and Gen. Liman with the N. England Forces to the number of 3 or 4000 men which we heard were on their march with some more cannon. Would to God they were permitted to come as their good will was not wanting. A party of Indians were seen advancing with great speed towards the road that leads to Fort Edward which confirmed us in our belief of a relief.

About 11 o'clock Monsieur Montcalm sent an officer with a flag, with a letter that was intercepted by the above mentioned Indians from Genl. Webb wrote by his *Aid-de-Camp* Mr. Bartman to Col: Monro acquainting him that his Excellency could not give him his assistance as the militia had not yet come up to Fort Edward, &c. The French officer delivered an other letter from Montcalm acquainting Col: Monro that he came from Europe and should carry on the war as a gentleman and not as the savages do but like a true Frenchman, both broke his word and Articles of Capitulation as will appear in the sequel of this relation.

During this interval the enemy made a shew of all their Indians, about 1200, on a rising ground about 250 yards distance bearing S:W: which (while) their engineers reconitred our old camp ground which was afterwards a great advantage to them. As soon as their officer returned they began their firs in good earnest which we returned with the utmost bravery. This day we split two of our heaviest pieces of cannon (*viz.* 32 pounders) and our largest mortar was rendered useless which was very unlucky for us as we could not be supplied with others in their place. This day Col. Monro published his orders to all in the fort that if any person proved cowardly or offered to advise giving up the fort that he should be immediately hanged over the walls of the fort and he did not doubt but the officers in the garrison would stand by him to the last and that he was determined to stand it out to the last or as long as two legs were together.

Sunday 7th The enemy continued plying us very hard with their cannon and bombs while the compliment was returned by us with all our artillery, still hoping for a reinforcement from Fort Edward. A shell fell into the south bastion broke one man's leg and wounded another; split one of our 18 pounders and burst a mortar. Several of the enemys shells fell near the camp S.S.E of our fort about 400 yards distance and on a line with the fort from the enemys two batteries, so that their shot missing the fort could strike the camp. It appeared that the enemy could throw their shells 1300 yards. A shell fell amongst the officers whilst at dinner but did no other mischief than spoil their dinner by the dirt it tore up. Another shell fell into the east or flag bastion and wounded two or three men.

Monday 8th We now began to believe we were much slighted, having received no reinforcement from Fort Edward as was long expected. The enemy were continuing their approaches with their entrenchments from the 2nd battery towards the hill on our old camp ground, where they were erecting a third battery, which would have greatly distressed us: There were frequently during these last 2 or 3 days smart skirmishes near our camp, but we beat them off the ground. This night we could hear the enemy at work in our garden, on which some grape shott was sent in amongst them, which had good effect as it drove them off, however they had got their 3rd battery almost finished by day light.

Tuesday 9th This day the enemies lines were finished, parallel to our west curtain in the garden, distance about 150 yards. Col. Munro, after a Council of War had been convened, wherein the officers were of opinion, that the loss of our heavy cannon *viz* 2, 32 pounders, 1, 24 pounders, two 18 pounders, one 9 pounder and 3 mortars bursting would render it impossible to defend the fort much longer, as the enemies batteries had increased and our metal failing us, and no help coming, wherefore it was thought advisable that a white flag should be hung out in order to capitulate; which was done accordingly, and the firing ceased.

The enemy very readily granted the capitulation: had Monsieur Montcalm been a man of honor, he would have performed his part; but instead of that such a scene of barbarity ensued as is scarce to be credited: After the articles were agreed on and signed, the officers left the fort to a regiment of the French Regulars who were ready at the gate, through which we marched with most of our valuable effects and arms to the camp and in the evening three companies of the 35th Regiment had marched out and the other three companies were on their march out of the breastwork, when we received orders to return to our posts again where we remained till next rooming.

Wednesday 10th. This morning the Marquis MontCalm being desirous of our being eye witnesses of how well he was able to perform his part of the capitulation (see the 7th Article), the Indian doctors began with their tomahawks to cure the sick and wounded. They began to seize on all the negroes and Indians whom they unmercifully draged over the breast work and scalped. Then began to plunder Col. Youngs and some other officers baggage on which Col. Monro applyed to Montcalm to put a stop to these inhuman cruelties but to no purpose, for they proceeded with out interruption in taking the officers swords hats watches fuzees cloaths and shirts leaving quite naked and this they did to every one they could lay hands on.

By this time the 35th Regt. had almost formed their line of march and the Provincials coming out of the breast work the French officers did all they could to throw them into confusion alledging as soon as the Indians had done stripping them they would fall on and scalp them which thru (*sic*) them in a panick that rushed on the front and forced them into confusion, the Indians pursued tearing the children from their mothers bosoms and their mothers from their husbands, then singling out the men and carrying them in the woods and killing a great many whom we saw lying on the road side. The greatest part and best of the plunder was brought to the French general.

Our officers did all in their power to quiet our soldiers advising them not to take notice but suffer themselves to be stript without resistance lest it should be construed as a breach of our part of the capitulation and those that were in the rear should fall a sacrifice to their unbounded fury. Those therefore that had been able to perserve their arms carried them clubed. The French it is true had a detachment of their men drawn up as is mentioned in the 1st and 6th Article of Capitulation but their only business was to receive the plunder by the savages.

Braddock Ballads

The poetical sensibilities of the nation do not seem to have been very strongly affected by the inception or by the failure of Braddock's Expedition. A few copies of contemporaneous verses having fallen in my way, however, they are preserved here, as part of the *res gestae*.

1.

(This jingling provincial ballad was composed in Chester County, Pennsylvania, while the army was on its march in the spring or early summer of 1755. During the Revolution it was still a favourite song there, the name of Lee being substituted for Braddock's. It has never, I believe, appeared in print before. There is no doubt of its authenticity.)

To arms, to arms! my jolly grenadiers!
Hark, how the drums do roll it along!
To horse, to horse, with valiant good cheer;
We'll meet our proud foe, before it is long.
Let not your courage fail you:
Be valiant, stout and bold;
And it will soon avail you,
My loyal hearts of gold.
Huzzah, my valiant countrymen!—again I say huzzah!
'Tis nobly done—the day's our own—huzzah, huzzah!
March on, march on, brave Braddock leads the foremost;
The battle is begun as you may fairly see.
Stand firm, be bold, and it will soon be over;
We'll soon gain the field from our proud enemy.
A squadron now appears, my boys;
If that they do but stand!
Boys, never fear, be sure you mind
The word of command!

Huzzah, my valiant countrymen! again I say huzzah!
'Tis nobly done—the day's our own—huzzah, huzzah!

See how, see how, they break and fly before us!
See how they are scattered all over the plain!
Now, now—now, now, our country will adore us!
In peace and in triumph, boys, when we return again!
Then laurels shall our glory crown
For all our actions told:
The hills shall echo all around,
My loyal hearts of gold.
Huzzah, my valiant countrymen!—again I say huzzah!
'Tis nobly done—the day's our own—huzzah, huzzah!

2

(The following lines are from the *Gentleman's Magazine*, Vol. XXV., (Aug. 1755). It would seem that they were first published as a broadside and sold through the streets.)

On the death of Gen. Braddock, said to be slain in an ambuscade by the French and Indians, on the banks of the Ohio, July 9, 1755.

Beneath some Indian shrub, if chance you spy
The brave remains of murder'd Braddock lie,
Soldiers, with shame the guilty place survey,
And weep, that here your comrades fled away.
Then, with his brother-chiefs encircled round, (his officers)
Possess the hero's bones of hostile ground.
And plant the English Oak, that gave his name, (Brad in old Saxon-English is the same as Broad, and Brad-oke the same as Broad-oak.)
Fit emblem of his valour and his fame!
Broad o'er this stream, (the Ohio), shall thus his honours grow,
And last as long as e'er its waters flow!

(From XXV. *Gent. Mag.*, Sept. 1755)

Apology for the Men who deserted Gen. Braddock when surprised by the ambuscade.
Ah! Braddock, why did you persuade
To stand and fight each recreant blade,
That left thee in the wood?

They knew that those who run away,
Might live to fight another day,
But all must die that stood.